CULTURAL
ANALYSIS

CULTURAL ANALYSIS

The Work of Peter L. Berger,
Mary Douglas, Michel Foucault,
and Jürgen Habermas

Robert Wuthnow
James Davison Hunter
Albert Bergesen
Edith Kurzweil

Routledge & Kegan Paul
London and New York

First published in 1984
Reprinted in 1985 and 1986
by Routledge & Kegan Paul Ltd
11 New Fetter Lane, London EC4P 4EE
Published in the USA by
Routledge and Kegan Paul Inc.
in association with Methuen Inc.
29 West 35th Street, New York NY 10001
Set in 11/12 Journal by
Hope Services, Abingdon, Oxon
and printed in Great Britain by
T. J. Press (Padstow) Ltd., Padstow, Cornwall
Copyright © Robert Wuthnow, James Davison Hunter,
Albert Bergesen and Edith Kurzweil 1984

Library of Congress Cataloguing in Publication Data

Cultural analysis.
Bibliography: p.
Includes index.
1. Culture. 2. Social change. 3. Berger, Peter L.
4. Douglas, Mary Tew. 5. Foucault, Michel. 6. Habermas,
Jürgen. I. Wuthnow, Robert.
HM101.C86 1984   306   83-17781

ISBN 0-7100-9894-4
ISBN 0-7100-9994-0 (pbk.)

Contents

Contents

Preface

The idea for this book grew out of a graduate seminar on theories of culture at Princeton University. In examining the writing of various contemporary analysts of culture — Althusser, Barthes, Bellah, Berger, Douglas, Eliade, Foucault, Geertz, Habermas, Lévi-Strauss, Lukács, Ricoeur — and in comparing this work with the standard social science literature on culture two conclusions became apparent. First, and of course obvious to anyone who has tackled some of these writers, was the need for interpretation and simplification in order to derive usable concepts and hypotheses from their work. Second, and of greater importance, was the conclusion that some fundamental reorientations were being presented here; moreover, there were some common themes even among these otherwise diverse perspectives on culture.

The present book is an attempt to clarify the contributions of four of these writers — Berger, Douglas, Foucault, and Habermas — with respect to the study of culture and to point up some of the converging assumptions that may be laying the foundation for a new approach to the study of culture. The writers selected were chosen because they represent four relatively distinct theoretical traditions, yet each has modified that tradition and moved in significant ways toward developing a new approach to culture. While some other writers have made contributions in this field too, the number to be discussed was intentionally limited so that each perspective could be examined in depth.

The book's focus is specifically on *culture*, a concept (it will be apparent) which remains subject to ambiguities of treatment but which retains value as a sensitizing concept for investigations into the symbolic-expressive dimensions of social life. This book differs from other treatments of these writers, therefore, in that its focus is on questions concerning the definition and content of culture, its construction, its relations with social conditions, and the manner in which it may be changing. We have sought to explain what each of our four theorists has had to say about these questions. As already implied, we have also approached these writers with the social scientist chiefly in mind, rather than the philosopher, humanist, or historian.

As for the role that each of the book's co-authors played in its preparation, Wuthnow was primarily responsible for initiating the project and for drafting chapters 1, 5, and 6; Hunter, for drafting chapter 2; Bergesen, for drafting chapter 3; and Kurzweil, for drafting chapter 4. Each of us read, commented on, and participated in revisions of all the initial drafts as well. So the final product is truly a collaborative effort.

Special thanks are due to the Problems of the Discipline Committee of the American Sociological Association which awarded a small grant for a conference to discuss our preliminary work on these theorists. This conference was held at Princeton University in May 1982. Much credit also goes to Robert Cox whose encouragement and insights were a special source of inspiration. He is the originator of the diagram which appears in modified form in chapter 5. His comments on Foucault and Habermas were also of particular value. Others with whom discussions on these writers have played a valuable role include: Angela Aidala, Stephen Ainlay, Keith Allum, Marvin Bressler, Karen Cerulo, Kevin Christiano, John Gager, Sarah Hewins, John Kuzloski, Ann Orloff, Don Redfoot, Wesley Shrum, Jeffrey Stout, Walter Wallace, and David Woolwine.

1 Introduction

While theories, methods, and research investigations in other areas of the social sciences have accumulated at an impressive pace over the past several decades, the study of culture appears to have made little headway. The major theorizing, as well as the bulk of empirical work, that has been done in the social sciences since the Second World War has tended to pay little attention to the cultural factor. The Marxist tradition has, of course, been notorious for its neglect of the cultural realm. Even in the more interesting variants of American and British neo-Marxism, culture often continues to be dismissed as little more than ideological subterfuge. The structural-functional perspective, as advanced principally by Parsons, identified culture as an autonomous system of action, but failed largely in its efforts to promote research investigations of this system. Symbolic interactionism, ostensibly concerned with symbolism and meanings, developed chiefly around the perceptions of individuals in microscopic settings rather than with the larger patterning of cultures themselves. Other perspectives in social psychology, while paying heed to cultural phenomena such as beliefs and attitudes, have been equally caught up with the individual psyche rather than devoting theoretical effort to the investigation of culture. In substantive fields the story has been much the same. The study of social movements has shifted increasingly toward examining the resource base from which collective behavior is able to emerge, rather than giving weight to the goals, frustrations, or legitimating symbols of challenging groups —

nuts and bolts have replaced hearts and minds. In the field of formal organizations, research has shifted away from norms and goals to the selective rationality of markets and environments. Studies of status attainment, one of the more popular topics in the social sciences, deal almost entirely with formal models of inter- and intra-generational transmission, even though (ironically) the concept of occupational prestige seems an obvious candidate for cultural analysis. Social networks studies focus exclusively on interpersonal linkages and exchange. Even in social psychology where the relation between 'culture and personality' still occupies a position of formal importance, research has come to focus more on life events, stages of development, support networks, and social roles than on the influences of culture. On the whole, it may be only slightly presumptuous to suggest that the social sciences are in danger of abandoning culture entirely as a field of inquiry.

All of this is of little concern as long as the alternative approaches and theories are able to get by without recourse to the idea of culture. But the denial of culture has been difficult to sustain in actual practice. For all its materialism, Marxism does continue to posit the existence of ideology and neo-Marxists raise questions about the legitimating assumptions of the state — surely aspects of culture. Social movements make use of symbolism and ritual and themselves become figments of the cultural world as they are given public definition and historical meaning. Formal organizations struggle to maintain the moral commitment of employees and clients and their behavior is greatly influenced by ideas and information received from other organizations. Status, in actuality, remains the product of negotiation and display in ways far more significant than mathematical attainment models have been able to explain. Networks exist only in so far as actors are capable of transmitting messages, overtly or inadvertently, to one another about their relative positions and intentions. Life events, feelings, and other aspects of the self coalesce as formative dimensions of the personality in no way other than through the mediation of symbolic gestures and reflection.

These examples not only indicate the numerous areas and

ways in which cultural factors surface in social life; they also give a sense of what culture is and how it may be defined. For present purposes, culture may be provisionally defined as the symbolic-expressive aspect of human behavior. This definition is sufficiently broad to take account of the verbal utterances, gestures, ceremonial behavior, ideologies, religions, and philosophical systems that are generally associated with the term culture. There are some special advantages as well in defining culture this way, as will become evident in subsequent chapters.

It will also become apparent, however, that theorists of culture remain sorely divided on how best to define culture and what aspects of it to emphasize. That this should be so is a reflection of how little progress has been made in the study of culture. With only a few exceptions, this field remains an impoverished area in the social sciences. Its importance, though debated, is sufficiently evident that efforts need to be made to promote the study of culture. But thus far, these efforts have been largely unproductive.

Limiting assumptions

Why has the study of culture failed to advance? To some, the answer is straightforward. Some time ago, according to this interpretation, social scientists discovered that culture actually made relatively little difference in human affairs and for this reason ceased applying their best efforts to its investigation. They turned from the ephemeral realm of attitudes and feelings to the more obdurate facts of social life — income inequality, unemployment, fertility rates, group dynamics, crime, and the like. For others, an equally straightforward explanation is probably evident. Moods, feelings, beliefs, values — the stuff of which culture is comprised — cannot be studied, however important, without great difficulty and expense. These phenomena are tough to operationalize and measure. Those who try, moreover, invariably face critics who argue that rich, personal, empathic description is the most that can be hoped for in the realm of culture, while those who rely on empathic description hold no match to social scientists in other areas who can wield precise statistics

3

and rigorous tests of formal propositions.

But these views are more *symptomatic* of conventional wisdom about culture than they are helpful as diagnoses of the problem. They reflect the very assumptions that have inhibited progress in the study of culture. These limiting assumptions need to be unmasked at the outset.

The first is the assumption that culture consists primarily of thoughts, moods, feelings, beliefs, and values. This is a common view in contemporary social science. Culture is that residual realm left over after all forms of observable human behavior have been removed. It consists of the inner, invisible thought life of human beings, either as individuals or in some difficult-to-imagine collective sense, as in notions of 'collective purpose', 'shared values', and 'intersubjective realities'. What people actually do, how they behave, the institutions they construct, and the physical exchanges of money and power in which they engage, however, are not a part of culture.

This view of culture has gradually evolved and been defended on the basis of selective readings of classical social theory until it is now a prevailing assumption in the social sciences. It is rooted fundamentally in the familiar, common-sensical Platonic dualism between mind and body. But it has taken on sophistication from modern theoretical work. From Marx the idea has been inherited that culture is an aspect of 'superstructure', separated as it were from the more objective and consequential elements comprising the social 'infra-structure', namely, means of production and social relations. From Weber a counterargument has been derived which asserts the importance of culture. But in the Weberian view culture is nevertheless a matter of 'ethic' and 'spirit', still differentiated from concrete social arrangements involving social classes, the state, and technology. From Durkheim the notion has evolved (particularly in the work of interpreters like Guy E. Swanson) that culture is a set of shared beliefs, often misguidedly oriented toward gods and other mysterious forces, but which in reality are mere reflections of the power configurations within societies. From Parsons one learns to separate the 'cultural system' from the 'social system', the one seemingly comprised of little more than the social scientists' assertions about collective values, while the other represents the actual realm of human interaction. In conventional accounts of social psychology, a world of 'attitudes' populated by mental and emotive predispositions is set off from the world of behavior.

The point is sufficiently evident. In standard social scientific discussions of culture the human world is divided in two, objective social structure on the one hand, subjective thoughts and perceptions on the other, and the cultural part is defined as the most fluid, unconstrained, and least observable category of non-behavior. Having defined culture in this way, it is not surprising that social scientists have found it difficult to make headway with the analysis of culture.

A second limiting assumption is closely related. If culture consists of thoughts and feelings rather than behavior, then the relation between these two realms is an obvious question to explore; hence come studies relating subjective perceptions to objective circumstances, attitudes to behavior, opinions to voting, ideology to revolutions, class consciousness to class, alienation to inequality, and so on. Yet the focus of these studies has not been to understand culture, but in essence to explain it away. It would scarcely do (for building an empirical social science) to explain the observable activities of human actors in terms of unobservable cultural predispositions. Indeed, studies attempting to do so have been disappointing in being able to pin down stable relations. Rather, it has proved more attractive to argue that patterns of observable behavior are the real sources of ideas.

To put the issue more clearly, studies of culture have been inhibited by the assumption that culture can only be understood by relating it to social structure. This is reductionism. Instead of treating culture as an interesting phenomenon in its own right, social scientists have reduced it to some other level. Instead of attempting to understand religion, one attributes it to differences in social class. Instead of dealing with the internal characteristics of ideology, one seeks its roots in vested interests. Now, there is value in this approach for certain purposes, just as there is value in reducing human behavior to the functioning of chemical impulses. But social scientists have generally resisted such attempts as far as social structure is concerned on the grounds that much of value is overlooked. They have been less conscientious in dealing with culture.

Cultural analysis has also been limited by the assumption that only individuals have culture. This supposition is another form of reductionism. At one level it makes sense, of course, to limit culture to individuals. If culture is indeed nothing more than thoughts and feelings, then, to be sure, individuals are the only ones who can think and feel. But in other areas of the social sciences advances have been made only by abandoning this assumption. Durkheim's classic study of variations in suicide rates was conceivable only by assuming that these rates were independently interesting apart from the actions of individuals. So with Marx. The study of capitalist class relations implied something of importance that even individuals were neither aware of nor able to control.

The study of culture has been restricted in two significant ways by equating it with the thoughts and feelings of individuals. It has been limited in scope. And it has focused on a limited question. The problem of scope is the more obvious of the two. The logical course of inquiry, if culture is strictly an attribute of individuals, is to probe into the subjective consciousness of individuals: find out what they think and feel; in short, study the construction of subjective meanings. This, of course, is an endless task if one wishes to do it well. One individual's views are likely to be quite different from those of the next. But more importantly, one misses the broader dimensions of social life — institutions, classes, organizations, social movements. To the extent that culture is a part of these at all, it exists only in the heads of individual members. The other problem — focusing on a limited question — has also been inhibiting. This is the question of consistency. To the extent that patterns within culture have been studied at all, they have been defined largely in terms of consistency: do logically compatible attitudes actually go together with one another in people's minds? But only individuals can be credited with consistency or inconsistency. This question makes sense only if culture is regarded as a property of individuals. And even individuals seem remarkably capable of withstanding inconsistent attitudes. Thus, for all the research that has been made possible by survey techniques and quantitative analysis, little has been learned about cultural patterns.

The thrust of these arguments is to suggest that cultural analysis has been inhibited, not so much by a simple failure to specify testable propositions or to employ rigorous methods, but by deeper assumptions about the nature of culture itself. These assumptions have relegated culture to the realm of subjective thoughts and feelings held by individuals and have attempted to explain them away rather than identify systematic patterns among the elements of culture itself. So defined, it is little wonder that culture has remained poorly understood, if not genuinely misunderstood.

What is needed before cultural analysis is likely to advance is a fundamental respecification of the premises concerning culture. Its definition, what its main elements and indicators are, its relation to social structure, and how its changes need to be rethought, as it were, from the ground up. This task has, in fact, begun and much insightful progress has been made, but the work thus far has occurred primarily on the fringes of established social science and has involved considerable borrowing from other traditions. To date, these emerging approaches have not been well understood or critically examined.

Four perspectives on culture

Over the past quarter century, four approaches to the study of culture have been pursued with growing interest and with some success. Largely outside the mainstream of social science, these approaches have been oriented primarily toward the realms of meaning, symbolism, language, and discourse. Each is rooted in deeper philosophical traditions themselves quite distinct and in significant ways alien to the so-called 'positivist' tradition of contemporary social science. The first, and perhaps most familiar of these, is phenomenology; the second, cultural anthropology; the third, structuralism; and the fourth, critical theory.

These approaches are largely European in origin and for this reason have remained relatively obscure to American audiences. As each has developed in recent decades, there has nevertheless been a growing (some would say, cult-like)

Introduction

amount of interest in them to the extent that it is probably fair to suggest that the major assumptions that are now beginning to reorient work in the area of culture stem largely from one or more of these traditions.

Each of these approaches has been the locus of important theoretical contributions. It is possible to find competing views within each, but each approach has produced at least one influential writer whose work on culture has made substantial contributions in its own right. This volume focuses on the contributions of these four writers: Peter L. Berger, Mary Douglas, Michel Foucault, and Jürgen Habermas.

Each writer has contributed significantly to the discussion of culture. Each has borrowed major assumptions from the theoretical tradition from which his or her work has emanated, but has also rejected certain elements of this tradition, borrowed ideas from others, and attempted to mold a more adequate framework for the analysis of culture. The purpose of this book is to introduce the work of each writer, to summarize their contributions to the analysis of culture, and to suggest common perspectives which point toward an emerging framework for the investigation of culture.

Peter L. Berger and phenomenology

Phenomenology derives ultimately from Hegel and reflects a rich tradition of philosophical theorizing about the human condition, as evidenced in the works of Edmund Husserl, Martin Heidegger, Jean-Paul Sartre, Alfred Schutz, and others. Much of this work is concerned with questions of ontology and epistemology; that is, with issues oriented toward the very basis of being and knowing. There is, in fact, a distinct theological flavor to much of this work in that it is deeply concerned with questions of ultimate meaning, existence, and transcendent being.

Applications of phenomenology to the social sciences stem primarily from the writings of Maurice Merleau-Ponty and, more importantly, Alfred Schutz. The work of these writers re-emphasizes the call that had been put forth earlier by Weber, Mead, and others to give special consideration to the role of subjective meanings in social life. It stresses the

8

'inter-subjectivity' or shared understandings on which social interaction is based and argues for descriptive research oriented toward a more empirically grounded understanding of the ordinary perceptions and intentions of social actors in daily life.

Peter L. Berger (with various co-authors) has emerged since the middle 1960s as a leading proponent of the phenomenological approach and, more generally, as one of the most thoughtful and well-respected theorists of culture. He has written voluminously on topics in a number of fields including the sociology of knowledge, religion, theology, modernization, sociological theory, and public policy. Utilizing and significantly revising the phenomenological perspective, he has created an impressive conceptual apparatus capable of dealing with such micro-sociological problems as the internalization of values as well as more macroscopic problems such as the cultural construction of institutions, ideologies, and changing societal patterns.

Berger was born in Vienna in 1929 and grew up the son of a businessman. Completing his secondary education in England, he emigrated to the United States in 1946 while still in his teens. He attended what was then called Wagner Memorial Lutheran College on Staten Island (majoring in philosophy) and upon graduation in 1949 entered the New School for Social Research abandoning his earlier plans of becoming a Lutheran minister. While there he studied with such figures as Alfred Schutz, Carl Mayer, and Albert Salomon and with students such as Thomas Luckmann — scholars who played a prominent part in shaping his intellectual career.

He completed graduate studies in 1954 (dissertation — 'A Sociology of the Bahai Movement') and after serving two years in the US Army as an interpreter and social worker in a psychiatric clinic and one year at the Evangelical Academy in Bad Boll Germany, took a position at the University of Georgia and then at the women's college of the University of North Carolina. In 1958 he moved to the Hartford Seminary Foundation as a professor of Social Ethics where he stayed until 1963. Here he began to publish prolifically. Among his more influential writings at this time were *The Precarious Vision* (1961) and *The Noise of Solemn Assemblies* (1961).

Though well received, these books stirred authentic commotion in ecclesiastical circles inasmuch as they challenged many core assumptions of the religious (particularly, Protestant) establishment of the day.

Between 1963 and 1970, having returned to the New School, Berger developed his thinking on the nature of culture and social reality and produced the works that gained him international recognition. In *Invitation to Sociology* (1963a) he set out the intellectual parameters and calling of the discipline. Many of the themes presented in this book were later developed in *The Social Construction of Reality* (1966, with Thomas Luckmann). This book's intent was to reformulate the substantive parameters of the sociology of knowledge. The central thesis of the book was that the worlds people inhabit are, within the limits of the natural environment and man's biology, *socially constructed*; therefore, the reality that people perceive and experience is socially (and differentially) located in society. The conceptual paradigm of this book also provided the angle of analysis for his next work *The Sacred Canopy* (1967), a theoretical treatise on the sociology of religion.

Until the late 1960s, Berger did not show much interest in politics. However, in the summer of 1969, at the invitation of Ivan Illych, he visited Illych's think tank in Mexico City. There he began to explore the theoretical connections between his previous work on culture and modernization, Third World development, and politics. At about this time he also left the New School for a professorship at Rutgers University. The result of his changing interests was, most importantly, *The Homeless Mind* (1973), with Brigitte Berger and Hansfried Kellner, and *Pyramids of Sacrifice* (1974).

In 1979 Berger left Rutgers for a position at Boston College and after one year took a chair at Boston University. In these years he began to move into new territory as well as return to previous interests. In the latter case, he extended his work in the sociology of religion and theology with *The Heretical Imperative* (1979a) and an edited book, *The Other Side of God* (1980). He also extended his thinking on the method of sociology in *Sociology Reinterpreted* (1981a).

Overall, Berger's career has been marked by an impressive

consistency, contributing voluminously to the discipline of sociology and in particular to the analysis of culture. The corpus of his work includes nearly twenty books and monographs and close to a hundred articles on literally dozens of topics. As a talented writer, a humanist, and most of all as an intellectual saboteur he has been a leader in reorienting contemporary perspectives on culture.

Mary Douglas and cultural anthropology

The British tradition of cultural anthropology, founded by Bronislaw Malinowski and carried on by such eminent figures as Edward Evans-Pritchard and Edmund Leach, has focused heavily on empirical materials from tribal groups. This work has paid special attention to the social functions of ritual, drawing inspiration from Malinowski and from Durkheim, and on classification systems — categories of thought and social demarcation — used to impose and maintain order in societies.

Mary Douglas is one of the leading theorists in the British tradition of cultural anthropology. Her work, like that of her predecessors, has been preoccupied with questions of social order. Drawing on a wide range of materials from primitive groups, she has formulated perceptive arguments about ritual, symbolic deviance, social boundaries, and comparative cosmologies. Her work has not been oriented toward formulating systematic propositions about culture or a pantheon of abstract concepts with which to describe culture. Nevertheless, a distinct set of arguments about culture runs through her work. She has received considerable acclaim for her work and her major writings have attracted large followings in a variety of social scientific and humanistic disciplines. Her insightful treatments of the manner in which cultural patterns are dramatized and affirmed provide an especially valuable complement to the more abstract formulations advanced by such writers as Berger and Habermas.

She was born in 1921 and, after studying at Sacred Heart Convent in London and Oxford University, took a job at the Colonial Office from 1943 to 1947. It was here that she became acquainted with anthropologists and developed her interests in Africa. At the close of the Second World War she returned to Oxford where she earned a Bachelor of Science in anthropology in 1948 and a doctorate in 1951, studying with Edward Evans-Pritchard. In 1949 and 1950, and again in 1953, she did field-work in the Belgian Congo. She became a member of the anthropology department at University College in London in 1951, teaching there for more than two decades before leaving in 1977 to become Director for Research on Culture at the Russell Sage Foundation in New York. In 1981 she was named Avalon Professor of the Humanities at Northwestern University. She has also lectured at New York University, Columbia, Yale, and Princeton.

During the first decade and a half of her career, Douglas's interests centered almost exclusively on Africa. The results of her early field-work were published as a short monograph entitled *Peoples of the Lake Nyasa Region* in 1950. Another monograph (co-authored with Daniel Biebuych), entitled *Congo: Tribes and Parties*, appeared in 1961 as a Royal Anthropological Institute pamphlet. Her first major book, *The Lele of the Kasai*, was published in 1963. Although this work was largely descriptive and ethnographic, it presaged things to come with insightful analyses of symbolism and ritual.

From the middle 1960s, her interests turned increasingly to broader theoretical and comparative issues. *Purity and Danger: An Analysis of the Concepts of Pollution and Taboo* (1966) earned her recognition within the broader social scientific community as a scholar with bold imagination and fresh insight about the structure of culture. Shorter essays produced during this period also reflected the broadening scope of her interests: 'The Meaning of Myth' (1967); 'The Social Control of Cognition' (1968); 'Heathen Darkness, Modern Piety' (1970); and 'The Healing Rite' (1970). In 1970 she published the book that won her international attention and which remains her single most important contribution to the theoretical analysis of culture. *Natural Symbols* was both an analysis of culture and a challenge to its contemporary expression. She continued her explorations in comparative cultural analysis throughout the decade. Part of this work was reflected in *The World of Goods* (with Baron Isherwood), published in 1979, and in *Risk and*

Culture (with Aaron Wildavsky), published in 1982.

Like Berger, Douglas has been of inspiration to hundreds of social scientists who have felt the need to grasp the symbolic world more effectively. Through her empirical work she demonstrates a technique for understanding symbolic patterns. And like Foucault and Habermas, along with Berger, she advances a perspective on culture which casts a critical light on contemporary conditions.

Michel Foucault and structuralism

Michel Foucault represents a distinct contrast with both Berger and Douglas. While their work stems from a cultural milieu that is at least assimilable, if not familiar, to students of mainstream social science, and is written with relative clarity, Foucault's work tends to be maddeningly obscure. It is filled with insightful reflections on the nature of cultural development and presents a provocative method of cultural analysis, but derives from a tradition of French scholarship which is as yet little known or appreciated by English-speaking audiences. Foucault works partly within the Durkheimian tradition, partly within the Marxist tradition, and partly within the structuralist tradition, but his rendition of all these traditions is unique.

He was born in Poitier, France, in 1926 and was educated at the Ecole Normale Superieure, receiving his doctorate in 1948. Here he came under the influence of Louis Althusser, who introduced him to Marxist structuralism; Jean Hyppolite, an eminent philosopher whose work was oriented toward Hegelianism; Georges Canguilhem, a historian of ideas; and Georges Dumezil, whose interests included the history of myth, art, and religion. After having joined the Communist party and taking an active role in the debates going on among French intellectuals concerning Marxism and the Soviet state, Foucault turned away from theoretical philosophy and became increasingly interested in the social sciences. In 1950 he earned a degree in psychology, spent the next two years studying psychopathology at the University of Paris, and then observed psychiatric practice in mental hospitals for the following three years. From there he went to the University of Uppsala in Sweden where he was a lecturer for four years. This position was followed by two years as director of the Institut Francais in Hamburg, Germany, after which he became director of the Institut de Philosophie at the Faculté des Lettres in Clermont, France.

Foucault's training in philosophy and in the history of ideas, together with his experience in mental hospitals, shaped the subject matter of his first book, *Madness and Civilization: A History of Insanity in the Age of Reason*. Published in 1961, the book won the medal of the Centre de la Recherche Scientifique and immediately became a best-seller in France. His next book, *Birth of the Clinic: An Archeology of Medical Perception*, appeared in 1963. Like the earlier study, it was concerned with the role of language and terminology in shaping mental perceptions and in the ways in which the very arrangements of space, tools, and social relations affected ideas.

From here, Foucault's interests turned to a decidedly more grandiose topic — the origin and evolution of the behavioral, social, and cultural scientific disciplines. Published as *The Order of Things: An Archeology of the Human Sciences* in 1966, this study dealt with the fundamental categories of language that make thought possible in the human sciences, categories concerning language and speech, history, value, utility, exchange, wealth, and labor, to name a few. Though frustrating in its scope, its obscure and truncated style of argumentation, and the unfamiliarity of its logic and method, this book has been touted by European scholars as a major contribution to philosophy and, of all his writings, is perhaps of most general relevance to social scientists, since it contains insightful analyses of the suppositions underlying social scientific work.

Sensing the need to clarify and systematize his methods of inquiry, both for himself and for his rapidly growing cadre of intellectual disciples, Foucault next published *The Archeology of Knowledge* (1969). This volume contains his most pro-vocative outline for a reorientation of cultural analysis. Its publication represented both a culmination of the work that Foucault had concentrated on during the previous decade and a turning point which would become increasingly apparent in subsequent work.

This shift was toward an increasing emphasis on power. In *I, Pierre Rivière . . .* (1973), *Discipline and Punish: The Birth of the Prison* (1975), and *The History of Sexuality* (1976), Foucault has stressed the extent to which knowledge is shaped by differentials of power and the ways in which it both dramatizes and mediates the application of power to social institutions. These themes have also been important in many of his more recent essays and interviews, a number of which have been collected in *Power/Knowledge* (1980a).

Compared with Peter Berger, Foucault's perspective borrows heavily from the structuralist tradition of French cultural analysis — the tradition generally associated with the work of Ferdinand de Saussure in linguistics, Claude Lévi-Strauss in anthropology, and Emile Durkheim in sociology. This emphasis is also apparent in contrast with Mary Douglas, although the differences are less pronounced. Foucault has denied allegations that his own work falls within the structuralist tradition, but observers have noted strong similarities — sufficient to have earned him the label 'neo-structuralist' — particularly in his emphasis on patterns and relations among the elements of discourse from which deeper rules and uniformities can be inferred. Structuralism, however, is only one of the traditions that has influenced Foucault. Both his earlier involvement with Marxism and his more recent interests in power demonstrate certain parallels with critical theory.

Jürgen Habermas and critical theory

Critical theory emerged in Germany in the decade following the First World War. Its chief figures included Max Horkheimer, Theodore Adorno, Erich Fromm, and Herbert Marcuse, all of whom drew heavily from Marxist writers such as Lenin, Trotsky, Luxemburg, and Bukharin. Unlike their predecessors, these scholars were deeply influenced by the events surrounding the First World War — the collapse of the international labor movement, the hardening of Soviet dictatorship, and the economic devastation that led to fascism. While embracing the Marxist critique of capitalism, they re-examined its philosophical foundations in hopes of making it more applicable to the current situation. Institutionally, critical theory became associated with the Institute for Social Research, a center at Frankfurt which had been established by a wealthy grain merchant to promote Marxist studies. As it developed through the 1930s and 1940s, the critical school became a blend of diverse intellectual traditions including both Marxism and German idealism.

The philosopher and sociologist Jürgen Habermas has emerged in recent decades as the major spokesman for critical theory. Born in 1929, Habermas grew up in the German town of Gummersbach where his father, who had been a pastor and director of the local seminary, served as head of the Bureau of Industry and Trade. He dates his intellectual development from 1945. In that year, due to the Nuremburg trials and other disclosures about the war, he came to realize he had been reared under a politically criminal system. He became openly critical of the German political and academic elite, and pacifistic in his views.

From 1949 to 1954 he studied philosophy at the University of Göttingen. Most of his professors had taught there prior to 1933, and he was alarmed to find no break in their thought due to the war, nor any self-criticism of their philosophical views. His first article was a critique of Heidegger's *Introduction to Metaphysics*, focusing on his failure to repudiate ideas put forth under Hitler. At about this time, Habermas also became interested in Marxist theory. He read Lukács' *History and Class Consciousness* with great enthusiasm. But in the end he concluded it was impossible to apply Marx or Lukács directly to the post-war period. It was this ambivalence that attracted him to Horkheimer and Adorno's *Dialectic of Enlightenment*, which he read in 1955 — his first exposure to the critical school.

After a period of teaching at Heidelberg, he took a chair in philosophy and sociology at the University of Frankfurt in 1964, remaining there until 1971, when he left to assume a position at the Max Planck Institute in Starnberg. During this period he gained international attention as a theorist of the student protest movement. This movement gave him hope that critical theory could have an impact on politics and also helped to sharpen his own views in relation to his forebears in the Frankfurt school.

Habermas has written voluminously since the early 1960s. *Theory and Practice* represents his earliest work. Five chapters of this volume were originally published in 1963 and one appeared in 1966. In this book he examines what he perceives as a degeneration of political theory from the study of ultimate goodness and decency, as conceived of by Plato and Aristotle, to the study of effective means for manipulating citizens, as typified in modern social science. *Knowledge and Human Interests*, initially published in 1968, followed this critique with a systematic effort to develop an alternative perspective for the social sciences. *Toward a Rational Society: Student Protest, Science, and Politics* appeared about the same time, the six essays of which it was comprised being articles published in 1968 and 1969. These essays were written at the height of the student movement and reflect both his interests in that movement and his larger concerns about the ideological roles played by science and technology.

With *Legitimation Crisis*, published in 1979 Habermas turned his attention from the more purely theoretical and philosophical issues which had dominated his earlier work to an investigation of the social and cultural problems confronting advanced capitalist societies. In subsequent works, he has focused increasingly on questions of culture. In *Communication and the Evolution of Society*, published in 1976, he took up the question of how best to analyze problems of legitimacy as well as problems concerning cultural evolution and self-identity. His effort in this volume to 'reconstruct' Marx's historical materialism also reflects an increasing interest in culture. Theories of communication, particularly the work of John R. Searle, and theories of moral development and cultural evolution figure prominently as influences in this work. These interests are also evident in his most recent work, *The Theory of Communicative Action* (1983).

Toward clarification and comparison

The contribution of these writers to the discussion of culture has been considerable — too considerable, and too heavily influenced by particular philosophical traditions to be grasped

17

Introduction

easily. Each writer — one American, one British, one French, one German — has attempted through formal argument, empirical investigation, or some combination of both to specify a framework for the analysis of culture. The perspectives generated represent geniune contributions. Each perspective departs in significant ways from the normal assumptions about culture that have dominated the social sciences. Each has borrowed, both eclectically and systematically, from traditions whose assumptions need to be carefully understood. Each has formulated an operating concept of culture and has applied this concept to the study of social change.

The differences among these writers are acute. Writing from different national contexts and from four distinct disciplines (sociology, anthropology, history, philosophy), each has attempted to create a conceptual apparatus with its own design and integrity. The theoretical traditions from which they have drawn inspiration specify different assumptions about epistemology, about the goals of cultural investigation, and about the social scientist's calling. In addressing culture, they have focused on widely disparate phenomena, from perceptual realities to schemes of political legitimation, from everyday life-worlds to epochs of cultural evolution, from primitive taboos to conceptions of insanity. In method their work runs the gamut from the intricately empirical to the ponderously philosophical.

There are nevertheless sufficient similarities in these perspectives to invite comparisons. All of them place heavy emphasis on language and communication, on systems of classification, on the symbolic-expressive, on culture. They struggle with issues of subjectivity and human perception. They reject possibilities of the social sciences being modeled after the physical sciences and, for this reason, have given close attention to the assumptions and purposes underlying the social sciences. They all perceive significant problems in modern culture which require critical reflection. These writers have felt compelled to grapple with the legacy of many of the same theorists — Marx, Weber, Durkheim, Freud, Mead, Nietzsche, Heidegger. Even the imprint of common events, owing to substantial parallels in personal biography, invites comparison: the Second World War, the

18

intellectual atmosphere immediately after the war, the formative years of the 1950s, the politicized climate of the late 1960s and 1970s.

In addition, significant strands are evident in these perspectives to point, however tentatively, toward possibilities of synthesis, or at least of selective borrowing, with considerable promise for the future development of cultural analysis. Comparison of their prevailing assumptions suggests that some convergence has already begun to take place as far as the direction of cultural analysis is concerned.

Specifically, two significant shifts of emphasis are evident in this work. The first is most evident in contrast with earlier theories of culture which dichotomized human behavior into two realms, one characterized as concrete observable behavior or social structure, the other as thoughts, beliefs, and ideas which could be understood by attributing them to aspects of the former. While this perspective continues to be reflected *in practice* to a considerable extent in Berger's writings (and is not absent from Habermas), it is nevertheless a view that all four writers have rejected as being reductionistic, based on a false bifurcation of the human condition, and counterproductive as far as understanding culture itself is concerned. Secondly, a shift is evident in these writers away from the traditional assumptions of phenomenology. That is, neither the quest for empathic understanding of the subjective moods and intentions of the actor nor the emphasis on rich description in phenomenology has been strictly adhered to by these writers. Instead, each has come increasingly to emphasize the more observable, objective, shared aspects of culture and to seek patterns among them. Language, ritual, and categories of classification have largely replaced subjective meanings as the focal points of cultural analysis. This shift is again more evident in the case of Douglas, Foucault, and Habermas than it is with Berger. But even Berger's phenomenology departs significantly from the assumptions that have been associated with this approach.

These shifts represent a major reorientation of cultural analysis from the way it has been understood in the social sciences. In the emerging framework, culture is understood as a behavioral phenomenon, or, more precisely, as an analytic

19

aspect of behavior. It is neither reducible to more concrete forms of social structure nor comprised of subjective meanings. As with other aspects of behavior, patterns among the elements of culture are themselves the principal focus of investigation. In differing ways, each of the perspectives to be examined gives valuable clues as to how that investigation should proceed.

In Chapters 2–5 the integrity and distinctiveness of each theorist's contributions are examined. The purpose of these chapters is to clarify the intellectual assumptions, perspective on culture, and contribution to the discussion of culture and social change of each writer. In Chapter 6 the similarities and differences are made explicit in order to highlight the framework that is now emerging for the study of culture.

2 The phenomenology of Peter L. Berger

Unlike Habermas, Douglas, and Foucault who are more closely identified with a 'school of thought', most writers classify Berger's work as simply, 'Bergerian'. In one sense, this is wholly appropriate in that his framework for the analysis of culture is couched in a sociological dialectic that is largely his own unique creation. Those who have attempted to locate his work within a broader intellectual tradition have characterized it as 'Weberian', 'neo-Weberian', 'phenomenological', — or even 'German humanistic'. Clearly these efforts are not unfounded either. Berger owes substantial intellectual debts to Weber and the Germanic tradition in intellectual thought. He borrows heavily from terminology associated with certain variants of classical phenomenology. However suitable it may be to classify him in these ways — indeed to classify him at all — upon close scrutiny, such labels are, in the end, caricatures for what is really an intensely diverse set of intellectual influences on his work.

Berger demonstrates a genuine eclecticism and a propensity for synthesis of the finest kind. What is more, his fluency in German and a working fluency in several other northern European languages have given him access to a wide set of literature otherwise inaccessible to the majority of American scholars.

The full range of individuals upon whom Berger has relied or whose work has in one way or another influenced his work is probably impossible to catalogue. None the less, a sketch of his intellectual heritage is possible. It would be possible, for example, to trace the influences on Berger's assumptions and concerns about the philosophical nature of man and society to the complex philosophy of Immanuel Kant; Berger's programs of reasoning to Georg Hegel and his followers. The writings of Marx have been a clear influence on his conceptions of individual and society. Perhaps more importantly, the debate with Marx, though not always explicit, has provided Berger with a consistent point of reference — if only negative (defining himself in contradistinction to Marx). The writings of Emile Durkheim and Georg Simmel have also been patent influences in his conceptions of social and cultural reality. Weber, of course, is Berger's principal source of intellectual inspiration. It is from Weber that Berger derives a basic understanding of the method and calling of sociology and a basic perspective on the nature of modern society, and indeed, an overall intellectual concern with the problems of meaning in a culture being transformed by the seemingly inexorable forces of modernization. There are, needless to say, critical ways in which Berger elaborates upon and even distances himself from Weber which will become apparent.

Among twentieth-century writers, several others have informed Berger's work on culture in significant ways. George Herbert Mead is particularly noteworthy. Of Mead's work in social psychology, Berger has said that it is probably the most important contribution to sociology from America. Jean-Paul Sartre and the existentialists as well as Karl Barth and neo-orthodox theology have also played an indirect part in shaping the philosophical backdrop to Berger's conceptions of man and culture. Of obvious importance in refining the philosophical basis of his methodological approach to the social sciences is the phenomenology of Alfred Schutz. Not least in significance in building a theory of man and culture and society are the numerous contributions of the German social philosopher Arnold Gehlen. To be sure, this does not exhaust the numbers of scholars who have shaped Berger's theoretical thinking.

It is important to note that he has always been careful to acknowledge his indebtedness to those from whom he has borrowed. One should not make something of Berger that he

does not make of himself. One notable feature of his eclecticism is its positive thrust. He borrows when it is deemed
useful. It is difficult to find in his work an effort to synthesize
for the sake of synthesis or to be exegetical. In his early work
he was much more careful to cite the works of others in
order to locate himself intellectually or to clarify his own
position relative to the position of another. Douglas, Habermas,
and Foucault are never cited in those works where there
would be substantive overlap. This may be partly due to the
fact that Berger was writing at a time when these individuals
were just beginning to gain recognition as scholars to be
contended with, though Berger rarely did it with those who
were major living forces in social theory, Talcott Parsons in
particular. Indeed, Berger has shown a distinct propensity to
shy away from an intellectual sparring with his contemporaries in the field. Though sometimes a source of frustration
to those attempting to place him, it would appear to result
from an economy of time as well as an aversion to pedantry.

While all social theorists implicitly or explicitly operate
with a particular philosophical conception of the human
species, with few theorists does it play so directly into a
theory of culture and into a particular methodology than it
does with Berger. Thus an adequate understanding of Berger's
theoretical work on culture and his methodological approach
to it must begin with a review of his intellectual assumptions.

Intellectual assumptions

At the base of Berger's work on culture is an understanding
of the biological and environmental constants which inhere
within the human condition. Based on the work of such
philosophers and biologists as Gehlen, Helmut Plessner,
Adolf Portmann and others, Berger maintains that humans,
unlike other animals, have no 'species-specific environment'.
Humans can inhabit, within the limits determined by their
organisms, any number of geographic and climatic environments. In addition, their instinctual apparatus, as compared
to the other higher mammals, is grossly underdeveloped at
birth. They suffer from what Gehlen calls 'instinctual deprivation'; they are 'unfinished', as it were. Humans do have

23

drives, naturally, but these are, in the main, undirected and unspecialized. Organismically, the human body is still developing biologically outside the mother's womb for the first year of life in ways that are completed for other mammals inside the womb. Thus our constitution at birth is one of 'world openness' and 'plasticity'. During this period of utter dependence, we interrelate with the human and natural environment in which we are placed and it is this environment which initially serves to delimit the wide range of socio-cultural formations that may develop.

The human condition, as a result of these anthropological givens, is inherently intolerable. The human organism simply cannot survive. Our biological constitution does not provide stable channels in which to direct our drives, but only the *imperative* that we must provide a stable environment which will protect us from the threat of extinction. What biology does not provide must be compensated for through non-biological means.

Reality construction

As both Hegel and Marx suggested, grounded in its biological equipment as an anthropological necessity is man's on-going *externalization* — 'The ongoing outpouring of human being in the world, both in the physical and the mental activity of men' (1967:4). 'Man is an acting being' (1965:201). Also built into the human condition as an anthropological constant is the predisposition to what Simmel called *sociality*. Solitary existence, after all, is existence at the animal level, as cases of children raised in isolation sadly exemplify. None the less, when these two anthropological features are understood together, one may see that people construct what was not provided for them in their biological constitution; they construct a world in its socio-cultural and psychological formations. Man, then, to Berger, is not only *homo socius*, but in sympathy with Marx's conception, *homo faber/homo pictor* — man the world-or culture-maker, including both the material and non-material dimensions of culture. Society, then, is a world-making activity.

The world that people create in the process of social

exchange is, following Durkheim, a 'reality *sui generis*'. It possesses a thing-like quality — the quality of objective facticity. But again the reality of this world is not an intrinsic quality, nor is it given once and for all. Culture must be constructed and reconstructed as a continuous process. It remains real, in the sense of subjective plausibility, only as it is confirmed and reconfirmed by oneself in relation with social others. Berger acknowledges with Marx that the process whereby man's world becomes an objective reality can reach an extreme in the process of 'reification'. What is in fact a human product is perceived as having a reality in and of itself, as an alien reality no longer recognizable as a product. In this situation man is alienated (in a strictly technical sense of the word, not in its popular, pejorative meaning). He merely 'forgets that the world he lives in has been produced by himself' (1965:200).

It is important to note what Berger regards as essential in culture. The very heart of the world that humans create is socially constructed *meaning*. Humans necessarily infuse their own meanings into reality. The individual attaches subjective meaning to all of his or her actions. In this sense one may understand one's acts as *intentional*: consciousness of something; directed toward something. In concert with others, these meanings become objectified in the artifacts of culture — ideologies, belief systems, moral codes, institutions, and so on. In turn, these meanings become reabsorbed into consciousness as subjectively plausible definitions of reality, morally sanctioned codes of personal and collective behavior, rules of social discourse and general recipes for daily living. Culture, then, is at base an all-embracing socially constructed world of subjectively and *inter*-subjectively experienced meanings. Without the intended and subjectively meaningful actions of individuals, there would be no such thing as culture. Culture, as artifact, emerges out of the stuff of subjective meanings.

Thus, the world that man inhabits has a sense of intelligibility and coherence to it: it makes sense. This 'reality' functions in the place of instincts, replacing the plasticity of the environment with ostensibly reliable structures. According to Berger, there is not only a biological imperative to build a world but a psychological imperative as well. The social world constitutes a nomos both objectively and subjectively. To be separated from this nomos is to be subjected to disorder, senselessness, and madness — in a word, meaninglessness. The following passage from *The Sacred Canopy* is instructive:

> Seen in the perspective of society, every nomos is an area of meaning carved out of a vast mass of meaninglessness, a small clearing of lucidity in a formless, dark, always ominous jungle. Seen in the perspective of the individual, every nomos represents the bright 'dayside' of life, tenuously held onto against the sinister shadows of the 'night'. In both perspectives, every nomos is an edifice erected in the face of potent and alien forces of chaos. (p. 23f)

The influence of existentialist philosophy here is patent. Early in his career, Berger carried through the existentialist agenda in maintaining that authenticity in one's life could only come by recognition that it is out of chaos that man must create a world and that the individual alone is responsible for his actions in this world. To hide from those responsibilities and choices behind the social fictions of society, the institutional imperatives of his roles, is to engage in 'bad faith'. This position was further intermixed with an earlier commitment to neo-orthodoxy. From his later work, it appears that with his neo-orthodoxy, he also repudiates this normative extension of his philosophical anthropology.

This view of cultural reality is indicative of other aspects of Berger's view of the human condition. Namely, there is an anthropological mandate for stable meanings that can be taken for granted. Clearly, the fundamental mandate is for *order*. Berger contends, there is 'a human craving for meaning that appears to have the force of instinct. Men are congenitally compelled to impose a meaningful order upon reality' (1967: 22). The larger social order is possible only through collective participation in symbols. The dominant order of a society is provided by a coherent, over-arching organization of symbols which provide a meaningful world for individuals to live in. A personal sense of order hinges on an appropriation of an identity or set of identities that, whether 'deviant' or 'normal', is reckoned with the larger social world.

In no way does Berger's argument imply a facile tautology as with, for example, structural-functionalism's notion of a societal need for 'functional integration': a system exists; an item is a part of the system; therefore, the item is positively functional for the maintenance of the system. The requirement for integration is not at the institutional level but at the *individual* level, the level of meaning, the way the social order is legitimated. And legitimation is variously and subjectively construed in society. This is not to say that delegitimation never occurs, or that delegitimation is somehow 'dysfunctional' with the attendant political implications that term carries. To the contrary, delegitimation does occur and whether or not it is dysfunctional (if one can use that term at all) is irrelevant. The distinction between a sense of integration for the individual and institutional integration is an important one. It is altogether erroneous to claim that a requirement for the former becomes a requirement for the latter. Berger does not make this analytical leap. Legitimation and delegitimation may occur concurrently without having to assess their functionality for the maintenance of the social structure. Legitimation and delegitimation are analyzed in terms of the changing definitions of reality in society.

The world in its socio-cultural and social-psychological formations, due to its socially constructed constitution, is inherently variable. Within the parameters of biology and environment, people have considerable latitude in the ways they may construct the world/nomos. A plurality of culture is then inevitable. Moreover, because of their constructed nature, these realities can never be as firm and dependable as those of the animal world. They are artificial and therefore inherently precarious. While humans continually strive to maintain their sense of arrangement, this sense is continually threatened by the marginal situations endemic to human existence. Dreams, fantasy, sickness, injury, disaster, emergency, mistake, all reveal the unreliability of the social world; all present a menace of various degrees to the paramount reality of everyday life.

Though Berger adopts a position of bracketing questions of epistemology and ontology (1966:14) in philosophical reflection, it is clear that his work is established in larger epistemological and metaphysical traditions in Western thought. Concerning Western social science, there are at least two major epistemological traditions: the humanistic and the positivistic. The humanistic tradition, on the one hand (especially as influenced by Kant) posits an intrinsic dualism in the world between different types of reality: the phenomenal and noumenal. The former (which would include the many dimensions of the natural environment, human and animal bio-chemistry and so on) is capable of being known and understood through the systematic use of the senses; the latter, which would include the social world, is capable of being understood principally if not exclusively through 'sympathetic reason'. The phenomenal is governed by 'laws of nature'; the noumenal is governed by 'laws of freedom'. The positivistic tradition, on the other hand, sees no qualitative distinctions in reality. All things are capable of being known, not only natural phenomena but human phenomena as well, through the techniques of positive science — the use of systematic techniques of observation and measurement. Berger's work, it should be clear, is grounded in a humanistic epistemology.

It is possible to distinguish two broad and more or less distinct ontological traditions in Western social science as well: a tradition that views the priority of being, its essence, in a 'material' base, and a tradition that views its essence in an 'ideal' or cultural base. Within each of these one may also distinguish between an emphasis on the individual and an emphasis on the collective dimensions. Those who attribute priority to ideals at the individual level typically focus upon individual consciousness whereas at the collective level the focus is upon cultural systems or 'collective consciousness'. In contrast, to those who attribute priority to the material, at the individual level, the beginning point of theory is typically the body and, at the collective level, it is the economic structure. Along these lines, Berger's concern with subjective and culturally objectified meanings points to an idealist ontological priority. It should be apparent that this is not a simplistic idealism. The interplay of human actors with a material world (natural and economic) has already been suggested. In fact, Berger's response to the classic 'chicken and egg' question is that the material is historically prior to the ideal. 'All consciousness, religious or other, [is rooted] in the world of everyday *praxis*' (1967:128). As he goes on to say, one should 'not conceive of this rootage in terms of mechanistic causality' (p. 128). What is here being called ontological priority is, in Berger's case, defined logically in terms of what is of greater prominence, not historically in terms of what came first. Moreover, given his focus on subjective meanings as the foundation of socially constructed reality, it is clear that the accent of this ontological priority is upon the individual as opposed to the collective.

Phenomenology and the social sciences

Berger's philosophical perspective bears on his methodology in specific ways. For one, the overwhelming (Kantian) emphasis on the centrality of the individual and individuals engaged in social interaction speaks to what Berger sees as the basic subject matter of sociology — not the only or necessarily the most important, but the basic subject matter. For Berger (as with Weber and Schutz), the common-sense knowledge of everyday life, the ways in which people organize their daily experience and especially those of the social world, is the background within which inquiry must begin. Moreover, this emphasis on the subjective meanings actors impute to their activity implies that actors themselves are 'rational' and therefore 'free' and not mechanistically determined. Such 'rationality' and 'freedom' is, however, inaccessible to the tools of positive science. Human activity (in the broader, Weberian sense of the term) must therefore be 'understood' (*verstehen*) as being meaningful to the actors in society; it must be 'interpreted'. Interpretive sociology (in the Weberian tradition) must therefore concern itself with an understanding of the *subjective meaning* or intentionality of those engaged in everyday life. This entails what Berger terms an 'interpenetration' of the relevance structures, meaning systems and bodies of knowledge of others bringing into the situation specific *scientific* knowledge and rules of procedure. The purpose of this task is to make these meanings clearer and to relate them (causally and otherwise) to other meanings and meaning systems. Stated differently, what is done in the act of interpretation is to 'transpose' the meanings of ordinary life into a different system of meanings, namely that of the social scientist. This constitutes 'an incipient *explanation*' of the situation in that 'the sociological interpreter now not only understands something, but understands it in a new way that was not possible before the transposition took place' (1981a:42).

In penetrating the world of everyday life, Berger contends that the tools of phenomenology prove indispensable. Unfortunately, phenomenology is like most intellectual disciplines in that it is conceived of differently by different proponents. Though influenced by a number of phenomenologists such as Wilhelm Dilthey, Edmund Husserl, and Maurice Merleau-Ponty, Berger's chief source of enlightenment was his teacher, Alfred Schutz. It is important to note that the brand of phenomenology Schutz proposes is of a particular sort.

It has been noted by Anthony Giddens (1977a) that there are at present two major variants of phenomenology: hermeneutic and existential. Although both variants share the same epistemological and ontological assumptions, they differ in terms of the central focus of cultural analysis — that is, between the individual and collective dimensions of cultural life. Hermeneutical phenomenology tends to focus on the collective aspect of culture as exemplified by its overriding concern with language. Texts provide the objective evidence for analysis; the objective is to explore and determine the nature and structure of communication. Of the proponents of hermeneutical phenomenology, Hans-Georg Gadamer and Paul Ricoeur are perhaps the most important. Existential phenomenology, in contrast, is oriented more toward the individual level of culture — that is culture as it has been internalized in the subjective consciousness of individuals. The object of analysis is the self as it creates and derives meaning in the world of everyday life. The work of Schutz, and therefore Berger, is plainly out of this camp. But a further qualification is also necessary.

Within existential phenomenology, as it has been described here, it is possible to distinguish between different types in terms of their relation to the empirical world. Every phenomenology can be described as empirical in that the concern is with everyday life. Yet how one approaches everyday life can be very different. On the one hand, phenomenological description can occur at a foundational level — describing the fundamental categories of consciousness as it pertains to everyday life. Schutz would be representative of this orientation. At another level phenomenological description can address problem areas. Berger would fall into this category in his efforts to describe modern consciousness or religious consciousness. At still another level, it may deal with specific problems in everyday life. Some of Berger's students would fall into this category as exemplified by studies of the aged blind. Corresponding to each level are broad techniques for accessing the empirical. At the foundational level the technique generally thought most appropriate is a reliance upon intuitive senses. Meta-data or the reliance upon data/conclusions generated by other studies is a technique successfully employed by Berger at the problem area level. Actual data collection whether through quantitative and/or qualitative means is most suitable for the analysis of specific problems. These categories are by no means exclusive in the methods implied.

Apart from drawing the finer distinctions in phenomenological analysis in order to locate and clarify Berger's own placement, the importance of this larger discussion is that whereas Weber's methodology operated out of an incipient and rough-hewn phenomenology, Schutz sought to refine Weber's methodology by clarifying his postulates and developing his concepts. To the degree that Berger depends upon Schutz for this sort of clarification of the interpretive method of sociology, Berger is the benefactor. This is obviously not the place to detail the intricacies of what is a very interesting though complex theoretical framework. Yet to the degree that the 'Schutzian model' informs Berger's work on culture it is appropriate briefly to outline a few of its key features.

All individuals inhabit a *life-world*, that is, a total sphere of experience circumscribed by a natural environment, manmade objects, events, and other individuals. Yet this world is not in most cases a single unity: consciousness is capable of moving through different spheres of reality; dreams, hallucinations, and the theatre provide examples. The life-world then consists of *multiple realities*. Among these is one that presents itself as the reality — the reality of everyday life, known in Schutzian terms as the *paramount reality*. The paramount reality is experienced in the wide-awake and presents itself as normal and self-evident, ordered and objective, and taken-for-granted as such. It further presents itself as an *intersubjective* world, a world of meanings one shares with others. Compared to the reality of everyday life, the other realities present themselves as *finite provinces of meaning*.

The reality of everyday life is shared with others. The most important experience of others is in the face to face situation. All other types of social encounter are derivatives of this face to face experience. In the face to face encounter, individuals cannot readily know the other's subjectivity; they must view and understand each other by means of *typifications*. The social reality of everyday life is comprehended in a continuum of typifications which are progressively anonymous as they are removed from the face to face situation. Together, people share a common *stock of knowledge* that differentiates reality and provides the necessary information to carry on in everyday life. This body of knowledge varies in relative degrees of precision and is organized around various concerns and priorities. In the main, however, this knowledge is determined by the individual's everyday pragmatic interests — by the *pragmatic motive*.

One can speak only of a phenomenological approach to the analysis of culture or phenomenological sociology in the most tentative of terms. Berger would agree with Merleau-Ponty that phenomenology stops where the mundane sciences begin. As Berger and Luckmann note in *The Social Construction of Reality*, 'phenomenological analysis [is] a purely descriptive method and, as such, [is] "empirical" but not "scientific" — as we understand the nature of the empirical sciences' (p. 20). For Berger, an empirical science must operate within the assumption of universal causality (1963a:122). Thus, while phenomenology does allow the social sciences to penetrate the world of everyday life and describe it systematically, it must move on to another level of reasoning.

In the Weberian sense, constructs or ideal types are then established in order to generalize different dimensions of the life-world. And naturally, it is from this process that sociological interpretation proceeds.

Berger's views of sociological interpretation are most fully developed in *Sociology Reinterpreted*. He does not argue for objectivity as defined by the positivists: that of reporting 'raw facts' in and of themselves. His view of objectivity is oriented around the interaction between values and scientific investigations and is grounded in what is known as the *phenomenological reduction*. Berger would agree that values do influence the problems and design of scientific research but that they should be controlled as much as possible so as not to distort sociological interpretation. That is, the researcher should *bracket* his or her own biases and opinions about the goodness or badness, rightness or wrongness, legitimacy or illegitimacy of the phenomenon under investigation. One must not pass judgment on the objects of inquiry. Questions of what 'is' and what 'ought to be' should be separated in the course of research. From a different angle, bracketing can be understood as an act of moving into a specific province of meaning or relevance structure (institutionalized in the scientific community) in which the researcher continuously strives to be open to the values and opinions of others, even if those values and opinions are considered personally offensive, and to systematically search for data that will falsify one's theories. Not to do these things, according to Berger, is to reduce sociology to another form of advocacy or to the defense of ideology. This is precisely the problem with Marxism 'in its various denominations'. Marxist '"sociology" [has] become a deduction from the *a priori* principles given in the ideology, an unfolding of a "truth" already known' (1981a:142). Thus Berger argues, given the ideological requirement for a proletarian class to exist, Marxist sociology has been compelled to find ways to 'discover' one. Because of the *a priori* principles of the value position, the possibility of falsification is undermined from the outset. At this point sociology ceases to be science.

This methodological defense extends not only to politics but also to religion. Questions as to the ontological validity of religious reality must be suspended in the social scientific study of religion. On phenomena of a political or religious nature, the investigator must remain 'atheistic' even if he has formulated opinions about them. As with Weber, Berger maintains that there is a place for values for the social scientist but that place is determined by his status as 'dual citizen'. It is in his role of private citizen that he is able to express his values on the issues of life. Moreover, Berger says, he *should* express those values. There should not be a carry-over of scientific objectivity to the ethical and moral quandaries of private life. The private sphere should be protected from the disenchantment of this form of coldly rational utilitarianism. As Berger maintains and as is apparent in his own published writings in the areas of theology and politics, this is not to say that sociology cannot or should not inform one's political, moral, or religious values. Sociology, as he contends in *Invitation to Sociology*, can be a prelude to a tolerant and even compassionate way of living in society. It can also help one formulate an *ethics of responsibility* — 'an ethics that derives its criterion for action from a calculus of probable consequences rather than from absolute principles' (1981a: 75). It does so in that it gives one an awareness of the extent of consequences, especially the unintended consequences of a particular course of action for those affected by it. These consequences can be gains or costs. None the less, when taking a value position, the social scientist should make it clear that one is doing so not as sociologist but as private citizen — as a Catholic, a Democrat, an American citizen, and so.

Berger's perspective on culture

Perhaps the most controversial methodological debate of the late nineteenth and early twentieth century in the social sciences (especially in Europe) concerned whether there really was a difference between the *Naturwissenschaften* and *Kulturwissenschaften* or natural and cultural sciences, and if in fact there was one, what was the nature of this difference and what were its implications for the actual performance of social scientific research. The effort to delineate the proper sphere of the cultural sciences has continued to be a concern to the present among some of the more philosophically oriented social scientists. For Berger, however, it is not an important issue, at least it is not something he addresses directly, at any length. In the main, Berger simply assumes that the nature, purpose and methods of the natural sciences are different from those of the cultural sciences. What they do share is concern for rigor, objectivity and a grounding in the empirical.

It is not entirely clear whether Berger ever set out to develop a systematic and integrated theory of culture. Whether he did or did not, what one finds in his diverse writings is something that comes close to such a theory (though not in detail, certainly in substance — in the breadth of vision). In his theoretical writings, he covers an astounding amount of territory. Given his range of interests (outside of cultural analysis) and his particular philosophical assumptions, this has naturally entailed a focusing on some dimensions of cultural analysis and an underplaying of other dimensions. Never having publicly stated that his goal was to establish such a grand theory, it would be inappropriate to judge against some abstract standard of exhaustiveness. We can approach his theory with a measure of tolerance — appreciating the numerous contributions to cultural analysis he has made rather than disparaging ostensible oversights.

Foundations

Berger defines culture as 'the totality of man's products' (1967:6). Defining culture in this way is to view it not only as material artifacts and non-material socio-cultural formations that guide human behavior (what we call society is a segment of culture), but the *reflection* of this world as it is contained within human consciousness. The subjective side of culture must be emphasized, for these products on the individual level serve as more or less lasting measures of human subjectivity. In different words, these products manifest the subjective meanings or intentionality of those who produced them. The fabric of culture then is the intersubjective meanings individuals hold concerning the world in which they live. Culture exists 'only as people are conscious of it' (1966:78).

Among the repertoire of human products, *signs* stand out as fundamentally important. While all of man's products implicitly reflect human subjectivity, signs are distinguished by their explicit intention to serve as a measure of subjective meanings. What is more, they are capable of being objectively accessible to others beyond the moment and situation in which they are initially expressed. They are capable of being detached from (transcending) the subjective states that spawned them.

In any given society one may usually find a number of sign systems — gestures, bodily movements, material artifacts, and the like. Language, which Berger defines as a system of vocal signs, is the most important sign system of a society. It is better than any other sign system in its ability to crystallize and convey subjective meanings. While language originates in the face-to-face situation, it is more detachable than any other sign system in that it can retain the meanings of individuals more accurately. One is also able to speak about things in which one never has or may never have any direct experience. Thus language is capable of becoming an objective reservoir of vast accumulations of meaning and experience which can be transmitted to others and preserved over time. Through the linguistic tool of writing (or more currently, audible recordings of language) one may even more effectively transmit and/or preserve these meanings.

Language arises in and has primary reference to everyday life — shared in common with others, oriented by practical concerns, and taken for granted as such. Due to its capacity to transcend the moment and the situation in which it emerges (the here and now), language joins different temporal, spatial, and social spheres of everyday reality and integrates them into a meaningful whole (1966:39). As a result, in conversation with others or in solitary conversation with oneself, an entire social world with a past, present and future can be available for reflection, discussion, manipulation and so on. Though language refers principally to the paramount reality of everyday life, it is also able to transcend it, to refer to and describe what Schutz calls finite provinces of meaning — and make sense of it in terms of the paramount reality. Describing an hallucination, interpreting a dream, explaining a terrifying experience provide examples. At the extreme, language can transcend everyday reality altogether in the encounter with a supra-natural reality inhabited by other-worldly beings and ordered by an entirely foreign system of values and principles. In this case, each reality can be explained and interpreted in terms of the other.

In terms of the relative temporal and spatial distance from the face to face situation in which meanings originate, the outer reaches, according to Berger, are found in *symbols*. Berger defines symbol as 'any significant theme that spans spheres of reality' and symbolic language as 'the linguistic mode by which such transcendence is achieved' (1966:40). Among the most important symbol systems historically have been religion, art, and philosophy. More recently the symbol systems of politics and psychology have gained increasing importance. Symbols or symbolic representations are highly abstract and loom far above everyday life yet they tangibly impose themselves upon everyday life in their capacity to inspire or to give meaning to individual or collective activity, to delegitimate other activity, and to bring to bear the force of social control. In a word, symbols and symbol systems provide an important ordering impulse to social affairs and to the collective views of the world. Thus they are an essential part of the reality of everyday life.

However brief, it is clear that Berger's view of language focuses on the broader themes: namely, the nature and functioning of language in culture as a conduit for human meaning. It is clearly different from a theory of language based in structural linguistics which emphasizes not meaning but the rules, patterns, and structures of language which make particular words meaningful. His perspective is consistent with, and in fact buttresses, a phenomenological approach to an understanding of culture.

Phenomenological sociology, as has often been repeated, focuses on meanings that people share intersubjectively, but that are also objectivated in a variety of cultural artifacts. It further attempts to describe social reality as a situation in which humans are constantly in the process of creating and recreating their worlds. As such, it presents an image of culture as fluid; an image of society as perpetually in motion

— even changing. Berger articulates this notion of fluidity in his more formal conception of the *dialectic*.

What Berger means by the term dialectic is something very different from that used by Plato, Hegel, or Marx. While this term assumes a more technical meaning in different contexts (as will be seen), overall it is roughly synonymous with the term interaction or interplay (cf. Wisdom, 1973). What is critical to emphasize is the sustained and unremitting character of this interplay.

Berger maintains that all reality is in a constant dialectic with itself. None the less, two dialectical processes are particularly important to human experience in the world and play a part in Berger's writing: a dialectic between the self and the body (or organism and identity), and the dialectic between the self and the socio-cultural world. The last is at the heart of Berger's theory of culture.

References have already been made to the dialectic between self and organism. At one level, there are the limitations that the human body places upon the individual at birth, the biological parameters which circumscribe the range of social possibilities open to any individual. Throughout the course of life the organism continues to affect one's world-constructing activity; yet, as Berger argues, the world one has created acts back upon that person's organism. It imposes limitations upon what is biologically possible to the organism (1966:181). Variable rates of longevity according to social class factors provide one example. Not only in terms of temporal limitations imposed upon the organism but in terms of the actual functioning of the organism, culture intrudes as well. Sexuality and nutrition provide the most obvious illustrations. People are driven by their biological constitution to seek sexual release and nourishment. The ways these are attained are highly variable — the body does not tell a person where to seek sexual release or what to eat. The channeling of these organismic drives is determined by socio-cultural factors. Thus the individual 'knows' that there is a 'right and wrong' way to achieve sexual release (e.g. Western prohibitions against incestuous and pre- or extra-marital sexual relations) and that there are 'right and wrong' foods to eat (dietary prohibitions for Muslims and Jews against eating pork).

Thus, while culture is spawned by and placed in a biological setting, culture reimposes its own constraints and patterns upon the organism and the interplay between the two continues giving rise to changes in each.

The dialectical interplay between the individual and the socio-cultural world is more conspicuous in Berger's writings for it is out of this dialectic that culture in its totality is constructed and maintained. This dialectic is summarized by the interaction of what Berger calls, three simultaneous 'moments' in a continuing dialectical process: externalization, objectivation, and internalization.

Externalization is the ongoing outpouring of individuals' physical and mental being into the world necessitated by their biological underdevelopment. Externalization, Berger suggests, is the essence of human being (1967:4). Because there is no biologically grounded structure of instincts which can channel thought and behavior, people are constrained to construct human structures which will perform the same functions. People's world-building activity is rooted in their biological necessity to externalize. To speak of an externalized product, is, however, to imply that it has acquired a measure of distinctiveness from the one who produced it.

This is the process of *objectivation*. Here the world, as Berger puts it, 'comes to confront him as a facticity outside of himself', as 'something "out there"', attaining the character of an external and 'objective reality' not as a reality only plausible to the individual but as one experienced in common with others (1967:8f). In the Durkheimian formulation, this world as an objective reality manifests itself most unmistakably in its coercive power, in its capacity to direct behavior, impose sanctions, punish deviance and at the extreme, destroy human life.

Internalization, the third moment in the dialectic of reality construction, is the process whereby the objectivated world is 'reabsorbed into consciousness' such that 'the structures of this world come to determine the subjective structures of consciousness itself' (1967:15). In this way the individual not only comprehends the objective socio-cultural world but identifies with and is shaped by it. As Berger has phrased it, the world becomes *his* world. Internalization occurs through

39

the process of socialization — a life-long process whereby individuals are initiated into the meanings of the culture and learn to accept the tasks, roles, and identities that make up its social structure. Socialization among other things, solves the problem of how one generation passes its world on to the next generation. Summarizing, Berger writes: 'It is through externalization that society is a human product. It is through objectivation that society becomes a reality *sui generis*. It is through internalization that man is a product of society' (1967:4). What must be underscored in all of this is that this dialectic occurs as a collective process within which the individual participates. It can never occur as an individual experience in isolation from the collectivity.

Berger maintains that it is only through an understanding of this inherently dialectical nature of man and society that one can understand any social phenomenon adequate to its empirical reality. The theoretical significance of this dialectical view of social reality is, as Berger himself posits, the integration of the fundamental insights of two seemingly opposed approaches to sociology, the Weberian and Durkheimian, namely: culture as subjectively meaningful activity; culture (social facts) as things. Both are correct, but each must be understood in terms of the other. Further discussion of the dialectical understanding of man and society and its relation to the phenomenological approach to the analysis of culture will be pursued later. For the moment it is expedient to turn attention to the heart of Berger's cultural analysis.

The social construction of culture

As previously noted, Berger makes the argument that people create culture as a substitute for what is denied them by their instinctually deprived organisms. A fundamentally important dimension of this social order is the *institution*. For his theory of institutions, Berger borrows heavily from Gehlen, but at the same time synthesizes elements of the theories of Schutz and Mead. Institutions originate out of human activity (behavioral or cognitive) which has become cast into a pattern or become habitualized. When these habitualized actions come to be commonly recognized by individuals in society as a specific pattern or type, institutionalization has occurred. Institutions are not only types of actions but types of actors as well. They posit that actions of a certain type will be performed by actors of a particular type. Institutions, as human constructions, function like instincts in that they pattern human behavior into stable and socially predictable routines. They also pattern human experience at the cognitive level with a sense of intelligibility and continuity. They provide the individual with psychological relief from having to constantly make decisions about what to do or to continually define and redefine a situation. Through institutionalization, courses of action are largely predetermined; a variety of situations are predefined. They function as a background of stability and predictability in which individuals may deliberate and even innovate.

Institutions not only regulate but they control human activity as well. Their capacity to control is inherent apart from any instrumentality of sanctions established to buttress them (through punishing those who deviate). A system of social control is only necessary in so far as the process of institutionalization is not entirely successful. Hence, the individual or group that does not 'buy in' to the established patterns of thought, discourse, or behavior of a society as a consequence of unsuccessful socialization, reasoned deduction, self-interest or self-preservation, and so on, will be confronted with the likelihood of sanctions. Institutions, then, like all of man's products, have the quality of objectiveness and persistence and they resist any attempts to be changed substantially or avoided. By virtue of their objectivity they are coercive, but many institutions carry mechanisms of social control to enforce their reality. Institutions are not simply maintained by their coercive ability but by implicit or sometimes formally explicit claims to legitimacy. They possess a degree of moral authority which implies that conformity is morally right and nonconformity is morally wrong.

Institutions further imply historicity. The small portion of human experience capable of being retained in people's minds becomes congealed in memory as recognizable events, objects, experiences, and so on. The critical role of language as the means through which these experiences are retained

41

and collected has already been observed.

Institutional meanings objectivated through language are strongly impressed on the consciousness of individuals from the moment they enter the social process. These institutional meanings tend to become simplified into easily grasped formulas; because people are often forgetful, these meanings are continually reimpressed (if even through unpleasant means) in the course of social activity. History and tradition emerge from this institutional/linguisitic foundation.

According to Berger, institutions must be seen from both a micro and macro social perspective. In the former case, his focus is upon *roles*. Roles, in this overall framework, are types or forms of activity rendered objective through linguistic means performed by a type of actor, one who identifies subjectively with this particular typification of conduct. Most importantly, roles *mediate* subjective meanings and their objectifications (institutions) in society for the individual. Roles represent the institutional order. As Berger notes 'by playing roles, the individual participates in a social world. By internalizing these roles, the same world becomes subjectively real [and meaningful] to him' (1966: 74).

At the cognitive level, roles mediate specific sectors of the common stock of knowledge. Knowledge is after all simply the 'objectivated meanings of institutional activity' (1966:70). Roles embody specified portions of the total available knowledge in society. All of this implies that knowledge is socially and therefore differentially apportioned in society. Knowledge is organized in terms of what is generally relevant and what is relevant only to specific roles. The division of knowledge in society, in other words, corresponds generally to the division of labor. An important part of this knowledge is that which represents specific roles through which individuals understand themselves and others. That is, identity formation is closely tied to ideas and the manner in which they are comprehended. Of this, more will be said shortly.

Concerning the macro dimension of institutional phenomena, the focus is upon the structural integration of different institutional sectors. The meaningful integration of the institutional order is not, according to Berger (contra Parsons), an objective, institutional problem *per se* but a *subjective* one. If a problem exists in the 'functional integration' of the institutions, it exists not as an organizational problem but as a problem of legitimation — justifying in a subjectively plausible way the nature and functioning of the social order.

The scope of institutionalization, Berger contends, is variable depending upon the general distribution of knowledge and the generality of meaning systems in a society. If the apportionment of general knowledge is wide and the system of values and meanings are shared by most, then institutionalization will be far-reaching. Institutionalization will be shallower in situations where the converse is true. The extremes of non-institutionalization and total institutionalization are possible to imagine, but impossible empirically. Empirical cases are concentrated toward the institutional side of this continuum — some slightly closer to one end than the other. Also conceivable is a pluralistic situation where the institutional order is fragmented — certain meanings and values (relevance structures) shared by some groups but not others. A process of institutional reverse or deinstitutionalization is also possible where structured activity, thought, or belief loses subjective credibility and individuals are left to reflect upon an open range of possible actions. What is important here is Berger's open acknowledgment that while institutions provide a background of stable definitions of reality, patterns of behavior, and so on, there is a foreground where individuals are capable of making choices, creating, innovating, and manipulating. This pertains in specific ways to Berger's conception of the social construction of *identity*.

The dialectic out of which culture is constructed is the same dialectic in which the individual acquires an identity. Berger acknowledges that the individual is provided with 'genetic presuppositions for the self' at birth. Yet at birth the individual is not provided with a subjectively and objectively recognizable identity. The character of the self is open-ended, not predisposed to any particular configuration but culturally relative in its formation. In a word, identity is like any other aspect of culture, indeed any other part of the reality of everyday life: it is a social product incomprehensible apart from the particular social context in which it was shaped and is maintained.

43

The phenomenology of Peter L. Berger

The larger dialectical process of externalization, objectivation and internalization is not a sequential but a simultaneous phenomenon at the collective and the individual levels. Yet in the life of every individual there is a temporal dimension in that at birth he or she is not a full participant of society but a potential one. The beginning point for the individual is internalization — the appropriation of the reality of culture into subjective consciousness. Through internalization, the individual becomes a member of society. The process through which internalization occurs is called socialization — 'the induction of an individual into the objective world of a society or a sector of it' (1966:130).

For a conceptualization of the process of socialization, Berger is careful to distance himself from Freudian or psychiatric models which implicitly or explicitly posit a normative conception of reality and of the self. More suitable to his task and to his phenomenological assumptions and agenda is Meadian social psychology — an indebtedness he acknowledges at every available opportunity.

Primary socialization is the first and most important socialization an individual undergoes and it is in this process that he becomes a member of society. The conceptual apparatus Mead develops to explain this process is well-known and unnecessary to elaborate here. The child learns to take on the roles and the attitudes of significant others. Gradually he is able to abstract the roles and attitudes of concrete significant others to a generalized other, society. This process is largely concurrent with the internalization of language. Language is the principal means by which an individual becomes a member of a social world and through which the world becomes and continues to be plausible. What Berger highlights in all of this is the fact that in the same process whereby the individual takes on the roles and attitudes of others, he or she also takes on their world. Identity as an objective location in a certain world can be subjectively appropriated along with that world. Society, identity, and reality in general are all solidified in consciousness in the same process of internalization/socialization.

Berger follows closely the intellectual cues offered by Mead and Cooley and the symbolic interactionist school of social-psychology. If roles are types of activity performed by types of actors, then each role has a particular identity attached to it. Since individuals ordinarily play out a variety of roles in everyday life, one may speak of an identity set. The occupational identity, however, carries a certain para-mountcy in this repertoire (1964a). While a certain degree of role discrepancy is socially permitted and psychologically bearable, there are strong social and psychological pressures to achieve a level of consistency in the roles individuals play and in the identities they therefore assume (1963a). Important to emphasize is the fact that roles and therefore identities are socially bestowed in acts of social recognition. One is that which a person plays; one is that by which a person is addressed. Identity, for Berger, constitutes what Mead calls the 'social self'. At the extreme, roles may become reified in the minds of people where individuals totally identify them-selves and others with their socially assigned roles or identities. They see themselves only as the embodiment of these typifi-cations. This is not always the case, however, for the actor is capable of establishing a sense of distance from the roles he or she plays in an act of reflection.

Berger notes what is usually absent from most symbolic interactionist writings, namely that socialization and the process of identity formation always take place in the context of a specific social structure. Inasmuch as roles mediate the knowledge and meanings of specific institutional configur-ations to the individual, the substance of identity will there-fore reflect the social structural conditions from which it emerges. Though Berger does not develop this line of thought at length, he does point to the way in which social class, racial and ethnic peculiarities, gender, and so on, play a critical role in the shape and substance of individual identity. Social structure also is a factor in the relative 'success' of the socialization process — success only defined in terms of the relative symmetry between objective and subjective reality (1966:173). Maximum success (greater symmetry) is more likely to occur in societies with a simple division of labor and minimal distribution of knowledge. Greater rates of 'unsuc-cessful' socialization are more likely in a society marked by a plurality of culture and identity — where the individual subjectively experiences himself and the world as one possibility among the many available. Alternation, the experience in which a new perspective of society and a new identity is acquired, is also more likely under these social structural conditions.

This latter situation points to the artificial and thus inherently precarious nature of reality in general and, for present purposes, identity in particular. The reality of everyday life of which personal identity is a significant part, is maintained as plausible only as long as it remains plausible in the ongoing conversations one has with others, especially significant others (1967:16). When the conversation is interrupted or held in abeyance for any number of reasons, the entire world begins to lose credibility. In Berger's use of the metaphor of the theater, the stage upon which the theater of everyday life is played is made of cardboard and threatens to collapse at even the slightest provocation.

The reference to the metaphor of the theater is not insignificant. It not only illustrates the inherently precarious nature of all social reality, it implies another problem. The metaphor of the individual as an actor playing out roles in a drama called society is one that in Berger's early works (*The Precarious Vision* and *Invitation to Sociology* most notably) is carried out relentlessly, almost to the point of stylistic ponderosity. In this he was not unlike some proponents of symbolic interactionism. One question that arises (unoriginally) is this: is the individual's identity nothing more than the sum total of the roles he plays in society? That is, does Berger have an oversocialized conception of the self? If one were to consider only the more salient themes in these books one might have to conclude that he probably does. A second look at this theoretical work, however, is enough to conclude that he does not. Internalization, Berger emphasizes, is only one part of the larger dialectic. Without an adequate grasp of the other two, one is presented with a picture of society as mechanistic determinism where the individual is solely the product of society. Though Berger would acknowledge society is the stronger partner in this dialectical relationship, he also contends that the individual is not passively shaped by his world. He is a participant in the process, co-producing with others not only the social world but himself as well. More important is Berger's repeated insistence that individuals can say 'No' to the institutional imperatives. The consequences may in the end be grim, but to deny that one has the capacity to say 'No' is to be, in the Bergerian sense, alienated from that which is humanly constructed. It is in the end an exercise in self-deception and 'bad faith'. Quite to the contrary of some opinion, the individual, while a product of society through socialization, is, according to Berger, capable of genuine acts of freedom (philosophically not sociologically defined).

Berger's treatment of institutions and identities is rounded out by his discussion of knowledge or *world views*. Knowledge as shared meanings about reality is, for Berger, the foundation of the world of everyday life as it is objectively defined and subjectively perceived. In the broadest sense, knowledge makes human beings and society as we understand them possible. More specifically, it allows individuals subjectively to integrate the institutional order and locate themselves and their personal relevances within it. Institution and identity, in other words, come together as a coherent reality. It is necessary to accentuate Berger's point that the knowledge by which individuals understand reality and orient themselves is primarily 'pre-theoretical' in nature. Formal theoretical systems of knowledge must be accounted for; yet, overall, theoretical knowledge is a small and by no means the most important part of the social stock of knowledge in a society. Pre-theoretical knowledge is 'common knowledge', usually organized into myths, beliefs, values, maxims, morals, and 'bits of wisdom', and is presented as simple formulae about everyday life. As this pertains to institutions, this knowledge 'constitutes the motivating dynamics of institutionalized conduct' (1966:65). It does so by determining the spheres of institutional activity and the range of possible situations that could emerge within them, by creating the types of roles to be played in any given institution, and therefore, by controlling for all such conduct. In doing this it also constructs the kinds of identities available making it possible for the individual to locate himself and others in the larger social world. Knowledge, again as shared meanings, is for Berger, at the heart of the

47

fundamental dialectic of society. In his words:

It 'programs' the channels in which externalization produces an objective world. It objectifies this world through language, and the cognitive apparatus based on language, that is, it orders it into objects to be apprehended as reality. It is internalized again *as* objectively valid truth in the course of socialization. (1966:66)

Beyond this pre-theoretical knowledge are more formal organizations of knowledge that concern the reality of every-day life (not including specific bodies of highly specialized knowledge which pertain to particular spheres of relevance). At the next level of theoretical sophistication are explanatory schemes that are highly pragmatic and directly relevant to concrete actions. Proverbs, moral maxims, and traditional wisdom provide examples. This knowledge may be further developed and transmitted in the form of specific myths, legends and folklore. Knowledge reaches even greater formality when it gains autonomy from institutions. The highest stage of theoretical organization is found in what Berger calls the *symbolic universe* — 'bodies of theoretical tradition that integrate different provinces of meaning and encompass the institutional order in a symbolic totality' (1966:95). Concep-tually, this term comes very close in meaning to a functionalist definition of religion; yet Berger is very careful to distinguish religion as a specific phenomenon from it. Religion, especially as it is conceptualized in a theological system, is one type of symbolic universe among other historically dominant forms: mythology, philosophy, and science, most notably. Religion as a symbolic universe, however, is a particular concern in Berger's writings (cf. Baum, 1980; Cairns, 1974; Harvey, 1973; Hammond, 1969; Wilson, 1969; Clanton, 1973).

Berger defines religion as a humanly constructed universe of meaning whereby a sacred cosmos is projected. The concept in this definition is the term *sacred* — a quality of mysterious and awesome power which is believed to reside in certain objects of experience (1978:26). Related to, but not equated with, the sacred is the supernatural. For Berger, the supernatural is a finite province of meaning set against the paramount reality of everyday life. Not simply a sub-universe within the mundane world, it is a universe which looms over and even envelops the common-sense reality. The sacred exists within the reality of the supernatural but becomes accessible through collective symbolizations of it. These symbols, by definition, are institutionalized into a symbolic universe or canopy over the world of everyday life. Religion thus represents the furthest extent of man's world building. 'Religion is the audacious attempt to conceive of the entire universe as being humanly significant' (1967:28).

Religion in its theological formulations is, again, one form of symbolic universe. Mythology shares many of the religious assumptions of the theological model but is, according to Berger, 'naive' in the sense that it does not go far beyond positing the universe as an objective reality. It differs from the theological model in terms of a lesser degree of theoretical systematization. Theology, philosophy, and science, unlike mythology, are the property of specialists and are therefore further removed from the common knowledge shared by most people. Science marks this development in the extreme. In its modern expression, science marks an extreme in the secularization of the symbolic universe. The preceding are merely ideal-types Berger offers. It goes without saying that, historically, symbolic universes appear in a large variety of modifications and combinations of these types.

The symbolic universe is a part of the social stock of knowledge in a society. Its significance in Berger's view rests not so much in its existence but in its function. Its importance rests in its capacity to help maintain as stable and plausible the reality of everyday life.

The problem of legitimation

If culture is socially constructed, it is also socially maintained. Overall, Berger's concern with the social maintenance of culture avoids the organizational problems of how to keep the behavior of social actors in conformity with particular societal goals or how to deal with those who for whatever reason deviate from normative expectations. His interest converges instead upon the cognitive problem of legitimation — the task of explaining or justifying the social order in such a way as to make institutional arrangements subjectively plausible. His articulation of this phenomenon is inclusive of but not limited to political institutions or agenda. In keeping with his conception of value-freeness, he also avoids any temptation to infuse normative evaluation in terms of what he considers legitimate and illegitimate. His usage is broadly cultural in its essential features.

In this broader formulation, Berger maintains that at bottom, all knowledge performs legitimating functions. Pre-theoretical knowledge is itself an incipient legitimation inasmuch as the world, when described, is affirmed in its structure. All other legitimations emerge out of this foundation. The symbolic universe is particularly important for its legitimating functions.

Social structurally this means that motivations and institutional configurations are located within a comprehensively meaningful world. The socialist state, for example, is justified in terms of its role in ushering in the Utopian 'goal of humanity' — lasting economic and political equality and justice for everyone. Ideology, as a special form of legitimation, must be understood within this context. Ideology, for Berger, has a specific meaning, narrower than those who define it as a system of ideas; wider than those who define it in political terms. An ideology in Berger's view is a set of ideas which is used to legitimate vested interests of sectors of society (1963a:111). In many cases reality is distorted in order to justify these interests. In most cases there is the deliberate effort to blend ideological thinking in with a larger symbolic universe. In this collective sense, the symbolic universe also orders history. By explaining the past and interpreting the future the present era gains significance. In the West this has often meant the positing of history into a theological scheme — history is moving in a particular direction and toward a specific endpoint.

Individually, the symbolic universe plays a similar role. For one, the discrepant experiences — the plurality of roles and sometimes competing priorities of everyday life — are, in the main, integrated into a meaningful whole. The dominant impulse, in any case is, one of integration. The stages of biography are also ordered in terms of socially relative schemes which allow the individual in reflection to assess whether he or she is living according to the 'nature of things'. Individual identity is legitimated in the same manner, by placing it in the context of a larger universe of meaning (1966:98f). The individual, for example, may sense that his other 'true self' grounded in a cosmic reality remains constant, though his or her experience in the world may contradict it.

In all of this, Berger maintains that the case of religious legitimation is paradigmatic. Unlike positivists or Marxists, he contends that religion historically and on the present scene is far from being epiphenomenal. This may be largely due to the fact that religion has and continues to provide powerful legitimations of the social world for virtually all societies. Religious legitimations are effective because they interpret the order of society in terms of an all-embracing, sacred order of the universe. The human factor is transcended by a supra-human reality; human history is placed within a sacred notion of time. Institutionally, the kinship structure reflects the cosmological family of which all beings including the gods are a part; human sexuality reflects divine creativity; the political structure extends into the human world in the divine power of the gods; indeed, political authority in society is understood as the expression of divine authority. Specific roles within these institutions are located in a parallel fashion. Identity then is also given cosmic significance. Another social psychological dimension of religious legitimation is that of theodicy. Following the Weberian formulation, theodicy for Berger is that which legitimates the marginal and anomic experiences that constantly threaten man's existence. Sickness, injury and death are interpreted as events in a larger cosmic history and as such are given an ultimate significance (1966:101). In the course of everyday life theodicy allows the individual to carry on life after the death of a significant other and to anticipate his own demise without being paralyzed in his daily routines by the terror of it.

Empirically, of course, there are innumerable variations in which legitimation occurs — variability that corresponds to the empirical conceptualizations of the symbolic universe. Though paradigmatic in the religious case, other types of symbolic universes perform the same legitimating functions with varying degrees of success. Culture, the reality of every-day life, is sustained in large measure by the social stock of knowledge — symbolic universes notably. This reality is further maintained by what Berger labels, 'applications of universe-maintaining conceptual machinery': therapy and nihilation (1966:133f). Both are global phenomena inherent in the symbolic universe. Therapy is an application of the legitimating apparatus of a given world to individual cases. It is oriented toward ensuring that actual or potential deviants stay within the parameters of the institutionally defined reality. Exorcism, psychoanalysis, and pastoral counseling illustrate the range of historical possibilities. In contrast nihilation is 'negative legitimation'. Its purpose is the same as therapy but its technique is different. Nihilation denies and delegitimates the reality of phenomena that do not fit into the dominant universe of meaning. This is usually expressed as an assigning of negative or inferior status to all phenomena that stand outside of officially accepted reality.

This entire discussion of culture maintenance presupposes one very important fact, namely that it occurs within a particular social setting. The reality of everyday life as it is objectively held in common with others and as it is subjectively grasped by consciousness depends upon the presence of a social structure within which this reality is taken for granted. The social base and social process necessary for reality maintenance is what Berger labels the *plausibility structure* — a term in the sociology of knowledge which has a rough parallel in the symbolic interactionist term, reference group. Though the concept can and does refer to macro-societal phenomena, the plausibility structure is organized around the individual's primary relationships with significant others. It is principally through interaction with significant others that reality is maintained as subjectively plausible. The vehicle of reality maintenance is, as Berger deftly illustrates in 'Marriage and the Construction of Reality' (1964a), conversation. Moreover, it is conversation with others that mediates the reality of the symbolic universe. When this conversation is interrupted or undermined, as in the case where a plurality of reality definitions are in simultaneous competition with each other, the reality itself ceases to impose itself as self-evident truth. Needless to say, the relative stability and coherence of reality for society as a whole and for the individual is directly related to the inner-cohesion and organizational strength of the plausibility structures.

It should be recalled that the overwhelming part of this 'pure theoretical' work on culture (contained in a variety of sources) proceeds not as a theory of culture proper, but as an implicit theory within the context of an attempt to broaden the orientation of sociology generally, and to redefine the conceptual apparatus and foci of the sociology of knowledge particularly. As such, it is not surprising that a number of spheres of culture and dimensions of cultural phenomena are not given proper consideration. For example, Berger does not deal with the place of rites and rituals in collective life and their significance for the individual. And while his familiarity with the social scientific research on the range of socio-cultural life is apparent, he does not pursue the implications of his conceptual insights for any of these areas systematically (religion being a notable exception). His own applications of this perspective to an understanding of social stratification, marriage and family issues, race and ethnicity, work and occupations, ethics and morality, deviance and social control have all been superb but they invariably leave one wanting a more complete exposition of the topic from this perspective wedded with the current research in the particular field. But the significance of Berger's work lies in a conceptual apparatus that uniquely contextualizes all of these substantive areas of culture, and does so in a way that appreciates the phenomenon of study as human phenomena. At the same time is capable of being subject to the rigor of empirical analysis. Indeed, within this theoretical work is an implicit call for theoretical elaboration and empirical application to the range of socio-cultural phenomena. And because of its suitability for empirical application, it is subject, as any scientific theory should be, to the rigor of empirical verification or falsification. Sadly, there have been far too few efforts to do any of this.

Berger's analysis of culture is significant for other reasons as well, though only one will be mentioned in this context. This refers to the actual substance of his approach. Briefly, one of the great weaknesses of American social psychology (role theory/symbolic interactionism in particular) has been its inability conceptually to account for social structure — to build a bridge between the micro and macro social worlds. Berger can be credited with shoring up this weakness and actually building the framework for a bridge between those two spheres. This is done in his general synthesis of a theory of institutions with a dialectical social psychology. The role (institutionally located, socially bestowed by significant others and subjectively appropriated into consciousness) is the key link. Knowledge (socially defined and objectivated but subjectively internalized) is the key mechanism. In this synthesis the inter-relatedness of intersubjective meanings, primary relationships, role, identity, institution, social structure and symbolic universe is firmly established. Among other things, this enables the social scientist to comprehend the various dimensions of culture simultaneously as social facts and intersubjective meanings. In this, social psychological reality and micro-sociological phenomena are adequately placed in the context of a particular social structure, yet social structure is not reified into a static, lifeless form detached from the social processes out of which it was originally constructed and continues to be maintained. Given the state of social theory at the time Berger published these writings, this was no small feat. In ways that many fail to recognize, theoretical sociology has not been the same since. As observed earlier, this dialectical approach was in effect an attempt to bridge two major paradigms in sociological theory: the social definitionist (the Weberian) and the social factist (the Durkheimian). Others have attempted the very same task but not with the success of Berger. Though it is clear even from this review that Berger leans toward the Weberian and the phenomenological tradition, his efforts remain perhaps the most promising attempts to achieve reconciliation between the two paradigms.

Culture and social change

Though oriented and perhaps even inspired by classical social theory, Berger approaches the relation between culture and social change from a unique angle, one derived from the sociology of knowledge. His pre-eminent concern is with the effects of modernization upon human consciousness. These effects, of course, are wide-ranging, influencing core assumptions about everyday life, an experience of time and temporality, the formation and experience of the self, the interpretation of symbolic universes of meaning (religion in particular), and the nature of political reality. Berger, in his characteristically sweeping and comprehensive fashion, covers all of these areas.

Of all of his intellectual forebears, it is chiefly from Weber that Berger derives his orientation. As with Weber, the infrastructure of modernization is rationality, especially as it is embodied in the economic and political apparatus of society. In this he sharply distinguishes himself from Marxist theory on the subject, a theoretical perspective that explains the peculiarity of modern institutions almost entirely in terms of the peculiarity of modern capitalism. For Berger, functional rationality is the determining variable in modern society, yet it is not simply a functional rationality which spontaneously emerges and is diffused in society. Of principal importance in the origin, evolution, and transmission of modernization is the rationalized, indeed technologized, economy and its related institutions. Of critical importance in the inner-dynamics of modernization are the rationalized political institutions of society, particularly the modern bureaucratic state. In the Weberian usage, Berger labels these the primary carriers of modernization. In short then, Berger defines modernization as 'the institutional concomitants of a technologically induced economic growth' (1973:9). Implied is the recognition that there is no completely modern society, but 'only societies more or less advanced in a continuum of modernization'. Modernity, a term which also fits prominently in Berger's theory, is simultaneously a period of a society's history and a cultural world distinguished by the institutional and symbolic configurations of a technologically induced economic growth.

Among the secondary carriers of modernization, socio-cultural pluralism of the modern city figures most prominently in Berger's theory of modern culture. Though secondary to technology and bureaucracy and indeed in its modern expression a distant consequence of them, pluralism he argues gains a notable autonomy of its own. While many have discussed the consequences of the technological economy and of bureaucracy, Berger (almost alone) is to be credited with bringing to light the incalculable effects on everyday life in the modern world of pluralism (Hammond, 1969).

Features of modern culture

Technology, bureaucracy and pluralism, then, are the dominant institutional features of modernity. All, Berger maintains, have distinct effects on human consciousness. Truer to the argument, each of them has a corollary at the level of consciousness. Together they allow one to speak of modern consciousness or, in turn, the symbolic universe of modernity. True to Weberian form, Berger maintains that technological production was initially carried in the West by industrial capitalism though this economic structure is presently only one among other possibilities. A number of key elements of the world-view of modernity are derived from technological production. Among these are the divisibility of the fabric of reality into components and sequences, the multi-relationality of these components (people, material objects, cultural objects, etc.), a problem-solving or tinkering attitude toward life (including social experience and identity), and a corresponding orientation of progressivity in the events and actions of life. Overall they foster an 'engineering mentality' toward life (1973:112). Berger's contention is that while this cognitive orientation is derived from some form of engagement with technological production, there is a carry-over into the rest of the individual's life (including the way he views politics, seeks education for his children, approaches his hobbies, and manages any psychological problems he may have).

Bureaucracy, carried by a large number of institutions in contemporary society, but particularly by the modern state, also has distinct consequences for the world view of modernity. Among these are the perceptions that society is organizable and manageable as a system, that the various elements of experience are capable of being ordered into a taxonomic structure where the affairs of daily life are to be carried out in a regular and predictable fashion, that human rights are related to bureaucratically identifiable rights. As with technological production, this orientation is originally derived from the various encounters the individual has with bureaucratic structures but is carried over into an overall perception of the world.

Underlying both technological production and bureaucratic organization and thus also carried over into the totality of experience is a basic functional rationality. This is not an intellectualization of the world but rather 'the imposition of rational controls over the material universe, over social relations and finally over the self' (1973:202). An interesting dimension of functional rationality is the rationalization of time-consciousness. According to Berger, both technology and bureaucracy in their modern forms presuppose temporal structures that are 'precise, highly quantifiable, universally applicable and . . . capable of spanning past, present, and future within the same categories' (1973:149). This is a form of temporality that is, in the main, completely foreign to the majority of traditional societies. The minutes and hours in a day and the days, weeks, and months in a year of the modern West contrast sharply with the typically broader temporal structures of most traditional societies — usually defined by the recurring rhythms of natural phenomena.

Pluralism, as Berger contends, manifests itself in several ways in modern societies. Its most important form is sociocultural pluralism — the pluralism of symbolic universes where values, morality, and belief systems of a sometimes very different character are placed in a position of having to co-exist. Historically, this kind of pluralism was carried by urbanization, but at present it is also carried by mass communications and public education. Objective pluralism, Berger argues, has a parallel in subjective consciousness in the plurality of life worlds. Whereas individuals throughout most of history experienced the world of everyday life as more or less unified and integrated, individuals in the modern situation typically have sectors of their everyday life confront them as different and sometimes discrepant worlds of meaning and experience. The life-world that people inhabit in the relatively modern society is usually segmented or pluralized to a high degree. At the level of consciousness, individuals are aware of those who maintain values and beliefs that may be different from one's own. This awareness has the general tendency of undermining the taken for granted status of one's own beliefs and values.

Two other dimensions of modern life weigh significantly in Berger's theory of modern culture. These are dimensions which constitute part of the structural backdrop of modernity, each having important consequences for specific dimensions of modern experience. The first is a social structural configuration; the second is a social structural process.

In concert with a large body of contemporary German scholarship (Habermas, not least), Berger contends that there is a general though clearly distinguishable split in the social structure of the modern world between the public sphere and the private sphere. The public sphere is dominated by enormous public institutions, the bureaucracies organizing such areas of human activity as government and law, business and commerce, labor, health care, education, communications, the military, and even religion. These *megastructures* dominate most of the areas of human activity, but not all of it. There is an area left over — what German scholars have called the private sphere, the sphere of the intimate. This sphere is constituted principally by activities surrounding the family, voluntary associations, and a network (of varying sizes) of primary social relationships. The individual in modern society is usually aware (though to varying degrees) of this dichotomization. In the course of daily life, the individual migrates back and forth between these spheres. The split between these spheres is most often recognized as the difference between the work world and home. Yet, it should be apparent, the individual confronts the public sphere through more than his or her occupation. Typically, the individual relates to this sphere in a variety of different roles: as taxpayer, citizen, consumer, and so on. Thus everyone, even those not employed in the public sphere, is confronted in many ways by it.

The public/private dichotomization in modern life emerges from a combination of the increasing size and specialization of the institutional structures that accompany modernization. Yet as Berger cautions, the boundaries that separate them are somewhat porous. The carry-over of public-sphere rationality previously mentioned is indicative of this, but so are the increasing in-roads made by the state into family life — in child care, family sustenance, and so on. Berger indicates that the public/private dichotomy has a number of important consequences for modern life but these are best understood as they interact with the structural process.

The concept *deinstitutionalization* is Gehlen's and can only properly be understood within Berger's adaptation of Gehlen's theory of institutions. Briefly, if institutions are those human constructions which shore up what the individual lacks in his or her biological constitution, providing a background of clearly defined channels of behavior and social relationship as well as an overall sense of intelligibility about the world, then deinstitutionalization is the process whereby that background begins to erode. The rules of discourse in social life, expectations of others' behavior and conduct, and stable guides to one's own personal behavior all begin to deteriorate. What could formerly be taken for granted in everyday life now appears as a range of possible choices for the individual. The fabric of everyday life begins to wear thin as a result of this process. Modernization, according to Berger and Gehlen, is characterized by an increasing trend toward deinstitutionalization.

Berger is careful to make clear that this process does not occur uniformly in modern society; it in fact bears special relation to the public/private split just mentioned. The megastructures of the public sphere typically confront the individual as highly imposing yet incomprehensible structures, often experienced as abstract, overly rational, and impersonal. In this sense, one may describe them as overly institutionalized. In very concrete terms, these structures are *alienating*. Deinstitutionalization, then, is not a problem of the public sphere but of the private sphere. And as Berger shows, most of the areas of life in the private sphere have been deinstitutionalized to one degree or another. Not least among these are the rules behind courtship and marriage, child-rearing patterns, the definitions of sexuality, rituals of everyday social relationship and discourse, leisure habits, and so on. In Berger's words, the institutions of the private sphere are all notably 'under-institutionalized'.

Such is the situation of modernity. Modernization in its structure and in its essence is a process that has radically changed the face of civilization and continues to do so in those parts of the world presently confronted by it. Unlike many of his ancestors in this intellectual tradition, Berger is very careful to make explicit the fact that this ideal-type process expresses itself historically in many ways according to the culture from which it emerges or into which it is exported. Countless variations can and do exist. The constraints modernization imposes upon the structure and culture of society do tend to be constant, however. Culture in its multiform expressions — institutions, symbols, and symbolic universe and consciousness — is radically transformed.

The special case of religion

A further dimension of Berger's discussion which has been implied but which deserves more careful review, if only because it figures so prominently in his theory of modern culture, is the deinstitutionalization of meaning that accompanies modernization, especially in its advanced stages. Though never explicit about this, Berger implies that deinstitutionalization is brought on by the convergence of a number of specific modernizing processes. The most important to Berger is that of pluralism, an endemic feature of both the public and private sphere. In the former, it expresses itself as different institutional worlds segmented from one another; in the private sphere, one sees the effects of sociocultural pluralism. Pluralism of both kinds posits different and often opposing interpretations of the world in close geographic and symbolic proximity to one another. Over time the tendency is for the normative claims of each to cancel out the normative claims of the other. The social base for any particular sphere of meaning and relevance is also undermined by the existence of others. The various plausibility structures, as they exist in the larger social world and as they intersect in the individual's life, are in implicit competition with one another. Social mobility, for similar reasons relating to shifting plausibility structures, also contributes to the deinstitutionalization of meaning (1964a). Rationality and its implications for critical reflectiveness play a noticeable role as well. The long and short of it is that in these specific processes (and perhaps others) deinstitutionalization occurs and, in this, the taken-for-granted certainties of everyday life are eroded. The definitions of reality that previously made the human condition possible, much less easier to bear, are gravely weakened. While the predicament this poses is serious for all symbolic universes, it is particularly menacing to the religious world view.

Most discussions of the relations between modernity and religion have focused on the social structural level and, in the main, Berger concurs with their conclusions: religious authority and religious symbols in the West have been routed out of one area after another of institutional life. The private sphere is religion's last bastion. In conventional social-scientific terms, this phenomenon is labeled the secularization of social structure; in Berger and Luckmann's terms, 'the privatization of religion'. Berger sees this phenomenon leading to the 'demonopolization' of religious traditions and therefore to religious pluralism. The pluralistic situation creates a market situation in which religious institutions must compete. 'The religious tradition which previously could be authoritatively imposed, now has to be marketed − . . . "sold" to a clientele that is no longer constrained to "buy"' (1967: 138). Ecumenicity, Berger argues, is a response to this situation and is not unlike economic cartelization − the market competition is rationalized 'by reducing the number of competing units by amalgamation and also by dividing up the market between the larger units that remain' (1963a: 87). Berger's concern, predictably, does not reside with the finer details of secularization of religion at this level, but rather at the level of consciousness and world view.

Berger defines secularization as 'the process whereby sectors of society and culture are removed from the domination of religious institutions and symbols' (1967:107). He considers it intrinsic to modernization. With regard to culture, narrowly defined, secularization is seen in the decline in the religious content of art, philosophy, and literature and in the rise of science as an autonomous and naturalistic perspective on the world. Because the plausibility structures for religious belief have now been relegated to specific 'enclaves' of the private sphere, religious conceptions and symbols tend to be plausible only when one is situated there, and even in the private sphere the plausibility structures tend not to be very durable. It is here that the 'crisis of faith', as a sub-case of the larger 'crisis of meaning' in modern culture, takes place. Faith, if a plausible option at all to the individual, becomes like everything else, a matter of choice or 'consumer preference'. Secularization at this level means that individuals come to view the world and their lives 'without the benefit of religious interpretations' (1967:108).

The irony of the situation is that secularization is rooted in a highly disenchanted Judeo-Christian heritage. Berger maintains that the '"disenchantment of the world" begins in the Old Testament' and is traceable through the emergence of Christianity and then through the Protestant Reformation. While scholarly opinion generally concurs with the Weberian thesis that Protestantism and secularization are historically connected, Berger maintains that the historical connection runs deeper — to 'the earliest available sources for the religion of ancient Israel' (1967:113). Religious developments originating out of this tradition are causal in the formation of the modern secularized world. It is in this sense that Berger argues that 'Christianity has been its own gravedigger' (1967:129).

The problem of plausibility is simultaneously a problem of legitimation. In the history of the Christian Church since the Reformation, Christianity's legitimacy has been continually assaulted. Pietism with its emphasis on individual religiosity rather than dogma, Enlightenment rationalism and its connection with Protestant liberalism, and the horror of the First World War constituted major assaults. Theology since Schleiermacher has offered one effort after another to cope with this situation and, in the main, coping has entailed 'cognitive bargaining' involving significant accommodation to the spirit of modernity (1967). Catholic and Jewish theologies have undergone similar contortions in attempting to cope with modernity (1977b).

The problem is not just one of institutional legitimacy but of the capacity of religion to legitimate. Historically, social arrangements and institutions typically received their greatest and most effective source of legitimation directly from religious symbols and authorities. Religion that has been privatized still has the capacity to legitimate the larger institutional order but its effectiveness as a 'sacred canopy' for society as a whole, one grounded in the cosmos, is greatly diminished. On the American scene these values have been 'hollowed out'. It would appear that Berger falls into the Durkheimian tradition in recognizing a general societal requirement for a 'collective conscience' or a symbolic universe that integrates the disparate definitions of reality into a symbolic totality for the individual (1973:109). In this regard Berger has spoken of secularism as a 'quasi-religion of the [American] republic' (1979a). Yet compared to the religious symbolic universe, 'the symbolic universe of modern societies will be a loosely assembled and far from stable constellation of reality definitions' (1963a:109).

The greater problem for Berger and one largely ignored by most of the social scientific community is the problem of legitimation at the social-psychological level — the problem of theodicy:

> Modern society has threatened the plausibility of religious
> theodicies, but it has not removed the experiences that call
> for them. Human beings continue to be stricken by sickness
> and death; they continue to experience social injustice
> and deprivation. The various secular creeds and ideologies
> that have arisen in the modern era have been singularly un-
> successful in providing satisfactory theodicies (1973a:185).

In *The Sacred Canopy* Berger offered a view of secularization principally as it is derived from the Western example. Though never stated explicitly, the image presented is one of a process that is more or less pervasive and historically inevitable corresponding to the spread and augmentation of modernization. It would appear that Berger has modified this view somewhat in recent years. In one forum he posed the question, has secularization 'resulted in a loss or decrease of religious experience or has [it] only delegitimated such experience in the officially established world view?' (1978: 36). Berger readily acknowledges that secularization does not mean that religious belief and practice disappear altogether. Even under the most hostile of conditions, strong religious impulses exist. Modernity, he posits, can even create conditions favorable to a temporary religious resurgence. Secularization occurs at different levels: at the level of consciousness (Berger's chief concern), it minimally entails the weakening of the plausibility of religious perceptions of reality among large numbers of people, especially true when the world view of secularity becomes established by the cognitive elites in society. At this point, the delegitimation of religious symbols and authority and hence the secularization of institutional structures is well on its way to becoming accomplished fact.

Modernity and the self

Modern culture is a historically unique phenomenon. Its consequences for the individual and for society as a whole are monumental. Everyday life in modern societies in Berger's view is radically different in its essential structure and complexion from that which is found in most societies that have not undergone modernization. For individuals and their world views, this presents something of a crisis situation — a crisis that becomes particularly intense for the individual in his experience of himself.

Berger views the self as a social product that the individual himself helps to create. As a human construction it is highly malleable — influenced strongly by the various institutional arrangements into which it is placed. Modernity, then, has very specific consequences for the self. The individual experiences himself or herself as he or she is perceived in the different spheres of life. Identity in the public sphere tends toward anonymity and impersonality; in the private sphere it is grounded in personal meaning and activity. In this sense the portion of self-identity tied to the role of 'worker' may be experienced as being 'less real' than identity as a private person or a family member. The carry-over of functional rationality also tends to approach personal identity and psychological difficulties as something to be tinkered with; as problems to be solved. From a historical and cross-cultural perspective, this is sufficiently noteworthy but in Berger's view, the consequences of modernity for personal identity are much more profound.

Among the many aspects of world view that have been deinstitutionalized in the modern setting, one of the more important ones is identity. In his review of Lionel Trilling's *Sincerity and Authenticity* (1973), Berger notes that pre-modern societies are typically characterized by a high degree of symmetry between self and society, between subjectively experienced and institutionally assigned identity. For most of human history, people's identities were tied directly to what they did. More specifically, work has long been not only a source of livelihood but also a source of self-identification. What is more, in most pre-modern situations, one's everyday activity, including occupation, was legitimated directly or indirectly by mythological or religious symbols. In many cases, identity was passed on successively from one generation to the next. One does what one's father does; one is who one's father is, and so on. This clearly did not mean that people were always happy about their place in life, but that they had a firm and stable identity, one they took for granted as the way things were.

Stable identities, Berger has argued, can only emerge in reciprocity with stable social contexts. Given the inherent instability of a pluralized and under-institutionalized private sphere, there can only be shakiness in the way people are defined and thus, define themselves. In *The Homeless Mind*, Berger identifies four characteristics of modern identity. First, modern identity is relatively differentiated, principally as a result of the plurality of social worlds which the individual experiences in contrast to the relatively coherent life-world structured in most pre-modern societies. Just as the discrepant realities of these social worlds are much more difficult to integrate, so too are the discrepant identities derived from these institutional spheres. Modern identity is also relatively open. While there are some aspects of identity which have a quality of permanence to them after primary socialization, there are others which do not. Vocation, for example, previously tied to kinship, has been deinstitutionalized. The modern individual is left to decide from a broad range of possibilities, 'who he wants to be'. Thus the individual is not only capable of planning an identity but is able to change into a number of identities through the course of life, and for this reason is 'conversion-prone'. As Berger notes, 'this open-ended quality of modern identity engenders psychological strains and makes the individual peculiarly vulnerable to the shifting definitions of himself by others' (1973:77). At the same time identity in the modern situation is unusually reflective. Borrowing again from Gehlen, Berger notes that a corollary of deinstitutionalization is the process of *subjectivization*. When assumptions of everyday life are rendered implausible and no longer taken for granted, conduct, relationships, morality, and the like, are transferred to the realm of choice. Individuals must necessarily turn inward to the subjective to consider, reflect upon and explore their new found choices. Subjectivization is the process of turning inward; identity itself becomes an object of deliberate attention. Subjectivity becomes complex and interesting, acquiring previously unknown depths. The final characteristic of modern identity is that it is unusually individuated. In this situation, Berger claims that individual subjectivity becomes the standard of reality and as such it attains an important place in the hierarchy of values. 'Individual freedom, individual autonomy and individual rights come to be taken for granted as moral imperatives of fundamental importance, and foremost among these individual rights is the right to plan and fashion one's life as freely as possible' (1979a:79).

The problem of identity in pre-modern and modern contexts can be put in different terms. The transition from pre-modern to modern society (particularly in the West) has been marked by a parallel transition in conceptions of identity; from honor to dignity (1970). Berger maintains that honor is a direct expression of status which functions to maintain boundaries between social equals and social inferiors. Honor also infers a certain standard or code of behavior and etiquette in varying social relationships. Dignity on the other hand pertains to intrinsic humanity stripped of all socially imposed roles or norms. 'All people regardless of race, creed,

color, gender, and so on share an essential dignity.' Both
concepts imply what is at the heart of the transition from
traditional to modern societies, namely, 'the concept honor
implies that identity is essentially, or at least importantly
linked to institutional roles. The modern concept of dignity,
by contrast, implies that identity is essentially independent
of institutional roles' (1973:90). In Berger's view honor, like
the term chastity, has become obsolete. 'At best, honor and
chastity are seen as ideological leftovers in the consciousness
of obsolete classes, such as military officers or ethnic grand-
mothers' (p. 83). With the disintegration of stable institutional
structures in which identities were formally imbedded, honor
naturally becomes meaningless. Identity, then (at least in the
West), becomes defined apart from and sometimes against the
institutional roles in terms of intrinsic dignity. Institutions
then cease being the place where the self is located but a
reality that distorts and alienates the self.

But freedom has its costs. Identity not firmly located in a
social structure, world view detached from the safety of a
sacred cosmos and undermined by weakened plausibility
structures and a social structure of vast and alienating proportions together constitute nothing less than the 'crisis of
modernity'. Consonant with the assessment of Sartre, Camus,
Riesman, Trilling, and others, Berger argues that modern man
suffers 'from a deepening condition of "homelessness"':

> The correlate of the migratory character of his experience
> of society and self has been what might be called a meta-
> physical loss of 'home'. It goes without saying that this
> condition is psychologically hard to bear. It has therefore
> engendered its own nostalgias — nostalgias, that is, for
> a condition of 'being at home' in society, with oneself and,
> ultimately, in the universe (1973:82).

The limits of modernity

Berger is not at all blind to the many advantages modernity
has brought about for the course and quality of life. He is, in
contrast to the majority of analysts of modern culture, one
of the few actively to celebrate modernity for those reasons.

But optimism aside, modernity engenders very real 'discontents' for those who are a part of it. The aggregate effects of these discontents is summarized by the notion of a metaphysical sense of homelessness. Modernity erodes precisely that which man's psychological and organismic constitution requires. Given Berger's assumptions, it is reasonable to predict that these discontents will have very real consequences in the social world. From the beginning of the modern era, these discontents have engendered formidable resistances in the shape of anti-modern ideologies and movements. Resistances to modernization in advanced industrial societies, Berger labels demodernization; those that occur in societies still undergoing modernization, Berger identifies as counter-modernization. Thus for example, much of the dynamic of the Third World can be understood in terms of counter-modernization (traditionalistic/nativistic and nationalistic ideologies); much of the political and cultural unrest in North America and Western Europe can be understood in terms of demodernization (counter-cultural ideologies, religious resurgence of certain types and neo-romanticist trends in art and literature). Modernization, then, has built-in limitations. It is neither an inevitable nor irrevocable process even though its inner dynamics appear inescapable.

One adjunct of Berger's work on modern culture has been a contribution to a larger body of social scientific research on what has been variously labeled the New Class, the knowledge class, or the cognitive elite. In Berger's view there is an intriguing connection between the discontents of modernity, demodernization, and the New Class. A number of scholars on the political right and left have written about the New Class or knowledge class and on a number of points there is agreement. Berger himself has adopted a broader conceptual framework concerning this phenomenon, one generally in line with whatever conceptual consensus exists. Most briefly, the knowledge class is a new class (post-Second World War), a feature of post-industrial society, and like all other classes, a relatively amorphous entity. What distinguishes this class from others is the fact that its members derive their livelihood from the knowledge industry — in the production, distribution and administration of knowledge or of symbols. Thus, it is not only made up of intellectuals (though they constitute an important part) but the larger educational community, those associated with mass communications, public sector services, and public interest groups. Though stratified within itself, it is overwhelmingly made up of middle- and upper-middle-class, college-educated individuals. The world view of the knowledge class tends to be secular humanistic. Because of its virtual control over the society's educational apparatus, technical expertise, mass media, its demographic concentration in urban areas, and because of its general affinities with the world view of modernity, it can in one sense be understood as the most modern class in human history. Yet as such it is, perhaps more than any other class, susceptible to the discontents spawned by modernity.

Berger was not the first to note that there is an affinity between intellectuals and left-liberal ideology of a socialistic or quasi-socialistic mold. This affinity extends beyond intellectual circles to the larger knowledge class, not in any uniform manner of course but certainly in a disproportionate way. On balance then, the new class is generally antagonistic to capitalism and 'big business' (1981b). Most of the explanations of this affinity, from Pareto, Schumpeter, Kristol, and Aron, suggest that their political values and ideologies are viewed as consistent with their collective interests. So Berger has argued along similar lines (1978). None the less, he also posits an additional factor for this alliance, one which is not usually addressed. Berger suggests that the discontents of modernity demand some kind of solution. Socialism or as Berger puts it, the 'socialist myth' has at its core an implicit protest against the discontents of modernity. 'Socialism is a faith in renewed community' (1977b). What is more, in its mythic form it has the capacity to synthesize modernizing and counter-modernizing themes. It fully incorporates the dominant ideas, values, and aspirations of modernity (including history as progress, the perfectibility of man, scientific reason as the means of liberation from illusion), but it goes on to include a Utopian/quasi-Utopian vision of the world (or at least society) as human community. In Berger's assessment, the weakness of this perception is that it views capitalism alone as the source of these discontents and that the abolition of capitalism would bring about these problems to an even greater intensity — 'the alienations of the socialist state, a political formation that (at any rate to date) has shown itself to be endemically totalitarian' (1977a:137). But the totalitarian outcome is not somehow accidental. In Berger's perspective, the essence of totalitarianism of the right or left is the effort to recreate a symmetry and integration that has been seriously challenged by the modern situation. The totalitarian vision, not unlike the socialist vision, is one that offers to ease the psychological despair of homelessness by promising to integrate the disparate worlds of individual and collective experience into an experience of 'at-homeness' (1972).

There is a certain theoretical liaison between Berger's general theory of modern culture and the mass society critique of the 1950s. Both theories point to a world where traditional beliefs and morals are in near-constant flux, where individuals are more estranged from others (part of a 'lonely crowd'), where each person assumes a multiplicity of roles, thereby losing a coherent sense of self, and yet is becoming increasingly rational in all spheres of life — similar in feeling to the notion of the 'regulated man' or even the 'organizational man'. Berger's analysis differs in significant ways too. He is not at all concerned about the impassioned 'search for status' in a society that has become heterogeneous and undifferentiated — a 'mass'. Nor is he concerned with a 'deterioration of high culture' into a bland, uncritical, low-brow culture. In this regard, Berger shares none of the conservative bias of the mass society critics, many of whom sought a defense of an aristocratic and privileged culture. Neither does he share the romanticist bias of a yearning for a bucolic serenity of the *Gemeinschaft* — quite to the contrary. The mass society critique also posited the transition from traditional to mass society as an inexorable, historical progression with little if any possibility of change, resistance, innovation, adaptation with creativity, and so on. Berger's approach is much more cautious in its sensitivity to historical variation. Moreover, it is not fundamentally 'Western-centric'. And while in places Berger's ideal types evade scientific scrutiny, on the whole they are still more prone to empirical verification and differentiation than are those of mass society theory.

Conclusions

Culture is, assuredly, a perplexing phenomenon — ubiquitous in presence, complex in detail, and as such overwhelming and incomprehensible in its totality and in its intricacy. Any attempts to grasp it all in analysis will, therefore, be frustrated from beginning to end. Social scientists are compelled from the outset either to explore one or several facets of culture carefully or to attempt to construct a theoretical scaffolding which endeavors to comprehend the essential elements of the whole. It is not always clear whether the few who attempt the latter are wise or foolish. Certainly some do a more convincing job than others. Berger as a generalist is plainly one of those whose performance has been brilliant. His undertaking has been ambitious and energetic in the sense that he attempts to cover an immense span of intellectual territory. This, of course, has its advantages and disadvantages. Among the disadvantages are that it can easily lead to a very thin covering of some dimensions of cultural life. Berger's work is not faultless on these grounds. One significant area is the connection between the micro and macro social worlds. As argued earlier, Berger can be credited with constructing a scaffolding between these two spheres of social life, but, although the connectives are in place and sturdy, the road is not yet sturdy enough to facilitate heavy traffic between the two. Too much is left to implication given the novelty of this bridge-building effort. What is especially called for is an elaboration of the problem of identity *vis-à-vis* the social structure. Berger's theory, it would seem, could profit greatly from a more systematic discussion of the different empirical relationships between the contents of socialization and different social structural configurations — the structural bases of personality.

Another area deals with his analysis of secularization. Berger acknowledges that religious systems, indeed any legitimating systems at all, have both cognitive and normative dimensions. The normative aspects are representative of the moral aspects of the symbolic universe. In Berger's work on secularization, however, he focuses almost entirely on the cognitive dimensions. The prophetic, judgmental side of religion in modern society, something of crucial import in the dynamics of contemporary religious phenomena relative to modern society, is neglected in Berger's work (cf. Hammond, 1969). Extending his theoretical paradigm to an understanding of moral change and the secularization of traditional moralities would then be a fruitful and important endeavor.

These are a few areas in Berger's corpus that could be developed more completely; there are others as well. Yet it would be inappropriate to fault him for the book or books he should have written.

Berger is often faulted, however, for two other reasons which are worth mentioning here. One is that his theoretical work remains at an 'elementary' (though not unsophisticated) stage. There are no systematic propositions or postulates offered, no testable hypotheses given, no operationalization of concepts. True theory goes beyond the kind of groundwork Berger provides and offers a systematic set of relationships that can be gauged in the empirical world as true or false. In fact, critics have argued, it is not evident how much if any of Berger's work can be translated into formal theory of this kind.

The other criticism is that Berger's work on culture in general, and on religion and modernization in particular, does not offer much that is new. The intellectual path Berger beats has been 'well-trodden' before, and though he is careful to acknowledge his forebears, he does not go very far beyond them. Only occasionally is one presented with a distinctly new concept. Why then, it is asked, is there all the fuss about Peter Berger? These criticisms have grounding in truth. For those stirred by formal theory, there is little to become excited about from a reading of Berger. There is little, to be sure, in his corpus that resembles a properly formed set of hypotheses. What he offers is not formal theory but an *orientation*, a new angle in the sociological perspective. And while it is true that he does draw from a large body of sometimes well-known theory and research, he presents his theory not so much as a synthesis, but as a distillation of this literature (cf. Wilson, 1969). One is made aware of the relevance of a disparate body of theory for an understanding of various dimensions of culture, the result being a unique way of looking at the data of everyday life. The paths are well-trodden, yet Berger succeeds in casting an interesting light upon these paths such that new insights are gleaned.

What can be said, in the final analysis, for the phenomenological approach to culture — or more precisely, Berger's representation of it? There is, among the critics of phenomenology and of Berger, a tendency to view phenomenology and phenomenological sociology as an enterprise in the vaporous and ghostly regions of the phantasmal world of human consciousness. This image is not entirely out of character. The transcendental phenomenology of Edmund Husserl with its concern for 'essence', the Platonic ideals of reality (such as the 'Transcendental Ego') comes close to fitting this description. Phenomenology is clearly rooted in Germanic intellectual idealism, and in some cases it avoids empirical reality altogether. Having said this, it is also important to note that much has happened in this tradition since the time of Husserl, most notably Alfred Schutz and Maurice Merleau-Ponty. This is clearly not the place to elaborate upon the intricacies of their respective works in phenomenology, the ways their conceptualizations differ from each other, from Husserl, Dilthey, and the other idealists, but let it suffice to say that they succeeded in making phenomenology much less foreboding — more empirical and thus more conducive to the empirical sciences.

In what way is phenomenology *à la* Schutz, Merleau-Ponty, and Berger empirical? It is empirical in the sense that it is concerned with human experience in everyday life. Its task is (most generally) to describe human experience as it is lived and not as it is theorized about — to account for social reality from the point of view of the actors involved. Consciousness as a web of meanings is a phenomenon of subjective experience; none the less, as Berger writes, 'it can be objectively described because its socially significant elements are constantly being shared with others' (1973:14). Moreover, as it has been noted, cultural objects 'manifest the intentionality of those who produced [them]' (1964a:202). In this way, human experience — subjective meanings, intentionality, consciousness, and the like — is empirically available for systematic description. Meanings are shared and it is from these shared meanings that the social scientist derives his concepts and ideal types. In Schutzian phraseology, 'the constructs of the social sciences are, so to speak, constructs of the second degree, namely constructs of the constructs made by the actors on the social scene'.

It is important to recall that phenomenology is only a descriptive method. It begins and ends there. It is only a prolegomenon for the social sciences which like all empirical sciences are concerned mainly with causality. Thus, cultural analysis, even for Berger, begins where phenomenology leaves off.

Berger insists that cultural analysis implies no preference for qualitative over quantitative techniques (1981a:46). The issue is what kind of method is best capable of obtaining the evidence being sought in a particular research endeavor. Quantitative methods, he maintains, have a place 'as long as they are used to clarify the meanings operative in the situation being studied.'

To concede with Berger that phenomenology can be empirical is not to argue that this approach is without problems. As seen in Berger's phenomenological description of modern consciousness, though it is empirical at base, it is not easily given to empirical verification or empirical differentiation. It is also unclear how reproduceability is to be facilitated: though meanings are shared in common and though intentionality is embodied in cultural artifacts, the social scientist's interpretations of these meanings can vary considerably. Moreover, there appear to be no built-in checks beyond the broadest postulates that guide the research act to ensure with any precision the validity of one's interpretation of the meanings operative in the situation being studied.

Another problem is that cultural products or artifacts are often objectivated in the social world in very different ways than their producers originally intended. Subjective or intended meanings, in different words, need not correspond with cultural products. Herein is strong justification to follow the cue offered by the structuralists, namely to view cultural artifacts as concrete observable objects not reducible to subjective meanings and to analyze them as such. Indeed, Berger's concept 'symbolic universe', as a total system of beliefs, values, morals and knowledge, as well as his adaptation of Schutz's concept 'finite province of meaning', suggest close convergence with the structuralists at this point. None the less, though consequences do not always correspond to original intentions, Berger would maintain that in the ongoing social process, intentionality is still operative in the way individuals relate to and interact with their world, and thus, the phenomenological approach should play a part in any analysis of social reality.

It is important to remember that the impulse behind phenomenological sociology from its beginning was that it was to be a corrective to various positivistic sociologies which had the endemic tendency to reify social phenomena. Positivism is especially guilty of this because of its tendency to construct third and fourth order constructs (e.g. through mathematical modeling) and to analyze social reality entirely with reference to these constructs. What one has is a conceptual apparatus that is removed from the social reality in successively distant degrees. The problem with positivism from Berger's point of view (and all of phenomenology) is that constructs that have been reified in this manner are unable to penetrate what is specifically human in human reality — a serious fault in a science that takes this human reality as its avowed object. In Berger's words, the difficulty in positivistic sociology is that 'even if it begins by modestly assigning to its constructs merely heuristic status, it all too frequently ends by confusing its conceptualizations with the laws of the universe' (1966:186f). As a corrective, phenomenology *à la* Schutz has suggested that the constructs social scientists employ must always comply with the 'postulate of adequacy'. This means that the concepts used in social scientific analysis and interpretation must be constructed in such a way that they are understandable to the actors engaged in the activity being studied. In other words, a concept or sociological interpretation is 'adequate at the level of meaning' if it corresponds to the common-sense interpretation of everyday life.

As Berger recognizes, an exclusive emphasis upon subjective

meanings leads to idealism; an emphasis on the objectivity of social reality leads to sociological reification. Both are distortions of social reality. These two, he maintains, are correct only when seen together. The virtue of the phenomenological approach to the analysis of culture, historically, has been in its providing a measure of balance to the positivistic tendencies dominant for so long in sociology. Berger's work itself does not achieve that balance to an entirely satisfactory degree. For many it leans uncomfortably toward idealism. His notion of the dialectic between individual and society and his own extensive work in the analysis of culture, however, do offer important clues for achieving such a balance.

3   The cultural anthropology of Mary Douglas

Like Berger, Mary Douglas approaches culture primarily from the standpoint of everyday life. Hers is a world of ordinary symbols, rituals, objects, and activities all of which dramatize the construction of social life. Although her training is in cultural anthropology, she has been less concerned than many of her colleagues with abstractions about values and world views, focusing instead on the more observable artifacts of culture in daily life — its goods, its views of what is clean and dirty, the ways in which people treat their bodies, and so forth. In this respect she goes one step farther than Berger in making everyday reality the centerpiece of her investigations. For him, it is the philosophical immediateness of everyday reality that serves as a vehicle for considering other, more abstract, more remote, modes of legitimation. For her, everyday life is itself the focus of interest. Accordingly, she has written most about such seemingly mundane matters as dirt, food, bodies, jokes, material possessions, and speech.

In all her work Mary Douglas has been concerned with classification schemes — the patterns or cultural structures — that give concrete symbols their meaning and are reaffirmed in ritual and speech. Deviance, dirt, and other things that are regarded as pollution are important for her because of what they reveal about systems and rules of classification. The very basis of cultural classifications, of order in social life, she argues, is the presence of symbols that demarcate boundaries or lines of division. These are the ways in which collectivities differentiate themselves from other collectivities (external

The cultural anthropology of Mary Douglas

lines) and subgroups or individuals are differentiated from one another (internal lines). It is, in fact, this concern for symbolic boundaries that underlies her most ambitious theoretical contribution, the attempt to describe whole societies and whole cosmologies in terms of the nature and clarity of various combinations of external and internal lines of demarcation — what she calls 'grid' and 'group'.

Her interest in classification schemes derives from questions about the ordering of collective life. Here she departs noticeably from Berger. His considerations on culture, while including such macroscopic concerns as the modernization of institutions, harken back repeatedly to the needs of the individual — for meaning and purpose, for a secure world in which to live, for a sense of personal coherence. Douglas, in contrast, favors questions about the kinds of cultural distinctions that are important for the functioning of whole groups, and the vehicles by which these distinctions are made known. This emphasis reflects her indebtedness to Durkheim. She has taken seriously the Durkheimian injunction to treat social phenomena as facts *sui generis*. At the same time, the world she describes is never far removed from the individual. It is the world in which self concepts are constructed; it is dramatized in the linguistic codes that the individual assimilates as a child; and it involves the individual as a moral actor who feels constrained and compelled by the valences attached to objects and actions.

Because of its concern for the concrete, the mundane, Douglas's work requires a somewhat different approach to understand and appreciate it. It is pitched at a relatively low level of abstraction, depends heavily on induction, and is defended on the basis of revealing examples rather than philosophical argument. Although Berger also relies heavily on induction and example, there is a clear sense in which the philosophical and theoretical assumptions of phenomenology have guided his work. With Mary Douglas, the theoretical underpinnings of her approach to culture remain more in the background. She is less consciously concerned with defending a metatheoretical approach than with deriving 'middle level' observations about the ordinary components of culture. In this, she represents a clearly different style from Habermas and to a lesser extent Foucault. Both of the latter have shown far greater interest in the most general assumptions underlying the social sciences and have gone to great pains to reformulate these assumptions at the most general level. For them, it is necessary to deal specifically with the content of these abstractions or, in the case of Foucault, to keep in mind his desire to chart innovative theoretical waters at the same time that he considers concrete historical problems. The avenue by which one comes to understand and appreciate Douglas's work, by comparison, is to consider her own examples and inductions, and then by extension and application to other cases — music, art, dawn and dusk, and so on — come to a point of being able to evaluate the generality of the conceptual apparatus with which she has worked.

Intellectual assumptions

Along with writers such as Erving Goffman, Kai Erikson, Robert Bellah, and Guy E. Swanson, Mary Douglas falls generally within the Durkheimian tradition in the social sciences. She emphasizes, as just mentioned, the collective nature of human existence; she is concerned with questions of moral order; she pays attention to the ways in which rituals dramatize moral order. More than any of the others, she has followed the Durkheimian method of drawing on primitive cultures to illuminate the general nature of these processes. She has also advanced that aspect of Durkheim's work which, in collaboration with Marcel Mauss and others, examined the nature of classification systems. Unlike Durkheim, however, her work displays less of the dualistic quality which led Durkheim to differentiate culture from social structure and in his work on religion to reduce the former to a functional adjunct of the latter. As a cultural anthropologist, Douglas has concentrated chiefly on culture itself, concerning herself with its internal patterns, rather than its ultimate causation or determination by other factors. In this quest she has naturally paid close attention to the work of Claude Lévi-Strauss and others in the structuralist tradition. But again she has borrowed selectively from this tradition while remaining critical of some of its more general assertions.

The Durkheimian legacy

Among the classical theorists who have shaped the social sciences, Durkheim is virtually the only one whose imprint can be recognized clearly in the work of Mary Douglas. And this is one of the characteristics which distinguishes her approach. While it is true that Durkheim's influence can be seen elsewhere, particularly on Foucault and to a lesser extent on Berger and Habermas, each of the other writers has been influenced less by Durkheim than by some other writer or tradition. In contrast with Berger and Habermas there is little evidence of phenomenology in Douglas's work. Unlike Foucault and Habermas she bears litttle affinity with Marx, And unlike Berger, there is less evidence of having been influenced by Weber.

Mary Douglas knew what Durkheim realized, that there is a social basis for human thought, and the brunt of her work has been applying that understanding to the belief systems of modern society. She feels, though, that 'Durkheim did not push his thoughts on the social determination of knowledge to their full and radical conclusion' (1978a:xi). This occurred, she argues, because of the assumptions Durkheim made. First, he thought primitives were different from moderns. 'Primitive groups are organized by similarities; their members are committed to a common symbolic life. We, by contrast, are diversified individuals, united by exchange of specialized services' (1978a:xi). Second, he believed in objective scientific truth, that is, the possibility of non-socially determined knowledge. She disagrees with both of these points. The difference between Durkheim's mechanical solidarity, the social glue of similarity holding primitive society together, and organic solidarity, the social glue of interdependence holding modern society together, while important, does not separate primitives from moderns. The mechanical-organic scheme cuts across both, as there are conditions of mechanical and organic solidarity in both primitive and modern societies. From this point of view secularization is just another cos-mology generated by a certain kind of social organization. Modern societies are secular because of their social organ-ization, which is not modern as opposed to primitive, but represents particular patterns of social relations. If primitive societies possessed the same form of social organization they would also have a secular cosmology, albeit in the form of primitive religion. Evolutionary movement, then, is not only not the same as movement from mechanical to organic solidarity, but it is not a move from religion to science either. The pygmies, a primitive society, do not have much, or any religious life, which Douglas attributes to their low level of social organization. A similar, more tightly organized primitive society, should have a richer religious life as a function of their different social relations.

As for science, she suggests, 'It is entirely understandable that Durkheim should have internalized unquestioningly the categories of nineteenth-century scientific debate since he strove to have an honorable place in the very community from which the standards of conduct emanated' (1978a:xvi). Here, then, is the heart of the problem of analyzing modern culture. A community's socially constructed picture of the cosmos, like science, is protected by not only being defined as sacred and dangerous, but more fundamentally, as truth — that is, as reality and *a priori* nature itself. For modern society this insight suggests that the very things we consider the most real — hence scientific — are, in fact, the most religious.

> The second essential character of the sacred is that its boundaries are inexplicable, since the reasons for any particular way of defining the sacred are embedded in the social consensus which it protects. The ultimate explanation of the sacred is that this is how the universe is constituted; it is dangerous because this is what reality is like. (1978a: xv)

Douglas welcomes the relativity implied in carrying the Durkheimian program to our own world. For her nothing is sacred. Scientific and hygienic explanations are just as much legitimations of social order as the primitive's gods and spirits. This assumption gives her the desire to unveil our ideas about hygiene, cleanliness, dirt, and pollution, and on a much broader scale, whole cosmological systems. From daily cleanliness rituals to world views, she makes the basic assumption that culture is rooted in daily social relations.

Structuralism

Her indebtedness to structuralism is weaker than is her debt to Durkheim, but she has examined its assumptions critically as a way of clarifying her own approach. As we shall see again in discussing Foucault, the grand design which Lévi-Strauss set forth in his structuralist reorientation of anthropology has been fraught with sufficient weaknesses and has paid off sufficiently little that few of the more recent generation of cultural anthropologists, including Douglas, have expressed enthusiasm for it. Yet she does go part of the way down the structuralist path.

She grants — although this assumption is not unique to structuralism — that all experience is received in a structured form. Like Berger, she assumes that reality must be symbolically organized ('constructed') in order for us to interpret it and take action in relation to it. With Lévi-Strauss, she also grants that the structuring of experience often comes about through a system of paired opposites: male/female, black/white, good/evil, purity/dirt. These are the kinds of distinctions that let us know when we have encountered a symbolic boundary. But she does not go so far as Lévi-Strauss does in suggesting that *all* classification systems are comprised of paired opposites or that the secret to comprehending these systems is to identify parallel patterns among these opposites. Generally she has refrained from looking at highly integrated patterns of this type in her own work, pointing at most to similarities between the surface content of symbols (bodies, for example) and implicit beliefs accompanying these symbols. For her, it is often problematic whether a symbolic boundary exists at all, and the interesting question therefore is to discover how clearly one is evident, how permeable or impassable it is, and how social activities dramatize its presence. Nor does she accept the structuralists' assumption that paired symbolic opposites correspond to some physiologically determined pattern in the human brain. While the brain may in fact operate on binary impulses, these are of little use in understanding why cultures actually get structured the way they do. She looks instead to the nature of social groups for answers. Where there is frequent interaction among a closed group of persons, for example, the messages necessary for co-ordinating group activity are likely to be manifest in behavior itself and, therefore, need only minimal articulation in codified speech or ritual. In a loosely knit collectivity, on the other hand, the infrequency and diversity of activities may require that more be spelled out in an elaborate, complex system of articulated symbols.

Her other difficulty with structuralism is its presumption to have identified a method of discerning the 'real' meaning of a myth or of some other cultural system. To assume that an anthropologist can figure out exactly what is being communicated, and why, by looking only at the arrangement of paired opposites in some cultural system, she argues, is clearly presumptuous. The reason is that there is never just *one* meaning that can be conveyed by a system of symbols. The anthropologist simply identifies one of a number of the possible meanings that can be conveyed, and while this 'interpretation' may be insightful for some purposes, it is always less than the set of rich meanings which are there in the social setting itself. In short, the anthropologist engages in a kind of *reductionism* by claiming to have discovered the one true interpretation of any myth. A better approach, she claims, is to become sufficiently immersed in the social situation itself, paying attention to all of the ways in which communication occurs, so that one is at least sensitive to the multiplicity of meanings present. She departs from structuralism, then, in rejecting its strongly positivistic assumptions, preferring instead to acknowledge with the hermeneuticists the relativity of meanings to the larger contexts in which they occur.

In practice she has been careful in her work not to 'second guess' either the primitive or modern materials with which she has worked. She makes no claims to have discovered higher truths or deeper meanings in these materials than their originators saw. But she has also attempted more than sheer description of these original or surface meanings. She seeks to discover why symbols occur in some settings and not in others, and why patterns among symbols are sometimes more complex than at other times. To answer these questions she has herself focused heavily on patterns or structures or relations among symbols, rather than on the specific meanings hidden in these symbols.

Douglas's perspective on culture

Her ideas on culture seem to have evolved gradually, beginning with field work in the Belgian Congo among the Lele in the early 1950s. Here she studied the role of animals in Lele religious symbolism (1957, 1963). These studies of Lele cults, pollution beliefs, and hygienic concerns made her realize that there were more general processes of classification and 'that a much closer fit between religious and other forms of organization could be revealed through studying higher level classification systems' (1978a:204). In *Purity and Danger* (1966) she presented many ideas on the social basis of pollution beliefs. Her thinking became systematic with the publication of *Natural Symbols* (1970) and *Cultural Bias* (1978b). In these books and some of the essays in *Implicit Meanings* (1978a) and *In the Active Voice* (1982a) she spells out her more general ideas on the link between culture and society. The work up through *Cultural Bias* represents an ever more systematic approach to the relationship between forms of social organization and whole cosmologies. Then, these general ideas are extended to new substantive areas. In *The World of Goods* (1979), written with Baron Isherwood, she explores the communicative role of economic goods, and in *Risk and Culture* (1982), written with Aaron Wildavsky, she looks at the environmental movement as a belief system generated in sectarian groups.

To explore systematically the full range of Douglas's ideas it will be useful to begin with her analysis of dirt and cleanliness.

Pollution and moral order

A simple artifact often holds the essence of a whole social system. For Marx, it was the commodity which held the secret of the capitalist mode of production. Understanding how a commodity is produced, exchanged, and attains value illuminates the essence of capitalism. For Durkheim, it was the simple Australian totem which contained the essence of religion. Understanding why such seemingly non-significant objects as carved sticks or stones were sacred was the key to understanding not only Australian aboriginal religion, but the elementary forms of all religious life. For Mary Douglas, the artifact is simple, obvious, and everyday, much like Marx's commodity and Durkheim's totem. It is dirt; ordinary plain dirt. Understanding what makes things dirty or clean is the basis in her work for understanding the innermost secrets of the moral order itself and the means whereby society periodically renews and reaffirms its basic social relations and collective sentiments.

Dirt. Why the 'ugh' and 'ick', and the compulsion to clean things up? At first glance it seems that things are dirty in and of themselves. We know dirty shoes when we see them, we know hands that need washing, stuff on the carpet, and spots on white shirts. But why are they dirty? If it is the 'dirt' itself which makes things dirty, why are bits of leftover dinner dirty when they fall on the floor, but clean when they are put into the waste basket, which is still on the floor, only in a different place? Or better yet, why are shoes dirty when placed on a table, but not when on the floor? In considering these examples, it soon becomes clear that it is not so much the bits of food or pieces of earth themselves that elicit the response 'dirty', but their *location*.

> We are left with the very old definition of dirt as matter out of place. This is a very suggestive approach. It implies two conditions: a set of ordered relations and a contra-vention of that order. Dirt, then, is never a unique, isolated event. Where there is dirt there is a system. Dirt is the by-product of a systematic ordering and classification of matter, in so far as ordering involves rejecting inappropriate elements. (1966:48)

From this point of view what is dirty is relative. It is not earth *per se* that is dirty, but earth on the carpet; it is not cigarette ashes *per se*, but their location on chairs. What is clean and dirty depends on a system of classification and the location of matter within that system. As she says:

> It's a relative idea. Shoes are not dirty in themselves, but it is dirty to place them on the dining-table; food is not dirty in itself, but it is dirty to leave cooking utensils in the bedroom, or food bespattered on clothing; similarly, bathroom equipment in the drawing room; clothing lying on chairs; out-door things in-doors; upstairs things downstairs; under-clothing appearing where over-clothing should be, and so on. In short, our pollution behavior is the reaction which condemns any object or idea likely to confuse or contradict cherished classifications. (1966:48)

Now generalize this point about dirt to whole systems of purity, and from purity to questions of the sacred and holy. 'This idea of dirt takes us straight into the field of symbolism and promises a link-up with more obviously symbolic systems of purity' (1966:48). In short, systems of classification form the basis of Douglas's approach to culture.

But what is the system here? There appear to be at least two things. First, society's normative rules, the do's and don'ts that not only regulate behavior but more fundamentally divide reality into forms and structures, the shapes of which constitute the basis of human thought, a point recurringly made from Durkheim and Mauss (1963) on primitive classification systems to Lévi-Strauss (1966) on the logical basis of primitive thought. Although we tend to focus upon moral rules themselves, there is, second, a more fundamental level at which order exists. This is the very definition of things, independent of, or *a priori* to, their moral evaluation. We live within what Peter Berger calls 'symbolic universes', referring to the fact that our taken for granted reality is socially constructed, constituting a 'sacred canopy' (Berger, 1967) which not only legitimates our experiences but defines the very nature of our existence. 'Legitimation not only tells the individual why he *should* perform one action and not another, the distinctly moral component; it also tells him why things *are* what they are. In other words "knowledge" precedes "values"' (Berger and Luckmann, 1966:93, 94).

While Being precedes its moral evaluation, it is also true that this very factual social reality — the myriad categories, classifications, types, labels, and definitions involved in naming things and transforming the formless void of unorganized experience into meaningful social reality also appears to be simultaneously infused with moral significance. It is not just that this is this and that that, but that this is in its right, correct, appropriate, and just place. In effect, social reality legitimates itself by its mere existence, independently of any larger set of rules, myths, or formally religious beliefs.

That which is dirty, unclean or deviant, is that which does not fit into its appropriate category.

> If uncleanliness is matter out of place, we must approach
> it through order . . . Defilement is never an isolated event.
> It cannot occur except in view of a systematic ordering of
> ideas. Hence any piecemeal interpretation of the pollution
> rules of another culture is bound to fail. (1966:53, 54)

Being dirty or clean, then, is not just a matter of factual location; it is not just a purely cognitive issue. It is not that scraps of food are clean when on the plate and dirty when on the table, but that they *should* be on the plate, and *not* on the table. There is a moral dimension to reality that makes the question of classification, and misclassification, also a question of right and wrong. The moral order is coterminous with social reality such that things have at one and the same time a factual and moral existence. When we say 'that's the way things are', we are not only making a factual statement about the mechanical appropriateness of nature, but a moral evaluation of that order.

The moral order is so infused into our structuring of reality that activities such as sorting, tidying, cleaning, and putting things in their place in general, act to reinforce not only the structure of social reality but of moral sentiments too. That moral component of assigning reality to different categories becomes particularly apparent when things get out of place. At that point we are socially obliged to reset the structure of things and thereby reinforce the fabric of social and moral order. Traditional religious rituals obviously have something to do with reaffirming social order, and as such are considered part of society's arsenal of ritual. But so does straightening our desk, brushing off our coat, and tidying up in general.

These mundane activities also carry ceremonial and ritual significance. The moral order enlists a cognitive classification system — the social assignment of things to their place — as a ritual mechanism for its periodic renewal. This is what Douglas realized. In theory, every activity that involves bringing some order is something of a social ritual, for the act of re-establishing order is one means for re-establishing society, which is itself nothing but ordered relations.

In *Purity and Danger* she makes this point by contrasting the propensity to see cleanliness as a matter of hygiene, with similar purity rituals in primitive societies, which are seen as magic and religion. 'Our practices are solidly based on hygiene; theirs are symbolic: we kill germs; they ward off spirits' (1966:44). Her point here is that modern pollution fears are as much magic and ritual as those of the primitives. The modern propensity to identify pollution rituals with hygiene reflects our use of conceptions of ultimate reality (science and medicine) to justify and legitimate social order.

If dirt is the by-product of ordering and classifying, and society is the source of rules and categories, then dirt is very much a normal part of social life, like crime and deviance. The presence of order — society — makes disorder possible. Rules, boundaries, categories, and all sorts of cognitive and moral classification systems create lines that are crossed and categories of things for which there are exceptions. Not everything fits, and what doesn't becomes deviant, odd, strange, or criminal. From this point of view crime and dirt are the same phenomena. Both represent something out of place. For crime, it is behavior which violates the normative and legal order; for dirt, it is matter which is not in its correct place. When things get out of place the normative and legal order is challenged and society re-establishes that order by taking ritual action. For individuals and crime there is punishment. For dirt there is a clean up (we often speak of 'cleaning up' crime, too).

Fear of pollution, then, is like fear of moral deviance. Shoes do not belong on the kitchen table and parents should not have sex with their children. Both involve things and behavior out of place, and as such, a threat to the larger moral structure from which their place derives. But deviance and dirt are normal and functional, and our reaction to them is one of the basic social mechanisms to renew and redefine social rules and boundaries. We find out on a daily basis what is what by the reaction of ourselves and others to the violation of social rules.

This idea, it is worth observing, has been taken one step further by Kai Erikson (1966), who argues that society need not wait for someone, or thing, to violate its rules. Society can have the same moral revitalization ceremony by simply treating people as if they had, in fact, violated the moral order. Through looking for scapegoats and the ritual persecutions of witch-hunts (cf. Bergesen, 1977; 1978), imaginary enemies and deviants are created and ritually punished for crimes they never committed. Erikson argues that this occurs in two general ways. First, other things being equal, a society will manufacture a relatively constant volume of deviance, like so many people being arrested for moral crimes, or so much political subversion discovered. Second, given what he calls a 'boundary crisis' in the moral order, the volume of deviance will dramatically increase, constituting something like a crime wave. The reasoning here is compatible with Douglas. Given a threat to a collectivity's boundaries or collective identity, it will respond by ritually persecuting people (scapegoating, witch-hunting, etc.) as a means of re-drawing the threatened boundaries. If a community is not sure of what it stands for, or of its collective identity, then the discovery of those who would oppose its central values is a means for reaffirming those very collective moral purposes. The political show trial, purge, and Congressional investigation, utilized to create subversives, are all ritual mechanisms in the periodic renewal of social order.

This process is also applicable to Douglas's understanding of dirt and pollution rituals. We often experience things out of place but do not react. Given some crisis in our social relations, however, we suddenly announce that 'this place is a mess' and proceed to clean it up. It is the social crisis, not things out of place, that suddenly makes the room seem messy and dirty.

In general, then, moral deviance, including the experience of dirt, is created in two ways. The first, the original

89

Durkheimian proposition adopted by Douglas, centers upon individuals crossing moral boundaries, or things being out of place, e.g. shoes on the table or people committing crimes. When this occurs people are mobilized to reset the order and reaffirm lines and categories by either cleaning up the mess or persecuting the deviants. Things are put back in their place. Here the effort and ceremony of cleaning up are much like the trial and purge. Both are ritual ceremonies which draw attention to the violated moral order, whether that be purported communist sympathizers in the State Department or a messy room. The second process involves the movement of moral boundaries. Here people do not violate the rules, but the rules are moved to reclassify people as deviant, subversive, or unclean. In this way the community can actually 'manufacture' deviance, which is exactly what a witch-hunt is all about. An aroused community persecutes people who have done nothing. The community need not wait for individuals to stray across the moral boundaries; the boundaries can be shifted to redefine individuals as being on the other side. Authorities can always declare some activity illegal or immoral and prosecute, no matter whether the same thing in a different place or at a different time was 'legal'. The community's rules shift when there is a crisis in its corporate identity or collective existence, creating an organic need to manufacture enemies to bring the community closer together.

The idea of dirt, filth, and uncleanliness representing things which defy their place is illustrated by Douglas when she tackles the old question of the biblical admonitions of Leviticus. At a general level the question is familiar to everyone: why did the ancient Israelites forbid eating pork? The most popular answer was because they somehow linked pork with disease. She dismisses this kind of argument as 'medical materialism', a term taken from William James. In other words, hygienic reasons are sought for obviously religious beliefs. Instead, she suggests the admonitions reflect animals, or categories of animals, which do not fit into a broader cosmological scheme.

The underlying principle of cleanliness in animals is that

they shall conform fully to their clan. Those species are unclean which are imperfect members of their class, or whose class itself confounds the general scheme of the world.

To grasp this scheme we need to go back to Genesis and the creation. Here a three-fold classification unfolds, divided between the earth, the waters and the firmament. Leviticus takes up the scheme and allots to each element its proper kind of animal life. In the firmament two-legged fowls fly with wings. On the earth four-legged animals hop, jump or fly. Any class of creatures which is not equipped for the right kind of locomotion in its element is contrary to holiness . . . Thus anything in the water which has not fins and scales is unclean (xi, 10–12). Nothing is said about predatory habits or of scavenging. The only sure test for cleanliness in a fish is its scales and its propulsion by means of fins.

Four-footed creatures which fly (xi, 20–26) are unclean. Any creature which has two legs and two hands and which goes on all fours like a quadruped is unclean (xi, 27), or creatures endowed with hands instead of front feet, which perversely use their hands for walking: the weasel, the mouse, the crocodile, the shrew, various kinds of lizards, the chameleon and mole . . .

The last kind of unclean animal is that which creeps, crawls or swarms upon the earth . . . Whether we call it teeming, trailing, creeping, crawling or swarming, it is an indeterminate form of movement. Since the main animal categories are defined by their typical movement, 'swarming', which is not a mode of propulsion proper to any particular element, cuts across the basic classifications. Swarming things are neither fish, flesh or fowl. Eels and worms inhabit water, though not as fish; reptiles go on dry land, though not as quadrupeds; some insects fly, though not as birds . . . If penguins lived in the Near East I would expect them to be ruled unclean as wingless birds. (1966:69, 70)

This analysis of Hebrew dietary laws has come under criticism from a number of scholars. One is Ralph Bulmer, who suggests that there are any number of 'real' reasons why the pig was avoided. He suggests, 'It would seem equally fair, on the limited evidence available, to argue that the pig was accorded anomalous taxonomic status because it was unclean as to argue that it was unclean because of its anomalous taxonomic status' (Bulmer quoted in Douglas, 1978:272). Note the logic here: it is the complete opposite of Durkheim's understanding of why things are designated deviant, criminal, or in the present case morally stigmatized as unclean. In the *Division of Labor* (1933) Durkheim wrote '. . . we must not say that an action shocks the common conscience because it is criminal, but rather that it is criminal because it shocks the common conscience.' Douglas's version would be something to the effect that we must not say an object (like the pig) is out of place because it is dirty, but rather, that it is dirty because it is out of place. Bulmer's version is just the opposite: 'the pig was accorded anomalous taxonomic status because it was unclean' rather than being out of place and therefore unclean.

Environmental pollution

In an essay written with the political scientist Aaron Wildavsky, *Risk and Culture* (1982), Douglas turns her attention to macro-pollution concerns in contemporary America. Her concern is to identify the social conditions which affect the selection of certain technological and environmental dangers, for 'the perception of risk is a social process . . . [and] society produces its own selected view of the natural environment, a view which influences its choice of dangers worth attention' (1982:6, 8).

The specific object of their attention is the environmental protection movement which arose during the later 1960s and mid-1970s, and identified a number of dangers to the environment, such as nuclear power plants, the industrial pollution of rivers and lakes, oil drilling on the California coast, and so forth. She claims confidence in the natural world has turned to doubt and asks why? Her answer is the growth in sectarian groups and their value systems. She argues sectarian groups have:

three positive commitments: to human goodness, to equality, to purity of heart and mind. The dangers to the sectarian ideal are worldliness and conspiracy. Put into sectarian terms, worldliness appears in big organization, big money, and market values — all deny equality and attack goodness and purity; conspiracy includes factions plotting secret attack, transporting evil into an essentially good world. Infiltration from the evil world appears as Satanism, witch-craft, or their modern equivalent — hidden technological contamination that invades the body of nature and of man. *We shall argue that these ideas and these dangers respond to the problems of voluntary organization: they are the daily coinage of debate in groups that are trying to hold their members together without coercion or overt leadership.* The remedies most easily proposed in such organizations are to refuse to compromise with evil and to root it out, accompanied by a tendency toward intolerance and drastic solutions. These organizations depending on the voluntary principle also tend to reject wealth. Nature in the wild, uncorrupted by social artifice, equivalent to a society without social distinction, is their preferred emblem of godliness and symbol of unworldliness. (1982:10, 11, emphasis added)

In this kind of analysis the origin of pollution beliefs (concern with dangers to the environment) are rooted in those groups who most vociferously expose them, rather than being seen as a cosmological concern of the society as a whole. Here whole cosmologies are reduced to the ideological positions of sectarian interest groups, and beliefs are seen as a product of conflict, and competition. This is quite a micro-orientation, and something of a shift from Douglas's previously stated commitment to more macro-analysis.

This brings us back to Douglas's desire to take Durkheim into modern society and expose all the clearly ritualistic and religious beliefs as just that: ritual and religion, and not real concerns with hygiene. It would seem, though, that the Durkheimian task is more difficult than it initially appears, for to use some Douglas on Douglas, as she used Durkheim on Durkheim, she has provided something of an analog to the 'medical materialism' in her own account of modern pollution beliefs. First, there is the general social scientific prejudice toward a more individualistic analysis of modern culture. Belief is often seen as ideology, and thus as the cultural expression of material interests of particular groups, rather than as the cosmology of the collectivity as a whole.

For instance, the idea of 'public opinion' and its concern for the environment is a perfect example of a kind of Durkheimian collective representation symbolizing the corporate reality of the national society. But, there is a modern propensity to regard the study of public opinion *sui generis* as a false reification of a collective reality, the public, which doesn't exist. What does exist, and what can be, and is studied, are the beliefs of concrete individuals, making the question of public opinion the study of the attitudes held by millions of individuals or, in Douglas's case, sectarian groups rather than a singular collective representation. When we study more primitive or traditional societies there is no difficulty in analyzing the relationship between their social organization and their cultural expressions. Gods, spirits, and sacred forces, the equivalent of today's 'public opinion', are all seen as the Durkheimian mirror of the underlying patterns of social organization. But, when it comes to analyzing modern society, then suddenly the gods are dead, or reduced to the psychological attributes of individual psychologies, or with, of all people, Mary Douglas, the organizational difficulties of voluntary associations. 'Border theories [the concern with environmental pollution] emanate from its social predicament of chosen voluntariness. *In the process of solving the formidable problems of voluntary organization*, it forms and declares its views about danger and conspiracy' (1982:189, emphasis added). Where is the Durkheim that so brilliantly illuminated her earlier studies of pollution and taboo? Pollution concerns now have been reduced to a kind of social glue to hold members to voluntary associations.

Historically, sectarian groups have tended to have the general ideological orientation Douglas describes, but this has more to do with their form of social organization than with problems of voluntary association. Revolutionary parties, religious organizations, and Utopian communities all have simple dichotomous cosmologies, of good insides and bad outsides. But these are a function of their organization as solidary corporate groups, where the black–white cosmology mirrors the clearly bounded, inclusive–exclusive, social organization of these groups. Environmental beliefs, though, are not limited to the groups which may champion them the most. They are general and as such part of the overall cosmology of the whole society.

If, as seems useful to suggest, environmental pollution concerns are more general than those of a few special interest groups, what are their social origins? The answer lies with the very Durkheimian analysis Douglas has made in her earlier work. Pollution concerns appear when social lines and boundaries are threatened, and since these environmental pollution concerns are national, they need to be examined in relation to national identity crises.

In general, pictures of nature represent ideas about ultimate reality, and as such are part of society's cosmology. To the extent that culture mirrors the social body in which it appears, the sudden appearance of a troubled nature should reflect social troubles in that society. The sudden concern with dangers to the environment, then, represents something of a 'pollution scare' that passed through the United States, and perhaps through a good part of the western world during the later 1960s and mid-1970s. Although groups like the Sierra Club, Friends of the Earth, and others championed these causes, the paranoia and concern over the environment was more general. There were national celebratory rituals, like 'Earth Day', bringing forth millions of people to affirm their concern with the environment and federal legislation to 'protect the environment'. This concern with the environment was institutionalized, and made a responsibility of the state itself. The national collectivity was clearly aroused, from the average citizen to the bureaucratic apparatus of the state.

This brings us back to the original Douglas question: why did this concern suddenly appear? Surely it was not because the environment suddenly became dirty. The amount of waste and dirt in the environment was probably increasing, but this had not generated a concomitant growth in environmental concerns. The environment was 'dirty' before the mid-1970s and dirty after, but the hysterical concern dramatically surfaced and then largely went away in just a few years. Why? The answer lies with Douglas's explanation of pollution concerns. 'As I see it, ritual pollution also arises from the interplay of form and surrounding formlessness. *Pollution dangers strike when form has been attacked*' (1970:126, emphasis added). The idea here is similar to Erikson's boundary crisis hypothesis.

The later 1960s and mid-1970s witnessed a number of national traumas including race riots, student protest, defeat in the Vietnam War, and the exposure of political wrongdoing in the highest office, the scandal of Watergate. These were traumatic years, and they also witnessed a turning point of American power in the larger world-system: American hegemony, so dominant since 1945, seemed by the mid-1970s to be declining.

> Looking back, the pivotal year in the American decline was perhaps 1973, a year that began with the United States' military withdrawal from Vietnam and the final collapse of the American dominated monetary system of fixed foreign exchange rates. It closed with the quadrupling of oil prices by the Middle East-led oil cartel. American political and economic hegemony had been successfully challenged. (Crittenden, 1979:1)

All of these social crises of the late 1960s and mid-1970s constituted a crisis in America's self-confidence, which manifested itself in a loss of confidence in a great number of social institutions (Bergesen and Warr, 1979), and in the environment itself. The social crisis was mirrored in the cultural sphere with a sudden concern over the very existence of nature. A crisis in the social base generates a crisis in its collective representations. Concern over the future of America was symbolized as concern over the future of the environment. The mid-1970s seem to have been years of shock and anxiety for the nation as a whole. The loss of confidence in the environment, and in institutions which deal with it, was, it can be argued, part of this 'loss of confidence' that passed through American society. Finally, it should be noted, that even this national analysis may be at too low a level of analysis, for the environmental movement was present in many western nations during this same period, suggesting that it was a function of shifting global social relations, and not just the dynamics of one country.

Symbolic boundaries and marginal situations

Douglas's analysis of dirt and pollution centers upon things or people who do not fit the classification system and hence are considered morally reprehensible. But she also points out that the boundaries of these classification systems generate feelings of awe, danger, and potency. To make her point she expands on the Van Gennep (1969) imagery of society as a house, with rooms being well defined status categories and corridors being transitional zones that are filled with fear and danger. But, she argues, along with margins, power also resides in a well structured social system.

> Where the social system explicitly recognizes positions of authority, those holding such positions are endowed with explicit spiritual power, controlled, conscious, external and approved . . . where the social system requires people to hold dangerously ambiguous roles, these persons are credited with uncontrolled, unconscious, dangerous, disapproved powers — such as witchcraft and evil eye. (1966:120)

It might be added that along with power, emotional states are similarly recognized. Executives, army officers, and bureaucratic positions in general, are thought to create people with either a narrow range of emotions, or emotions clearly under control. Artists, poets, and people with more vaguely defined roles are conversely thought to be capable of a wider range of emotions.

If 'intelligence' is considered a disposition similar to the imputation of power or emotion, then the imputation of intelligence that is uncontrolled and unconscious creates a state commonly referred to as something like 'genius'. Intelligence reflects ability, and unbounded and uncontrolled ability gets very close to our idea of genius. As such, we tend to think of occupants of more ill-defined roles, like artists, poets, or musicians, as carrying out their role from an un-bounded reserve of potentialities — genius — whereas occupants of more well-defined roles are seen as gathering their ability from identifiable sources, like training, experience, schooling, and so forth. Where abilities are bounded, there is also a sense in which the source of those abilities is definable. The military general is good because of battlefield experience; the professor, because of a degree from Harvard; the executive, because of organizational experience (he 'knows the ropes'). But the poet is good because he has something ill-defined — inspiration — and the composer of music is good because he is a natural genius. It would be hard to convince anyone that it was the classical training in music that made Mozart or Beethoven what they were, or that art school made Picasso a great artist. These are clear cases of genius, and a similar military genius, say Napoleon, would also be attributed abilities above and beyond what was learned from the academy. The point here, it seems, is that when behavior transcends the accepted expectations of a role, we attribute it with extraordinary powers and abilities, like the idea of genius.

Douglas also argues that 'pollution is a type of danger which is not likely to occur except where the lines of structure, cosmic or social, are clearly defined' (1966:136). This position represents the strand of Durkheim's thought which derives from the *Elementary Forms* and holds that a sense of power and potency goes with the presence of a strong corporate order. Here the gods are sacred, powerful, and dangerous. She seems to be arguing, though, that power, potency, and danger are generated *both* by the presence of a well-bounded social order and by the presence of social breakdowns, marginal situations, and ill-defined areas, such that both form and nonform generate the same social experience. It might be that positive rites, such as celebrations and ceremonies, are intended to reaffirm corporate social reality and negative rites, such as pollution beliefs, pertain to boundaries and ill-defined areas. But this hypothesis oversimplifies: there are moral interdictions against touching, seeing, and polluting sacred religious objects which are collective representations of corporate society, not the margins of social life.

How then can order and disorder generate the same beliefs? Possibly a strong corporate order is accompanied by ritual and pollution beliefs to reaffirm its collective reality, with the margins of the system having an extraordinary sense of potency and danger because the contrast between form and nonform is so great. Further, given a boundary crisis (the Erikson concept), a strongly bounded system will generate more of a ritual response (manufacturing deviance and dirt) than a society with weaker boundaries and less corporate reality. Conversely, a weaker corporate order will have less ritual and fewer pollution beliefs, as there is less collective reality to renew; and if all its social relations are somewhat ill-defined, the presence of ambiguity at the boundaries will be less threatening and hence not emit such a sense of power and danger. Finally, given a boundary crisis, there will be less of a response, as there is less corporate reality to be threatened and ritually reaffirmed.

Danger in the margins: dawn and dusk

As Douglas suggests, the margins of social life create a variety of experiences. Large breaks in the continuity of social reality, like death, are filled with dread and horror. Smaller gaps create feelings of anomie or identity crisis, and temporary breakdowns in the organization of interaction can create very mild identity crises, like embarrassment (Goffman, 1967). There is also a certain *ecstasy* that can be experienced during temporary breakdowns in social reality, a very minor loss of self that is not significant enough to create the negative feelings of severe anomie, but out of the ordinary enough to create a momentary sense of danger and excitement. Ecstasy, argues Berger (1967:43), involves a sensation of 'standing, or stepping outside reality as commonly defined.' This is like anomie, but not quite as severe. It is as if one is at the edge of organized reality and can feel the anomic terror of uncertainty and confusion, but if taken in mild proportions, this can be experienced as ecstasy rather than anomie. Too much of a break is terrifying. Just a little bit is exciting and ecstatic, and sometimes dangerous and frightening.

As an example, the experiences of dawn and dusk might be considered from this perspective. Here there is a sense of danger, sacredness, and ecstasy. People sometimes gather at dawn and dusk, watching the sun rise and set in quiet and reverence, as if in the presence of some larger cosmic force, certainly something beyond the experience of daily taken-for-granted reality. When camping, people may stop what they are doing; sit on a hill, silently, sometimes with others, sometimes alone; and watch the sun rise. They don't spend the whole morning watching the sun move across the sky. It is as if there is a certain fixed period in which it is proper to watch the sunrise, and then there is a call to return to the chores and necessities of everyday living; breakfast has to be made, tents folded, and sleeping bags rolled-up. As the crack between night and day is traversed, the roles, rules, and identities of daytime are activated and people are drawn back to their social obligations. Dusk also generates out of the ordinary experiences. Here the feeling is more of eeriness, but it may also be a quasi-religious experience like dawn. People go to watch the sunset, and again this is done quietly, almost reverently, as if in the presence of something sacred that requires a demeanor of silence and respect. Again there is a suspension from the duties and obligations of daily life. Traditionally, dusk is understood as an in-between time, and this idea holds the sociological secret for the experience of eeriness or sacredness that both dawn and dusk generate. A common ending in Western films is for the hero and heroine to ride off into the sunset. If this is examined more closely it can be seen why riding into the sunset constitutes an appropriate end of the film. To ride into the sunset is to ride into a crack, or gap, between the social worlds of night and day, and as such, to be suspended from the obligations of either world (if they ride into the night, there is the question: where will they stay, or will they sleep together, and if they ride off in the daytime there are the bad guys and a possible resumption of role obligations). Riding into the sunset is safe, because it is riding into nowhere, and as such, is a perfect way to terminate plot development. They are, in effect, riding out of reality itself, or at least out of the socially constructed reality of the movie.

Within the framework developed by Mary Douglas, dawn and dusk can be treated as in-between times, between the social worlds of day and night. The experience of awe or ecstasy that is generated is a mild form of anomie, a loss of self that is not as traumatic as falling through larger cracks in social reality. At dawn and dusk people experience the break or crack between the socially constructed cosmologies of day and night, which are by definition discontinuous spheres. The point here is the one Douglas makes about the corridors between the rooms being filled with a sense of danger and dread. Day and night are like two rooms, with dawn and dusk being the corridor which joins them. There is no way of going from one room to the other without passing through the corridor and experiencing the mild fright and anomie of this in-between time. 'Danger lies in transitional states; simply because transition is neither one state or the next, it is undefinable. The person who must pass from one to another is himself in danger and emanates danger to others' (1966:116). Day and night are separate social worlds, part of the 'sacred canopy', to use Berger's phrase, whereby we relate to ultimate cosmic reality. These cultural constructions — day and night — are discontinuous, and the break between them is what creates the experience of a momentary loss of self that we acknowledge as an out-of-the-ordinary experience.

The movement from day to night is not like turning on a cosmic light switch. The change in light is continuous and gradual, not discontinuous and abrupt. It takes a few hours for the sun to set, and it begins to get light long before the sun actually breaks the horizon. There is a smooth transition where shades of light or dark appear gradually. The anomic break, then, is in the social categories of day and night, which do have a break, not the physical light, which is continuously changing. Where the social sphere of day meets night there is a necessary crack, a place where the social membrane is so thin that the anomie of unorganized and unstructured life seeps through and bathes us in mild anomie or ecstasy.

There is, though, a sense in which the quality of the light itself generates anomic feelings. Douglas suggests that stickiness can create mild identity crises, because sticky things are neither solid nor liquid. They are in-between, and as such when sticky things get on our hands they create a visceral reaction which seems very threatening because it blurs the boundary between self and its larger environment. Stickiness provides a continuous link between the individual and the larger world, and as such threatens the separate identity of the self. Now, the colors of dawn and dusk are similarly in-between the black of night and light of day. The colors are more opaque, rose colored, and as such blur the distinction between the well-defined worlds of night and day. Distinctions are lost, signposts gone, and people momentarily enter an ill-defined in-between world that is neither light nor dark, day nor night. In short, there is anomie. People do, however, remain connected to their institutional roles at dawn and dusk, making the crack in the mythical cosmos somewhat removed from daily, institutional experiences. Here the uncertainty of this transitional state flows over the well structured world of occupation, family, and community which insulates us from the severity of the naked crack in the sacred canopy. As such we do not experience a full blown identity crisis, but more of a euphoric experience, where for a moment we are suspended by at least one layer of the many layered social realities out of which we are socially integrated.

Language as ritual and ritual as language

For Mary Douglas, what began as an inquiry into the origins of dirt and cleanliness ends with a general discussion of boundaries and their ritual reaffirmation. In this scheme the general question of *ritual* looms large. It is the linchpin to her whole scheme, serving as the intermediary between the society below and the culture above.

But what exactly is ritual? To this question Douglas starts with the sociologist's usual understanding of ritual as action devoid of personal commitment to the values being expressed. But, 'to use the word ritual to mean empty symbols of conformity, leaving us with no word to stand for symbols of genuine conformity, is seriously disabling to the sociology of religion' (1970:3). Instead, Douglas argues that ritual is a viable means of communication, and 'it will help us to understand religious behavior if we can treat ritual forms, like speech forms, as transmitters of culture' (1970:21). For her, ritual 'is preeminently a form of communication' a kind of language which communicates social information, and as such helps replenish society's collective sentiments. As such, ritual should be treated like speech, which also transmits culture and is generated in social relations.

To develop a conception of ritual she turns to the British sociolinguist Basil Bernstein and his notion of 'elaborated' and 'restricted' linguistic codes.

> Bernstein starts with the idea that there are two basic categories of speech, distinguishable both linguistically and sociologically. The first arises in a small-scale, very local social situation in which the speakers all have access to the same fundamental assumptions; in this category every utterance is pressed into service to affirm the social order. Speech in this case exercises a solidarity-maintaining function closely comparable to religion as Durkheim saw it functioning in primitive society. The second category of speech . . . is employed in social situations where the speakers do not accept or necessarily know one another's fundamental assumptions. Speech has then the primary function of making explicit unique individual perceptions, and bridging initial assumptions. (1970:22)

In terms of their actual organization restricted codes utilize a smaller lexical pool and more simple and rigid syntax. Elaborated codes provide a larger lexical pool and a wider range of more complex syntactical alternatives. Restricted codes limit the ability of the individual to communicate very specific meanings. What is spoken is general, known to all, and as such part of the group culture. Douglas, like Bernstein, follows the sociolinguistic tradition of Sapir and Mead in which society is thought to be transmitted primarily through its internalization of speech.

> As the child learns his speech or in our terms learns specific codes which regulate his verbal acts he learns the

requirements of his social structure. From this point of view every time the child speaks the social structure of which he is a part is reinforced in him, and his social identity develops and is constrained. The social structure becomes for the developing child his psychological reality by the shaping of his acts of speech. (Bernstein, quoted in Douglas, 1970:24–5)

Here the transmission of culture occurs through the individual carrying society in speech. But language also acts in a more direct fashion, independently of its effect upon the psychological realities of those who use its codes. When an individual speaks in a restricted code he or she is performing a linguistic ritual, which acts to renew common sentiments independently of reinforcing his or her social identity.

A restricted code, because of its very restrictedness, forces others to utilize their commonly held group assumptions to decode what is said, and this, in turn, brings these assumptions to life, and as such reaffirms the group which they constitute. If groups are comprised of shared assumptions among individuals — a common culture — then the activation of that culture is an activation of the group. It is important to realize that this process works independently of intentions. It is not so much that the individual desires or intends to reaffirm group sentiments, but when a restricted code is utilized group sentiments are automatically reaffirmed, for when one speaks in code others *must* utilize their baggage of shared assumptions to understand what has been said. Restricted codes are so brief that without some prior knowledge it is virtually impossible to decode what has been said.

Douglas's analogy of language and ritual is important. Ritual carries or transmits collective information, like language. But, it is also true that language acts like ritual, and its structure — its codes — are part of society's arsenal of ritual utilized in the periodic reaffirmation of social order. To speak is to perform a ritual, and partake, intentionally or not, in the affirmation and reproduction of basic social relations and commonly held values.

The importance of the Douglas-Bernstein linkage of language, ritual, and social solidarity is that it permits an examination of changes in group life that are associated with changes in the amount of ritual activity. There should be more ritual and more restricted codes where the solidarity of the group is higher. Increases in group solidarity or corporateness should generate more ritual of all sorts as there is more social order to periodically reaffirm. Douglas's focus is upon variations in the immediate context of individual speakers. But solidarity is also a property of the group, and not just a matter of 'uniting the speaker to his kin and his local community' as Douglas refers to it. Solidarity is a group property, referring to strongly bonded integrated collectivities, and as such is a concept for the comparative analysis of different groups and not just different pressures upon the individual. Her emphasis is sufficient for analyzing differences between individual speakers, but limits explanations for ritual in general.

Another difficulty arises when she identifies 'small scale, very local' situations as the origin of restricted codes. This makes comparative analysis difficult, for at the societal level restricted codes become limited, by and large, to primitive societies or local neighborhoods in modern society. Small-scale and very local is simply not a collective property of modern national societies. Douglas also argues that industrial society with its

> geographical and social mobility . . . detaches [people] from their original community . . . [and] here are the people who live by using elaborated speech to review and revise existing categories of thought. To challenge received ideas is their very bread and butter. They (or should I say we?) practice a professional detachment towards any given pattern of experience. (1970:31)

This purportedly modern use of language is contrasted with language in 'most primitive cultures in which speech forms are firmly embedded in a stable social structure. The primary use of language here is to affirm and embellish the social structure which rests upon unchallengeable metaphysical assumptions' (1970:28). That speech should be used to 'review and revise existing categories of thought' in modern society and merely 'embellish social structure which rests

upon unchallengeable metaphysical assumptions' in primitive
society seems like the same sort of ethnocentric nonsense she
herself debunked in *Purity and Danger*. Her progress made in
showing how modern hygienic practices are sociologically
similar to those of primitive societies seems to have been
completely forgotten when it comes to the 'wonders' of
language. It would seem that language is used as much for
embellishing the modern social order with its own unchallengeable metaphysical assumptions as that of our so-called
primitive brethren.

This problem arose, it seems, from her reliance upon the
linguist's emphasis on the individual speaker and the social
relations in which he or she is embedded. From the point
of view of the individual speaker this may make sense. From
the point of view of the group as a whole it is a definite
limitation. The resolution of this problem is to move the
level of analysis from the immediate social context of the
speaker to the overall corporateness or solidarity of the
group, community, or nation as a whole. Codes, as cultural
patterns or procedures, can be seen as properties of the
group, like its collective representations, and as such determined by the organization of the collectivity as a whole, not
just the immediate social pressures on the speaker. To broaden
the analysis of codes, therefore, the relationship between
the organization of groups and the kind of codes that are
prevalent should be examined, bypassing the immediate
context of the individual speaker.

Douglas's linking of linguistic codes, ritual, and social
solidarity can be expressed in two simple propositions:

Proposition 1   The greater the group's level of solidarity
or corporateness, the more restricted the linguistic code.
Proposition 2   The lower the group's level of solidarity
or corporateness, the more elaborated the linguistic code.

The importance of this association between language and
ritual is that the same theoretical logic can be applied to
various kinds of linguistic codes. There are a great variety
of symbolic systems which communicate meaning and
as such can be considered languages. Their codes should
shift between being more elaborated and restricted depending

upon the overall solidarity or corporateness of the group in which they are produced. From this point of view one can decode the 'language' of music, art, and food much like one decodes speech.

Music is obviously associated with ritual, as religious ceremonies frequently have musical accompaniment. But music is also a ritual in its own right, whether or not it is performed on explicitly religious occasions. Music is a collective enterprise and a distinctly social creation. Tones, and their arrangement in scales and metric sequences, are not a mere repetition of nature. Even the human voice, while natural, when used for singing involves social constraints such that it will hit certain notes and make certain acceptable sounds. Music, then, while involving the sounds of nature, so modifies them that the resultant structure is a cultural construction.

Music, like speech, is a language. Sounds or tones are basic elements that are combined according to the grammar of melody, harmony, rhythm, and composition. As words form sentences, sounds combine to form phrases, motifs, and larger musical wholes. It also appears, following the lead of Douglas, that musical codes function as linguistic rituals and change with shifts in group solidarity. In periods of higher solidarity and greater group consciousness there should be music of a more restricted nature, and during periods of lower solidarity and less group consciousness the musical codes should become more elaborated.

For an example, the history of Black American music from slavery through the 1960s might be considered. Slavery can be considered a time of strong well defined collective identity for the black community, which accordingly generated restricted musical codes, like spirituals. It is important to point out here that the idea of elaborated and restricted codes is relative. They are not absolutes, but points on a continuum, and so when spirituals are described as being restricted, this means that they are *more* restricted than the jazz and blues codes which followed. Spirituals were an obvious code. Biblical images of Moses, David, Pharaoh, and the Israelites were well known symbols for relations between slaves and masters. The restrictedness of spirituals is seen in the very structure of the music. Spirituals involve a regular pulsating rhythm in which a number of voices are merged into a singular voice, as if the group itself were singing. They also involve a narrower range of tones than the wide range of jazz, or the deliberate off-key singing in blues. Spirituals involve a much simpler melodic and rhythmic structure than jazz and, sung in congregations and choral groups, involve group music dealing with the concerns of the community as a whole, not individual problems, as in the blues. Harmony is also important, for here individual tones are submerged or transformed into a single tone, a group sound.

New musical codes appeared during the early years of the twentieth century. With the beginning migration of blacks from the south to the north, the overall solidarity of the black community began to decline, as people were now on the move, more dispersed, and pursuing personal goals on a much more individualistic basis than was possible under the more formal structuring of black existence during slavery. With this decline in solidarity the musical codes became more elaborated, accentuating the discrete purposes and goals of the unique individual rather than the collective concerns of the group as a whole. This manifested itself in the appearance of jazz and the blues, which first appeared during the early decades of the twentieth century. Jazz is perhaps the ultimate elaborated code, as there is no prescribed syntax. Improvisation is the imperative, and sounds can be combined in any way that pleases the artist. The range of tones is greater than spirituals, and there is, in general, less emphasis upon harmony. The classic jazz musician is the singular individual, Louis Armstrong, Miles Davis, Charlie Parker, or John Coltrane, although there were also big band jazz and smaller ensembles. But jazz is more a matter of individual expression, whereas spirituals involved a blending of individuals to create a choral sound. The blues, while having more structure than jazz, is still a more elaborated code than spirituals, as it deals with personal problems and is most often sung by individuals. There is also a great deal of variation in the singing of notes in the blues which represents a wider range of syntactical alternatives. Perhaps the most famous is the so-called blue note, the third and seventh scale degrees which are used either natural or flattened, and which are frequently played deliberately out of tune.

From Douglas's perspective the emergence of jazz and blues is to be expected during those periods in which group solidarity is declining. If the solidarity of the group were to increase, there should be a similar change in the mode of communication toward more restricted codes, and this is what happened in the 1960s with the heightened black consciousness and solidarity of the Civil Rights Movement. During this period soul music emerged. Although derived from gospel music, soul music was not religious like spirituals, but more social, for dancing and entertainment. In general the music celebrates love: found, lost, continuing, and unrequited. Soul music, unlike jazz and blues which preceded it, is largely performed by groups. Like spirituals, basic rhythm and harmonics are important. The collective orientation of soul music can be seen in lyrics which deal with issues of black pride, group solidarity, and the struggle for civil rights. It should be noted, though, that more often soul music lyrics dealt with questions of love, although here the themes seem much more general than the very concrete images of the blues. Like spirituals, soul music has a regular pulsating rhythm, a hook line that is repeated, and a narrower range of tones than jazz and a narrower range of lyrics and images than the blues. In short, it has a more restricted code. The passing of the 1960s also saw a decline in the importance of soul music proper and a disintegration of some of the more well-known groups.

Another kind of language is *art*, also a means of communication and a conveyor of collective information. If words are the building blocks for speech, and tones for music, then colors and shapes serve a similar purpose for art. Artistic syntax involves rules of composition, perspective, compatible and incompatible colors, and so forth. Art 'speaks' as colors and shapes are combined to make statements, which like speech and music, can be deciphered in terms of elaborated or restricted codes.

Art styles represent what is common to a number of artists. A style is like a code. Changing art styles, then, represent changing codes. In general, abstract art is a more restricted code, because it represents a reduction and simplification of vocabulary and syntax. Abstraction is a blueprint or outline of something that could, in principle, be spelled out in full. It is a reduced form of communication, which is exactly what the restricted code represents. Realism, on the other hand, is a more elaborated code, as more extensive art materials are employed to spell things out in more specific detail. Realistic art is a more explicit form of communication, as the meanings are contained within the actualities of structured color and form. Abstract art is more context dependent. It requires interpretation, or decoding, as the restricted gestures are capable of any number of alternative interpretations. What makes these objects art and not, say, spilled paint, or child's play, is their location in a social group which consensually understands that these are the codes of communication.

In general, then, abstract art would be expected to appear in communities having a greater degree of shared assumptions or a greater degree of solidarity, and more realistic art would be expected to appear when solidarity is weaker and when the community is looser and more poorly defined.

Douglas's hypothesized relationship between solidary communities and restricted codes can be seen, for example, in the changing styles of post-1945 Modern Art. From the point of view of Douglas and Bernstein, the world of New York Art resembled the close-knit British working-class neighborhoods where Bernstein found his restricted code in speech. In the art world, painters, patrons, museums, and critics all lived in close proximity and shared a common social life, and therefore, it would seem, produced an in-group form of 'artistic communication' in the form of a very abstract art, Abstract Expressionism. As the New York School grew in popularity and fame in the 1960s its collective assumptions became ever more well known, and as such there was less need to spell things out explicitly. As the in-groupness of the art community grew, the artistic communication became ever more restricted. The Abstract Expressionism of the 1940s and 1950s became more restricted with Minimalism in the 1960s, and finally so abstract and minimal, that the art object virtually disappeared with the appearance of Conceptual Art in the later 1960s and 1970s. The conceptual artist did not paint or sculpt, but provided 'documentation' which was only meant to illustrate his theory, which was the real object of artistic production. Here the role of critic and artist became fused, as the art producer was also the creator of the theories of his productions. Actually, his art and theory are one and the same thing, a situation which has caused great consternation over whether Conceptual Art is really art, philosophy, criticism, or literature.

But modern art did not stay with the very restricted object-free-art of the Conceptual Artist. There was a shift in styles (codes) and a rebirth of realism, what was variously called in the later 1970s and early 1980s, photo-realism, neo-realism, or super-realism. This was a much more explicit art; things were no longer hinted at, but spelled out in full. Why this sudden change from the restricted code of abstraction to the elaborated code of realism? The semantic machinery of art as a language may have reached a point of disequilibrium, because the art object itself had virtually disappeared, forcing a new cycle of realism, of more elaborated codes. A second answer, however, derives from the changing social context of these codes. If the sense of centrality and importance of New York itself was shaken, or began to decline, as many observers claimed, there should have been a shift away from the confidence of ingroup communication — like the restricted artistic codes of abstract art — to a more explicit code, like the elaborated realism of Super Realism. As the importance and centrality of a community withers, its commonly held assumptions similarly dissipate and the burden of meaning falls back on the system of signs. What is to be artistically spoken can no longer be hinted at, or activated by an abstract clue or gesture. It must be said in full by the coherent ordering of realism and the declining importance of abstraction in New York Art.

Decoding a meal

'Eating, like talking, is patterned activity, and the daily menu may be made to yield an analogy with linguistic forms' (1978:251).

Speech, music, art; all seem plausible as kinds of languages. But what of food, and its structured presentation? Douglas suggests that the organization of food and menus constitutes a means for encoding social information. Eating, like talking, is a means of communication. It is socially organized and highly structured; individuals do not eat when they want, but at culturally prescribed times — lunch, breakfast, and dinner. In some sense eating is a daily ritual and like other rituals is related to the larger social context in which it occurs. The ingestion of food is a biological necessity, and so is the presence of so many calories and possibly different kinds of food. But what foods serve as protein or carbohydrates and how they are prepared and presented is a matter of culture, not biology.

> Fox never appears on our menu, nor dog . . . but in parts
> of Russia foxes were reckoned a delicacy, likewise dogs
> in China . . . We may shrink from the thought of eating
> insects or singing birds, but we know that grubs and
> grasshoppers, blackbirds and larks are served as food
> elsewhere. (1978a:55)

Food is socially selected and structured from our choice of which animals and plants to eat, to how they are to be prepared and presented. At each point culture enters into the consideration as to what will be eaten and how. As such there is an order or structure to eating. This structuring of food can be deciphered and decoded, much like the earlier examples of music and art. Douglas suggests that the menu can be examined in terms of structuralist categories and binary opposites. Meals can be contrasted with drinks, and solids with liquids. In this fashion one can look at the categorical structure of any meal, much like one would look at the structure of myth.

The social organization of a meal is also a ritual ceremony. Meals are times when the family gathers, and seating arrangements reflect the status hierarchy of the family: father sits here, mother there, children over there. The assembled family is like any community coming together to periodically reaffirm group sentiments, and the organization of meals is like the organization of speech. As daily speech has its ritual aspects in elaborated and restricted codes, so do daily eating habits. Breakfast is the most atomistic meal. People arrive on their own, often fix their own food, and are allowed to express personal interests and needs, like reading the newspaper or being non-communicative and even a little gruff. These behaviors represent a degree of role distance from the meal as a formal social event. During breakfast it is not as important that seating arrangements reflect family hierarchy. There are rarely 'family breakfasts'; people sit anywhere around the kitchen table. Family members come and go on their own, and no one seems to mind, which is not so at dinner, where children have to ask permission to leave the table, even if they have finished eating. The family unit remains a cohesive entity throughout the meal, reflecting the greater ritual importance of dinner over breakfast. At breakfast there is also less ritual preparation of the table — no table cloth or cloth napkins, rather the formica of the kitchen table, or a more battered and scarred wooden table, reflecting its use in food preparation and other activities. The totemic object of the dinner ritual, the dining room table, is clean, a better quality of wood, more highly polished, and ritually guarded with a white cloth. In sum, breakfast is accomplished with less social organization, endowed with less ritual, and as such a much more individualistic meal. It is more an aggregation of discrete individuals rather than a corporate whole. This individualism is captured in the familiar call, 'What do *you want* for breakfast', which is contrasted with, '*We are having* pot roast for dinner'. At breakfast one is asked his or her opinion, not so at dinner.

Lunch is something of an in-between meal. More ritualistic than breakfast but less than dinner. Its increased sociability over breakfast is seen in the tendency to want to have lunch with others; one goes to a great effort to find a lunch date rather than eat alone. Similarly there is more ritual in the preparation of the food, and in its preparation. But dinner is the most ritualistic meal. Here the family unit is formally assembled. There is order and structure. People have places, and the exact location of glasses, plates, knives and forks is important. Napkins are another device for ritual cleanliness. Pollution rituals are also more prevalent at dinner; parents remind children to wash their hands before sitting down to eat. One dresses up for dinner, or at least brushes up loose ends, like tucking in shirt tails, combing hair, or washing one's face. There is also a general prohibition against discussing certain topics that might be divisive, but more importantly would reflect individual opinions and therefore the separate realities of the individual over their membership in the corporate familial group. Light dinner conversation is a sign of group membership.

Douglas's understanding of codes as ritual and food as a means of communication can also be applied to the manner in which food is presented. Food can be seen as analogous to words, sounds, colors, and shapes; that is, the basic building blocks through which information is conveyed. The syntax is contained in the rules for presenting the food. The point here is that people don't eat randomly; some things are eaten before others, and some in different combinations with others. The manner in which food is presented is a language that individuals participate in, much like speech. Sometimes we are conscious that a fancy and formal meal is making a statement, but often we are not, and take the rules for granted.

In general, two patterns can be identified. Food can be served in a sequence of courses, as during formal occasions, where, say, a salad is served and cleared, followed by an entrée and dessert. When food is presented in formal courses, the code is more restricted, in that there is a more formal structuring of the sequence of foods. This comes first, then that, then that. These rules rigidly structure and control the ways in which food is ingested, much like the heavy rhythm and harmonic structures that control individual voices or certain styles of art that constrain painters to present their pigments in particular patterns. This formal structure limits the discretion of the individual in picking exactly what he or she wants and in what proportion, much like the more rigid syntax of the restricted speech code limits the range of words that can be spoken. Eating and speaking are similar. Both are structured and convey social information. A restricted linguistic code limits the lexical pool and narrows the ways in which an individual can combine food in a meal. Individual foods are like words, and their arrangement is like grammar. In a more restricted code there is less choice and more imposed order. This holds for meals as well as sentences.

A more elaborated food code is found when the meal is placed on the table and people are allowed to pick and choose which foods they want and in what proportions. Here the syntax of the meal allows for greater individual freedom in choosing foods, in sequencing them, and in establishing the right proportions. The elaborated code is more flexible and allows the individual to express more personal intent, which is more or less what happens when one chooses just how much of this and that to put on the plate.

This structuring of meals in code may also vary with the solidarity or corporateness of the group. As with all codes, the more solidary the group, the more restricted the code. Remembering Douglas's central point that it is not so much tradition versus modernity, but kind of social organization, we would expect cultures with strong group solidarity to utilize food more often in ritual, like say, India with its caste prohibitions on eating and touching various kinds of food. In a culture with a very low level of group solidarity, we would expect little structuring of meals and little concern for the purity of arrangements, or the sequencing of food.

Culture and social change

Just as Douglas moves from minute discussions of dirt to more general discussions of pollution and purity, so she moves from relatively static, localized considerations of food, meals, and other codes to a broad examination of the cultural classifications which inform the role of goods in modern society in general. These aspects of her work involve her not only in criticisms of the cultural features of modern technology, social movements, and religion, but in constructing a theoretical scheme of her own with which to contrast modern culture from its predecessors and to discuss its evolution.

Goods in modern culture

In the *World of Goods* (1979) she generates an anthropological critique of the individualism of the economists' lonely consumer.

> To name one more familiar grief with economic theorizing: the idea of the rational individual is an impossible abstraction from social life. It is clearly absurd to aggregate millions of individuals buying and using goods without reckoning with the transformations they affect by sharing consumption together . . . Man is a social being. We can never explain demand by looking only at the physical properties of goods. Man needs goods for communicating with others and for making sense of what is going on around him. The two needs are but one, for communication can only be formed in a structured system of meanings. (Douglas and Isherwood, 1979:5, 95)

Economic goods are part of a larger cultural system, and like other aspects of culture they carry meaning and have identifiable social functions. The giving and acquiring of goods is a means for anchoring meaning in social life. 'Goods are neutral, their uses are social; they can be used as fences or bridges' (1979:12). The point here is not just the conspicuous-display-to-dramatize-social-position idea of Veblen, but that goods are social markers used to construct and demark social reality in the first place. We desire goods not just to fill material needs, but to decipher our social surroundings, locate our social self, and transmit knowledge about who and what we are. In this regard, most social scientists don't take Vance Packard very seriously. But he understood the very sort of point Douglas is trying to make. When he wrote about the sexual implications of buying certain car models, the point is not so much how advertising persuades, although, of course, it does, but that the meanings we derive from goods are part and parcel of the ways in which meaning is acquired and transmitted in the first place.

In developing her analysis of the cultural role of goods Douglas utilizes a scheme introduced in *Natural Symbols*, what she calls 'group and grid' analysis to reinterpret Max Weber's Protestant Ethic thesis concerning economic goods. She begins by suggesting that rather than examining religious factors as the explanatory variable, we should look at the social relations which gave rise to the Protestant Ethic. 'How the spirit of the age is generated is precisely what we want to discover' (1979:31). Her strategy is to treat the Protestant Ethic as another cosmology, no different from those of more primitive people, and as such generated by the social relations in which it appears. For example, the Catholic belief in a glorious afterlife, as contrasted to the Protestant sense of worldliness, is, she argues, not unique, but found in many cultures that promise heaven as a reward for deeds in this life. The Vikings had Valhalla and the North American Indians had a happy hunting ground. Further, 'the wild extravagance of the princely and ducal courts was undoubtedly less due to a lively faith in the world to come than to a rational and calculating overconsumption, an investment in conspicuous loyalty that might, with luck, pay handsome dividends' (1979:33).

This may be so, but it should be pointed out that she is reasoning exactly like the economists she criticized earlier. The problem is that everything can be made to be in someone's interest, and she searches for real reasons for what could be seen as more purely symbolic or ritualistic behavior. One may not want to label this conspicuous consumption as irrational, *à la* Weber, but the alternative need not be a search for hidden rationality. Certainly there is some calculation and rationality involved, but by looking for rationality in what seems clearly ritualistic she is conceding the game to the utilitarian outlook of the economists and their fellow travelers. It would seem the social world of pre-Reformation Europe was one of extensive social layers and demarcations (social lines and boundaries) with the conspicuous display of goods one of the mechanisms to anchor these lines and cleavages. This is the very point of her argument about the social role of goods as markers: the more there is to be marked, the more markers there will be, whether that be Hindu India or Europe of the Middle Ages.

Nevertheless, her basic observation is brilliant. Speaking of pre-Reformation Europe she notes, 'At that time individuals were not saving, but corporate groups were; the Protestant ethic takes over from pre-Reformation other-worldliness when the balance of power is reversed and when corporate groups lose out to the claims of individuals' (1979:35). The sixteenth century marks the beginning of the transition from the corporate world of medieval guilds, church, and nobility to the individualism of competitive capitalism and the citizenship of modern nation-states. She argues that the rise of Protestantism, at least as a cosmology, reflects the transformation of group life, and not the other way around. In this sense her argument is similar to Marx, although she takes a more Durkheimian position, focusing upon the corporate group rather than class relations.

The dominance of the corporate orders of pre-Reformation Europe provides an independent variable which she theoretically links to the other-worldiness of their consummatory behavior. Corporate groups, that is, collectivities with their own purposes and goals

> can claim to represent not only the longest view, but also the public interest . . . [further] . . . if we were to place different societies along a hypothetical scale from weak toward strong, the stronger the group the greater its capacity to accumulate assets in its own name and the less the power of its constituent members to accumulate for themselves. (1979:36)

She concludes that, 'the otherworldliness of a doctrinal bias is dependent on the strength of group' (1979:38). Interestingly, the growth in the strength of the state in the twentieth century has provided another corporate group that demands altruistic sacrifices and accumulates capital at the expense of its constituent individuals.

There is another important aspect to strong corporate groups:

> Because its legal existence is eternal, it can make its demand in the name of unborn generations . . . No individual acting on his or her own behalf can entertain dreams of such a long-term future. Only the group can develop a full-fledged otherworldly morality, for the group outlives its members. (1979:37)

This is the transcendent quality of groups that is associated in the Durkheimian tradition with the experience of the

118

sacred, holy, and spiritual. The idea of the religiously eternal is generated from experiences with 'eternal' social relations in the form of corporate groups (Swanson, 1964). From this point of view, groups could be arranged along a corporateness continuum and the transcendent claims of their religious doctrines examined. We would also expect that the more corporate the group the more individual activity is linked to some kind of transcendent reality.

More corporate polities seem to have political ideologies (civil religions) which have a longer span to their transcendental claims. For instance, single party socialist states utilize an ideology which links the daily actions of Party, and State, to the evolution of History as a transcendental force. The present is seen as the outcome of a pre-ordained struggle between historical forces. This can be contrasted with the less corporate polities of many western states. For instance, the legitimating mythology of the United States begins in an almost offhand sort of way, when the Declaration of Independence states, 'When in the course of human events it becomes necessary . . .'. In general, the most corporate polities should have the most direct link in their political mythology between history and their institutions and, further, that history should be animated by transcendental dynamics which drive it forward. The least corporate polities should have the most tenuous linkage between their political existence and history, and history should not appear as 'forces' rumbling through time and space but more as coincidence or *ad hoc* events of the moment. The casual reference in the American Declaration of Independence, 'When in the course' is somewhere in-between, employing the transcendent idea of history, but not providing any underlying logic for that historical progression nor for the appearance of the American polity at any particular point in time and space.

Group and grid

Douglas's perspective on groups is derived from Bernstein's understanding of the social contexts that affect the types of codes people speak. Her interest is in how individuals are controlled by society. Following Bernstein's lead, she makes two distinctions, group and grid.

> *Group* means the outside boundary that people have
> erected between themselves and the outside world. *Grid*
> means all the other social distinctions and delegations of
> authority that they use to limit how people behave to
> one another. (1982a:138)

From these two dimensions she creates a fourfold table:
strong grid strong group, strong grid weak group, weak group
weak grid, weak grid strong group. Strong grid involves
moral and normative prohibitions which limit or highly
structure individual interaction. As grid weakens,

> individuals have more scope to deal with one another as
> they wish. The move away from the insulation of strong
> grid is not necessarily a move to disorganization and a
> lack of rule. To permit the maximum possible number of
> contacts fairly entered, their conditions known and
> their performance accessible, a new form of control
> emerges: the invisible control of fair-comparison rules.
> (1979:39)

These rules range from courts of chivalry to the stock or
cattle market. Regardless of the historical period, the purpose
of these rules is to 'regularize competition' and ensure a
'fair contest'.

> In weak-grid, weak-group societies, instead of group values
> being imposed on the individual, the latter's personal
> responsibility is crystallized in the triangle of honor,
> shame, and luck . . . Instead of accepting their allotted
> station in a given scheme of things, as where grid is strong,
> each family is involved, for its very survival, in the effort
> for advantageous alliance — martial, defensive, or financial.
> (1979:40)

In this world of individualism, 'when luck, shame, and
honor have replaced the avenging ancestors as controlling
ideas, we have moved away from a society that is regulated
by reference to any hereafter to one explicitly concerned
with this world' (1979:41). This, of course, sounds very
much like the Protestant Ethic and with this in mind, she

goes on to reclassify the four types of economic orientation listed by Weber in terms of her group-grid scheme.

The *peasant* social order epitomizes strong grid, where peasants are insulated from other groups in society. Here, 'the system strongly classifies them into the periphery of the main society, so that they can neither compete with one another nor unite against oppressors. They would save, but their low level of output makes it difficult' (1979:42). Conversely, where group is strong 'the individual store is constantly raided for group purposes' (1979:42), and *traditional society* involves both strong grid and group. 'The individual saves little, but the group accumulates wealth. Guild halls and cathedrals get endowed and built. The otherworldly doctrine is one of the ways in which this pattern of behavior is made intelligible and acceptable' (1979:42). This would be the pre-Reformation doctrine Weber contrasted with the Protestant Ethic cosmology which followed. Finally, weak group and weak grid involves the most private accumulation. 'The individual *capitalist economy* . . . extolling the virtues of honesty, industry, and solvency which uphold the rules of interaction — is somewhere fairly low along the line of grid, possibly a little to the middle, if the common rules of commerce which are agreed upon attest to some strong group consensus' (Douglas and Isherwood, 1979:42, 43). Perhaps the least restrained — weak group, weak grid — are *adventurers* who are less constrained by the ethics and rules of conventional business practice. One thinks here of pirates, Spanish conquistadors, nineteenth-century American robber barons showing a strong disregard for business ethics, and marginal areas of contemporary economic life, like offshore banking, some aspects of organized crime, and the most speculative of business ventures. In sum, Douglas suggests Weber's different economic orientations can be seen as different cosmologies generated by different group-grid relations.

What started out as a simple discussion of dirt, and later extended to acquisitive orientations, ends with a general scheme linking the axial features of whole cultural systems to variations in their social organization. In *Cultural Bias* (1978b) Douglas briefly links the group-grid scheme to cosmologies in general: to how nature is contrasted with

121

culture; questions of space, gardening, cookery, medicine, and time; attitudes to youth and old age; human nature in general; sickness, health and death; personal abnormality and handicaps; personal relations; punishment; and definitions of distributive justice.

At this level she is attempting to grasp whole social systems, and not just individual pollution beliefs, the linguistic base of ritual, or orientations toward economic goods. Most generally, 'when the social group grips its members in tight communal bonds, the religion is ritualist; when this grip is relaxed, ritualism declines. And with this shift in forms, a shift in doctrines appears' (1970:14). For her group and grid represent two different ways in which society can 'grip' its members.

> Group is obvious — the experience of a bounded social unit. Grid refers to rules which relate one person to others on an egocentric basis. Grid and group may be found together. In this case the quality of relations is ordered and clearly bounded. (1970:viii)

As mentioned before, she then cross-classifies group and grid, creating her fourfold table.

> Three sectors . . . predispose toward ritual in its most magical and concentrated sense. Where grid is strong and group weak, magic is at hand to help the individual in a competitive society . . . where both group and grid are strong, magicality supports the social structure and moral code. Where group is strong and grid weak, magicality protects the borders of the social unit. Only in the area of zero organization are people very uninterested in ritual or magic. (1970:144)

In theory these ideas of grid and group are general, but they seem most applicable to the social organization of small-scale primitive societies. Consider, for instance, her explanation of the origin of witchcraft cosmologies. 'If we have social units whose external boundaries are clearly marked, whose internal relations are confused, and who persist on a small scale at a low level of organization, then we should look for the active witchcraft type of cosmology' (1970:113). Here she seems to be thinking of primitive or traditional societies, and not the social organization of large-scale industrial societies. This might be all right if witchcraft cosmologies were found only in societies whose 'internal relations are confused' and who persist on a 'small scale with a low level of organization', but they are not. Modern societies, which exist on a large scale with a high level of organization and well-defined role relations have also been plagued by witchcraft in the form of political witch-hunts, ranging from the Reign of Terror during the French Revolution, through the Stalinist Show Trials of the 1930s to McCarthyism in the 1950s and the Chinese Cultural Revolution of the 1960s. Douglas's 'four characteristics of the witchcraft cosmology: the idea of the bad outside and the good inside, the inside under attack and in need of protection, human wickedness on a cosmic scale, and these ideas used in political manipulations' (1970:114) are also the characteristics of the modern political witch hunt. Images of the People, the Nation, Democracy, or Socialism, constitute collective representations of the modern political community. This is the 'good inside ... under attack and in need of protection' from all sorts of subversives, spies, and alien ideas which represent the 'bad outside' and 'human wickedness on a cosmic scale'. The latter manifests itself in the historical dimension of the depicted struggle between, say, socialism and capitalism, where the ritual discovery of imperialist agents, wreckers, and saboteurs during the Soviet Show Trials of the 1930s and 'those taking the capitalist road' during the Chinese Cultural Revolution represent not just individuals gone astray, but human manifestations of cosmic — historical — forces. As mentioned previously, the ideology of one-party states represents a cosmology of historical progress, making opposition an instance of historical regression, 'capitalist restoration', and as such truly human wickedness on a cosmic scale. Finally, someone charged with subversive activity or dangerous thoughts has certainly been used for 'political manipulation', as we think of Stalin and his purges to eliminate enemies, Mao attempting to perpetuate his revolutionary vision and his struggle with Liu Shao-Chi, or the career of Senator McCarthy.

The central problem, then, with Douglas's explanation of

witchcraft cosmologies is that states which seem to have the most active witchcraft activity (Bergesen, 1977) are the ones with very strong and well-defined state bureaucracies which in turn organize and structure a great deal of daily life — hardly a situation of confused internal relations; in fact, almost the opposite. Also the single-party state is neither small-scale nor decentralized; again, almost the opposite.

Douglas seems to have reasoned that confused or ambiguous social relations generate ritual — which in many situations, like the Erikson boundary crisis hypothesis, is true. But, she also lists strongly bounded groups as a precondition for witchcraft, and since these are found in both primitive and modern societies, whereas confused internal relations, small scale, and low level of organization seem limited to more primitive societies, it may be that strong group is the key variable for explaining witchcraft. Also, if it is the gripping nature of social relations that generates ritual, then the category strong grid strong group, since that seems to grip the most, should generate the most active witchcraft cosmology: but it does not. Modern witch-hunts are most prevalent in single-party states where the strength of the state undermines strong social relations among individuals. Strong grid and strong group are actually antithetical dimensions of social organization and as such not found in the same social formation. Studies of highly corporate (strong) groups suggest that they are prone to subvert the power and legitimacy of institutional structures which link individuals (grid) in the processes of creating a one-to-one relationship between the atomistic individual and the all powerful corporate group. Studies of highly corporate groups such as religious orders and revolutionary parties (Coser, 1974) and Utopian communities (Kanter, 1968) suggest a similar hostility between the interests of the corporate body and the extended relations and obligations between individuals. In effect, there may be strong group and weak grid, or strong grid and weak group, but probably not strong group and strong grid.

The key limitation of the group-grid scheme is its egocentric nature, which derives from its origin in Bernstein's thinking about the social pressures on individual language users. Here both group and grid are meant to characterize immediate environments, of the face-to-face kind, and not the institutional or corporate organization of collectivities themselves. Douglas is quite explicit about this.

> If I speak of group, then, though the group may be ever so big, so that all the members cannot possibly know each other well, there would have to be in all parts of it a pressure from face-to-face situations to draw the same boundaries and accept the alignment of insiders and outsiders. A unit such as 'England' or 'the Catholic Church' would not qualify as 'group' in this sense. (1982a:201)

What of the origin and function of ritual? The linguistic analogy was important for two reasons. Ritual carries meaning like language, and as such is probably generated under the same conditions that generate linguistic codes. But Bernstein focused upon the individual speaker and his immediate social environment which might have made sense for his original British neighborhoods, but is a limitation when the inquiry turns to ritual and whole cosmologies. At this point we are dealing with broad cultural systems and need theoretical ideas which are capable of grasping the social organization of whole collectivities, not just the face-to-face environments of individuals.

There is another importance to the linguistic analogy; namely, it is probably more significant to understand that language acts like ritual than that ritual acts like language. This means that the explanatory task is not to see ritual as language and rely upon the sociolinguistic studies of conditions which generate patterns of speech, but to see language as ritual and look for the different patterns of social organization which generate more or less ritual. For instance, when studying linguistic codes it makes sense to inquire about the social milieu of individual speakers. Here we follow the individual and vary his environment. But, consider a more large-scale ritual — a public ceremony, religious festival, coronation, or national holiday. Here it makes more sense to focus upon the ritual itself, independently of the individual participant. We want to know why there are witch-hunts, feast days, sacrifices, and not why individuals partake of them, although that can be asked too.

Large-scale rituals seem to have more of a life of their own, existing as independent entities, and are not as closely tied to the individuals who carry them out as are linguistic codes. Codes have a life too, as they have a structure and organization of their own, and as social facts exist independently of individuals who bring them to life when they speak. More important codes are generated by certain kinds of social organization, not just pressures on individuals. It is the Durkheimian point about social realities having social origins. Here social organization generates ritual, whether that ritual be various kinds of linguistic codes or large scale public ceremonies of the more obviously religious kind.

What then of group and grid? One solution is to view them as aspects of the development of the overall corporateness of collectivities. It was Swanson's (1964) notion that when Durkheim spoke of societies *sui generis* he was referring to collectivities that had a corporate life of their own independently of their individual members and constituent groups. When a collectivity moves toward becoming a corporate actor it shifts from being a mere aggregation of members to a unitary whole. Following Swanson, corporateness can be considered a continuum, with collectivities varying in the extent to which they are organized to realize their distinctly collective interests and purposes. Although the idea of group and grid may equally 'grip' the individual, they are not equivalent dimensions of social organization. Group, emphasizing the well-boundedness of group life, seems to represent a more highly corporate order than grid, which pertains more to collectivities as aggregations of partial interests linked together rather than unified corporate wholes. Grid, it would appear, is an intermediary stage of corporate organization where the collectivity exists as a structuring of individuals rather than a single corporate actor.

This brings us to the question of corporateness and ritualistic cosmologies. Ritual carries collective information (the analogy with restricted codes) and thus reaffirms the collective reality of group life. Following Durkheim, ritual is understood as being performed to gods, spirits, and other collective representations which stand for or mirror the collectivity as a corporate whole. The more a collectivity exists as a corporate entity the more collective reality there is to be periodically reaffirmed, and hence the more ritual. Corporateness and ritual are not only positively correlated, but causally linked. The more corporate the collectivity, whether a small group, formal organization, or national society, the more ritual there will be to reaffirm these collective sentiments. This also means more restricted linguistic codes, whether speech, music, art, or food. Groups that are mere aggregations of separate interests should have less ritual, but as the group becomes more and more of a corporate entity the amount of ritual should increase.

First, there is weak group weak grid, a social arrangement with very little organization of any kind. It would be vaguely bounded and have weak ties among its members. As such there would be little external social reality present, and little need for ritual, with so little to reaffirm. Weak group weak grid would have the least ritualistic cosmology. Second, there is strong grid weak group. Here a collectivity exists as the linking or binding together of constituent sub-groups or individuals. The collectivity is an aggregation of parts bounded through multiple role reciprocities and strong rules.

> Where grid is strong and group weak, magic is at hand to
> help the individual in a competitive society. He trusts
> implicitly his know-how, his private destiny or star, and
> in the power of the rules . . . the cosmos is morally
> neutral and basically optimistic . . . [his] work is not
> controlled by independent ghosts or witches, or evil men.
> There is no sin: only stupidity. (1970:144, 137)

This sounds very much like the cosmology of Western societies, in which the individual and his institutions are strong (strong grid) and not totally subordinated to the state (strong group). The presence of ghosts, witches or evil men seems more relevant to primitive and traditional societies, but the same sort of phenomena is present in contemporary states where the gods and cosmic forces have taken a more secular form. In more corporate states, (strong group weak grid) political ideologies, like the sacred forces of history or nature, present themselves as cosmic forces which are periodically threatened by 'ghosts, witches or evil men' in the form of subversives, enemies of the people, spies, traitors, foreigners, and aliens.

As mentioned before, there is good reason to believe that the third category, strong group strong grid, does not exist empirically. Finally, there is the fourth category: strong group weak grid, comprising well-bounded highly corporate societies. In the modern world these are best represented by single party states and authoritarian regimes. Here the power of the state is supreme and there is an extensive state apparatus to insure the enforcement of state purposes above those of constituent groups and individuals. These states have the most corporate reality and hence the most ritualistic cosmologies. One-party states, for instance, are constantly plagued with boundary and purity concerns. Worries over infiltrators and enemies are common, and so is the periodic mobilization of the state's machinery to ritually root them out.

Modernity and religion

Finally, Douglas has employed her theoretical framework to address the purported effect of modernity on ritual and religion. There is something of a consensus in the social sciences that modernity has been hard on ritual and religion. Some call it a solvent, dissolving not only traditional ascriptive ties but also ideas of gods, spirits, and the supernatural. Modern culture is supposedly a secular world, where science has replaced religion and provides an ever changing and updated cosmology in accord with the latest empirical findings and theoretical speculations. What is left for religion and ritual is at best a source of comfort for those made insecure by modernity, and at worst some sort of false consciousness. That is a rough indictment of religion and ritual, and one that has existed at least since the Enlightenment if not earlier.

For Douglas, though, this perspective goes too far. From her point of view as long as there is collective life there will be ritual and religion, myths and collective representations, ceremonies and rites. Modernity changes the shape of society, but there are still social relations, and rituals for their renewal. Social change, then, does not mean the demise of religion. Until social relations disappear altogether, religion and ritual will play a role. The point is that religion is generated in social relations, which change, but do not disappear, with modernization.

Modernity was supposed to have had three negative effects on religion, and she dismisses them all. First, the 'prestige and authority of science . . . is supposed to have reduced the explanatory power of religion' (1982b:8), which she dismisses as a nineteenth-century relic opposing science and religion. She argues instead that people now understand that religion and science apply to different kinds of problems and hence pose no tension for each other. Second, the bureaucratization of life is supposed to have reduced the sense of the unknown and sacred. But, she argues, bureaucracy flourished in ancient Byzantium or the Vatican of the fifteenth century and so did religion. Religion and a bureaucratized world are not incompatible; at least they haven't been in the past. Third, we are now supposed to have little direct experience of nature, at least when compared with the past. Here she suggests that science has substituted a new sense of awe, as 'the sense of wonder in nature is deepened by the discoveries of science, and the sense of a game against nature to wrest a living from impersonal forces is still provided by bureaucracy' (1982a:11).

For Douglas, then, secularization is not new, but a cosmology generated by a certain set of social relations. As mentioned earlier, there have been primitive societies that one could characterize as having a secular cosmology. Social change may bring new social forms into being that have never existed before, and in that sense religion will change. But to the extent that we are still dealing with questions of group or grid, these will dictate the cosmology, not whether the society is new or old, big or small, traditional or modern.

She further suggests that a big part of the problem in modern society is the belief that culture (religion) is autonomous from social relations. 'When a scholar proclaims that nature has been demystified by modernization, I know that I am going to witness some mystification of culture' (1982b: 12). A safeguard is to:

> treat cultural categories as the cognitive containers in
> which social interests are defined and classified, argued,

negotiated, and fought out. Following this rule, there is no way in which culture and society can part company, nor any way in which one can be said to dominate the other (1982b:12).

If modernization *per se* doesn't bring about the demise of religion, it is still the case that social change does involve a shift in ritual and alternative symbolizations of social relations. Changes in social morphology are accompanied by shifts in the morphology of a group's collective representations, and Douglas suggests a great number of ways in which social relations are symbolized. For instance, she focuses upon the biological body as a symbol of the social body, with her central proposition being that bodily control will be as strong as in concern over the propriety of laughing, breaking wind, belching, publicly yawning, and so on. If social control is weak, the body will be relaxed, informal, untidy and sloppy, as with loose-fitting clothes or shaggy hair. Academics and artists, she points out, symbolize the less formal definition of their role with a 'display of carefully modulated shagginess according to the responsibilities they carry' (1970:72). She also suggests that where there is explicit social control over individuals, a positive value will be placed on consciousness. Trances and trancelike behavior or other situations involving a loss of control over the body will be frowned upon in more highly structured situations.

The body can also serve as a symbol for concern over group boundaries. Where there is concern about entrance and exit to the social body there will be concern about bodily orifices. Spittle, blood, milk, urine, feces, and tears, which have traversed the boundary of the body, can serve as symbols for concern about entering and leaving the social body. Similarly, ideas about the relationship of the heart, head, and sexual parts can symbolize social hierarchy or relations between groups and institutions. In short, the biological body is a perfect *tabula rasa* on which the form and structure of society can be written.

Douglas also argues that moral revitalization movements involve a shift from external to internal symbols.

Probably all movements of religious renewal have had in

common the rejection of external forms. In Europe manicheeism, Protestantism and now the revolt of the New Left, historically they all affirm the value of the follower's inside and of the insides of all his fellow members, together with the badness of everything external to the movement. Always we find bodily symbolism applied, from the values placed on internal and external parts of the body, on reality and appearance, content and form, spontaneity and established institutions. (1970:52)

Here social change seems to involve the delegitimation of the ritual props of the old order and an affirmation of internal states as symbolic alternatives.

Conclusions

Although it is impossible to succinctly summarize the complex thought of Mary Douglas, a few generalizations are possible. At the center of her work is the fundamental Durkheimian belief in the role of ritual and symbol in the production and reproduction of social relations. Further, much of this work load is carried by daily rituals that are hardly considered religious at all. Cleaning, tidying, and putting things in their place, along with the linguistic structure of everything from speech to meals, constitute the ritual lubrication which permeates daily existence. That we have not seen them as such further points to their very 'religious status' as sacred ideas. It is always easy to find the religious and symbolic in the lives of people different from ourselves. When it comes to our own social relations we enshroud them in myth just like our primitive brethren. But they are still there. From Douglas's point of view social relations are like clay. We mold them this way or that way as we make, or shape, our society, social order, class structure, state apparatus, or mode of production. But whatever the shape, however redistributed the rights, power, and surplus value, there is still some kind of social order — still some clay, — and that clay is reaffirmed and reproduced by ritual, regardless of the shape it is in. Religion doesn't disappear with modernization; it just reappears in new forms, from the cleanliness rituals of daily life to the political ceremonies of contemporary civil religion.

Rite, symbol, and myth do change, however, and to account for that in a systematic and theoretical way Douglas has devised a categorical scheme, group-grid, which enables her to analytically look at social relations in any social context. Most importantly, these analytical dimensions are linked to differences in cosmologies, so that a comparative study of culture and belief is possible. She has extended not only our understanding of what constitutes ritual, but in the connection of ritual and linguistic codes provides a new way of understanding all sorts of symbolic systems.

4 The neo-structuralism of Michel Foucault

Michel Foucault's essential concern is with the culture of the West, although he does not accept the categories which customarily are used to describe it. What Foucault is really writing about is all of man's thinking and the institutions that both perpetuate and inhibit this thinking. Foucault's subject is all of history, but history seen in terms of the shaping of modern culture, in terms of the dominant forces of power and knowledge. It is a history encompassing events as they affect all the individuals of a time rather than the ruling classes alone. Foucault's 'essential concern', as Alan Sheridan (1980:82), his translator and interpreter, states, 'has always been to understand the present, the present as a product of the past and as a seedbed of the new'. Clearly this coincides substantively with Peter Berger's notion of culture as being 'continuously produced and reproduced by man'. But Foucault, unlike Berger, Mary Douglas, or Jürgen Habermas, never looks at culture as an analytic or empirical category, or at the communication of groups; these are themselves the subjects of his analyses. Yet like them, he proceeds from the assumption that reality is socially constructed.

By now, Foucault's ideas have proliferated, so that some of them are no longer attributable to him alone. This is due to the fact that the interdisciplinary nature of his contributions has allowed every academic discipline, as well as the popular media, to adapt some of the ideas, so that there must have been a few thousand book reviews, in publications ranging from highbrow philosophy to the *Daily News*. *Madness and*

Civilization was of much interest to psychologists, psychiatrists and social workers; *The Birth of the Clinic* to doctors, health administrators and other professionals; *Discipline and Punish* has been read by most criminologists and penologists; and scholars in the humanities continue to address his theoretical works, *The Archeology of Knowledge* and *The Order of Things*, because they center on notions of language and discourse. Inevitably, *The History of Sexuality*, dealing with Foucault's ideas of power and knowledge rather than with sex, as the title would suggest, was reviewed in the journals of all these disciplines. This was due not only to the topic, but to the fact that by 1976 Foucault had become the foremost Parisian celebrity and his books had been translated into nearly every language. For the last few years, whatever Foucault says or writes makes news (cf. Cooper, 1981; Dreyfus and Rabinow, 1982).

Intellectual assumptions

Foucault's intellectual assumptions cover the broadest range. Some are responses to his immediate cultural milieu; others derive from the ideas his peers were discussing; and many have to do with the all-encompassing nature of his enterprise — the discovery of the origins of knowledge. In the Preface to the first edition of *Histoire de la Folie*, and in his inaugural address at the College de France, Foucault paid special tribute to three teachers: the philosopher Jean Hyppolite, who tried to use Hegel's philosophy as a means to understand the present and to make modernity the test of Hegelianism; George Canguilhem, whose studies in the history of ideas tended to stress discontinuities; and Georges Dumezil, who analyzed the myths, art, religion, law, and institutions of early European societies in terms of cultural totalities. At the time, he already had distanced himself from another teacher (Louis Althusser) and from the Communist Party which he had joined briefly in the late 1940s. But Marxist influences continued to permeate his intellectual formulations and ideas; Durkheimian assumptions were to be subsumed; and, increasingly, structuralist and deconstructionist ideas intruded.

The neo-structuralism of Michel Foucault

From existential phenomenology to structuralism

Immediately after the Second World War, French intellectuals, attempting to come to terms with the recent past, and exposed for the first time to Husserl's and Heidegger's phenomenology, began to address the many questions surrounding freedom and repression from a perspective informed by the latters' thought. Foucault, a student at the Ecole Normale Superieure, thus, was more than a passive bystander to the many questions surrounding the importance of experience, to the debates about the links between literature and its impact, and to the quarrels between Camus, Merleau-Ponty, and Sartre. Their political disagreements which at first were addressed as theoretical questions alone, touched on all the central issues, including beliefs about Soviet society and intentions, and about the political direction France was to take. Sartre's arguments for a time were found most persuasive, so that his existentialism became the guiding ideology for the French intellectual milieu, although there were continuing discussions about its viability. Because his theories were so linked to his politics, when at the XXth Party Congress in 1956 and Khrushchev's denunciation of the cult of personality, the repression in communist societies could no longer be denied, Sartre joined those who had questioned the validity of his own politics, and denounced Soviet practices. Foucault had left the party before and never directly entered the existentialists' fray. But because Sartre's politics had been so closely identified with his theoretical concerns, when his politics shifted, the theory also lost much of its legitimacy. Thus, when Lévi-Strauss presented the possibility of a new solution to the problems of existence — structuralism — in a culture where intellectuals' ideas always are picked up by a larger public, these ideas fell on fertile soil (cf. Kurzweil, 1980). This is not to say that there is a direct connection between the decline of existentialism and the rise of structuralism, but only that structuralist promises were welcomed for extrinsic as well as intrinsic reasons. Foucault did not immediately discuss structural linguistics or anthropology, nor the practicability of Marxist humanism or of communism. But he claims that he had been getting bored

135

with philosophy (namely Marxism); that his friends increasingly were painters, writers, and musicians rather than philosophers; that this had made him turn to the human sciences, and particularly to psychology.

Although the cultural influences on Foucault, particularly Sartre's leadership and the pull of Lévi-Strauss's theory as a means of 'deradicalization', should not be exaggerated, Foucault profited greatly from having matured during a period of extraordinary intellectual and social ferment and from having been with so many outstanding individuals who fertilized each others' ideas. Whether or not Foucault is deemed a Marxist, the influence of Marx on all French intellectuals is as undeniable as is that of Durkheim and Nietzsche. Foucault has made Marx's thought his own, or at least his means of criticizing society. He is concerned with false consciousness, not descriptively or theoretically, but in practice, insofar as he undercuts, or debunks — as Peter Berger would say — every accepted knowledge and belief. Unlike Althusser, who talks of a theory of practice, Foucault is critical of all ongoing practices with the help of his theoretical discourse which, itself, is a 'practice'. Unlike the humanist Marxists, who foresee a revolution after which the various crises of capitalism will be over, Foucault's predictions are more subtle and indirect. One can almost say that not only is he *not* waiting for a revolution, but that his thought itself has almost revolutionized our thinking about history. Only almost: his work has been as unacceptable to conventional historians who study specific periods, nation-based events and evolutions, demographic changes, etc., as it has been to their Marxist counterparts who observe the development and decline of capitalism. His books have rarely been reviewed in the historians' professional journals.

Foucault's history is also indebted to the *Annales* school and particularly to Fernand Braudel. The latter has emphasized what he calls 'submerged history', that is history which is hidden underneath the customary telling of events. He traces changes over the *longue durée*, namely over vast sweeps of time, stresses the importance of geography, and contrasts the influences of medium-term and short-term events. The publication of his *La Mediterranée* (1966), which created much controversy among French historians after the Second World War, also questioned conventional history, thereby lending support to those Marxists who studied history in terms of its progression from one epoch to another. Foucault, however, goes beyond Braudel, insofar as he mediates between Braudel's categories, between records of elite and popular culture (the latter tends to be dominated by the former), and draws attention to the exclusions, prohibitions, and limits through which modern culture historically came into being.

All of Foucault's teachers and contemporaries, as well as Foucault, take the influence of Durkheim for granted. This influence does not need to be acknowledged. Particularly the notion that human beings tend to classify and to connect ideas, thereby creating relationships specific to their culture (addressed directly by Lévi-Strauss in *Tristes Tropiques*, 1968), derived from Durkheim and Mauss's *Primitive Classification* (1963). The emphasis on the connection of ideas, and on the human need to unify knowledge in order to understand the universe, which was Lévi-Strauss's original impetus for his *structuralisme*, is an underlying aim of all of Foucault's work. Durkheim's spirit wafts over French sociology and social thought; thus, the credit due him is understood. This is so, in spite of the fact that Durkheim considered laws as instituting a society's moral code expressing collective sentiments and thus solidarity, whereas Foucault questions the basis of this solidarity, in so far as he focuses on the disciplinary fragmentations that began with the increasing importance of scientific knowledge.

The structuralist heritage

Though starting from a very different angle, Lévi-Strauss's promise to get to the roots of culture, long before there was any science, and attempting to find the origins of the binary relationships constituting this culture, also was to provide the means for Foucault's ends. Lévi-Strauss (1963, 1968) himself has looked to Saussure. Because he had found structural similarities in the kinship systems of different Brazilian-Indian tribes, he set out to apply Saussure's linguistic theory to help explain some of the contradictions he noted between natives' systems of terminology and attitudes and between their systems of nomenclature and social organization. Lévi-Strauss was inspired particularly by the very technical components of structural linguistics, and by its scientific approach. Empirical observation, the accepted method of anthropologists, fell short in his estimation of exploring symbolic relationships fully — both on the macro-level, where they were said to exist between languages and cultures, and in tribal societies whose rich mythology, so evident in the telling of myths, tended to be studied apart from social structure. It was this attempt to graft structural linguistics on to anthropology that inspired the structuralists in other fields to contribute their own expertise to the enterprise. Lévi-Strauss's imaginative leap in thought struck a responsive chord: others too were becoming increasingly disenchanted with the fragmentation of knowledge into academic disciplines and the seemingly widening abyss between theories based on objectivity and those advocating subjectivity.

When the search for unconscious structures did not yield results, Saussurean linguistics began to be bolstered by additional theories. Thus, interpretations began to center around applications of Roman Jacobson's (1971) notions of binary relationships between *phonemes* — the smallest units of sound — and *morphemes* — the smallest units of meaning. Later, Roland Barthes in *Elements of Semiology* (1968) went further, adding elaborations from André Martinet's (1960) and Louis Hjelmslev's (1959) linguistics in order to conceptualize total language experience (*la langue moins la parole*). This approach sought to interpret every sign associated with spoken and written language. When Barthes subdivided language into its scheme, norms, and usage, postulating *articuli* to emphasize some language aspects over others, and when he attempted to account for textual idiosyncrasies by way of *idiolects*, Foucault paid attention. Barthes' project was not so different from his own. Thus, when Barthes found that he still had to account for the dual nature of code/message and for double meanings in writing as well as in sound, Foucault examined how these issues would connect to the origins of knowledge. These questions were the focus of *The Order of Things* and *The Archeology of Knowledge*.

The very discussions of structuralism by its 'elaborators', brought out their own ambivalences, their frustrations about the elusive thought structures, and made for their later disaffection — when the promised structures continued to remain hidden. Because structuralism was both a method and a theory based on the success of this method, it was difficult even to define. The inherent problems, therefore are evident in even the best of definitions, such as the one given by Barthes:

> What is structuralism? It is not a school of thought, or even a movement, for most of the authors habitually associated with this word do not feel in any way bound together by a common doctrine or cause . . . The aim of all structuralist activity, in the fields of both thought and poetry, is to reconstitute an object, and, by this process, to make known the rules of functioning, or 'functions', of this object. The structure is therefore effectively a *simulacrum* of the object which . . . brings out something that remained invisible, or, if you like, unintelligible in the natural object . . . The simulacrum is intellect added to the object. (1964:213)

If intellect was the ingredient that would help unveil the unconscious relationships and the rules that went into constituting all structures, then their emergence should have been assured, for the individuals engaged in the search certainly possessed the most extraordinary talents. But Barthes, after spending ten years on his *Elements of Semiology*, conceded at its publication that the origins of writing had not surfaced; Lévi-Strauss returned to anthropology; and Foucault's *The Order of Things* and *The Archeology of Knowledge*, as will be seen, were abandoned in favor of studies of power and sexuality. He increasingly adopted ideas from Nietzsche and 'deconstructed' social texts similarly to the way Derrida deconstructed literary ones.

Alan Sheridan, in *Michel Foucault: The Will to Truth* (1980:37), supports Foucault's contention that his interests were completely outside structural linguistics, that he absorbed its language almost without realizing it, and that for this reason some of the terminology in the second edition of *The Birth of the Clinic* has been changed: language, for instance, became discourse; signifier/signified was largely dropped. Sheridan also extends Foucault's (1970:xiv) 'request to the English-speaking reader' that they 'free him from a connection to structuralism', having 'used none of the methods, concepts, or key terms that characterize structural analysis'. Of course, the inquiries of the other so-called structuralists are very different from Foucault's own; nevertheless, the preoccupation with structural linguistics, and the attempt to adapt some of its principles to the methodology in other areas of study, was a manifestation of what has been called *The Age of Structuralism* (Kurzweil, 1980). Certainly, when Foucault maintained in *The Birth of the Clinic* that the doctor's diagnosis and his treatment can be subsumed in a clinical method 'distinguishing between sign and symptoms', when he talks of 'the signifier (sign and symptom) as ... transparent for the signified, whose essence — the heart of the disease — is entirely exhausted in the intelligible syntax of the signifier ... and when the symptom abandons its passivity ... to become a signifier of the disease', it seems appropriate to connect him with structuralism.

Foucault's perspective on culture

The Archeology of Knowledge is Foucault's only book listing the word culture in the index. Still, all his works deal with culture in the broadest sense. For him the transmission of knowledge is central to culture and this process is never linear: it is linked to power in conscious and unconscious ways; it is insidious, sporadic, and ubiquitous; and it transcends national and 'cultural' boundaries. At the same time, he does not accept anthropological theories of cross-cultural transmission, since these as well would be 'unilinear'. As summarized above, Foucault's anthropology is more inclined to favor Lévi-Strauss's even though his connections to it are more methodological than substantive. His focus is on the knowledge in what might be called pre-industrial, industrial, or post-industrial societies rather than on the knowledge emerging through the telling of tribal myths. In any event, it is important to recall that Foucault emphasizes knowledge rather than culture as a category, although his many works on the history of systems of thought and of knowledge all are about Western culture — about how its emergence at the end of the Middle Ages determined its current state.

Central to Foucault's work is a focus on discourse. From it flows his many insights, including ones derived from the relations between different discourses, between theory and practice, and between the desire for knowledge and 'profit' accruing to the ones who know. Foucault's search in the historical record avoids acceptance of taken-for-granted truths, thus discovering previously ignored or neglected beliefs and the practical consequences to which they lead. The very depth, as well as the speculative nature of Foucault's endeavour, of course, make it antithetical to sociological inquiries based on empiricism. His system, by its very nature, must remain open-ended. Such a system does not lend itself to verification or falsification, leaving little common ground between Foucault and empirical sociologists.

Madness and medicine

Essentially, Foucault laid the ground for his subsequent works, however unconscious and loose its thrust still remained, in *Madness and Civilization*. Historical investigations relying on myriads of records describe the emerging connections between madness and psychiatry at the end of the Middle Ages. That was when leprosy, the scourge that had led to the construction of over two thousand leper-houses between the thirteenth and seventeenth centuries, disappeared; when madmen in their *Narrenschiffe* were still conveyed from town to town, leading a wandering existence. Foucault illustrates how society dealt with both types of deviants at the time, how it segregated the lepers so that they would disappear from sight and yet allowed the fools freedom to move about in their confining vessels. They could see the world, but could not attend church, might be whipped, or chased in mock races; and being on a ship controlled by sailors, also, 'made them prisoners of their own departure' (1965:10–11). Foucault's minute descriptions focus on contradictions

141

incorporated in the treatment of these deviants; at the same time, he shows the changes that occurred as a result of social conditions which ignored them as individuals. That the *Narrenschiffe* were eventually abandoned, and that the mad were then thought to be better off in segregated institutions, he argues, was as much connected to the availability of empty leprosariums as to the new knowledge about madness that was slowly being accumulated. Even the definition of madness, Foucault argues, always depends upon the elite, and upon the composition of this elite, as well as upon its need for outcasts. Thus, madness is a judgment rather than a fact. What is novel in Foucault's treatment of deviance is linking it to moral issues — a theme he expands on in every one of his subsequent books — when he keeps reiterating how the fate of fools, criminals, and other outcasts was less important than the act of their exclusion, and how this exclusion, itself, would symbolically purify society.

Foucault's historical reconstructions rely on every possible source: town records, biographies, national archives, unpublished letters found in attics, novels, poetry, etc. In this, his affinity with the work of the *Annales* school is evident, although he goes beyond them in his generalizations, and even more in his reliance on language rather than on events. He also depends more strongly on literary works than they do. In part, this may result from his focus on individuals within their times, rather than on the times or the individuals themselves. This emphasis, in turn, makes for the realization that at the end of the Middle Ages everyone was fascinated by madness, by its ambiguity, and by its existence at the edge of experience. Aware of the classical literature, Foucault finds that preoccupations with madness abounded and were helpful in dealing with anxieties about death. Foucault avoids the usual social science explanations which link this anxiety to the gradual loss of religion. Instead, he argues that writers and artists endowed the madman with more insight than they did the sane. In the sixteenth century, when madness had already replaced death as the root cause of anxiety, the madman seemed to be able to look into the future and, therefore, was frequently cast in the role of prophet.

Foucault also shows how this view of the mad as having

privileged access to a symbolic and completely moral universe changed at the end of the Middle Ages. This change coincided with the decision, however tentative it might have been at first, to confine the mad. How this decision itself had to do with the creation of the Hôpital Général, in 1656, which among other things, was charged with preventing 'mendicancy and idleness as sources of all disorder' (1965:57), he then documents. The use of confinement to create a cheap labor force, as a more commerce and industry-oriented society increasingly condemned idleness and sloth, is a theme he develops further in later works. But here he states for the first time that madmen, like the poor, became subject to the rules of forced labor, were considered as morally defective as all the others who could not or would not work.

Like other categories of individuals who did not fit in — the beggars, vagabonds, criminals, and sick — the mad were now available for discussion by the powerful. Since the mad were confined as a result of their uselessness, Foucault indicates why, at first, all the 'useless' were segregated together, and were categorized only later on, when rehabilitating them for work became specific topics for experts' discussion. Eventually, he documents, there was a convergence of aims between such diverse specialists as psychiatrists, doctors, lawyers, and politicians. But in *Madness and Civilization* he relies primarily on description to pull together facts which, given the disciplinary fragmentation of modern society, tend to be examined separately. Hence Foucault connects the conditions of horror to which the mad were condemned to their domination by hospital directors whose 'power of authority and direction, administration and commerce, police and jurisdiction, correction and punishment', allowed them to use 'stakes and irons, prisons and dungeons' (1965:59). And he shows how the mad, chained, exposed to rats, in wet and sewerless cells, often acted as if they deserved mistreatment and brutalization, although the conditions of their confinement might themselves have contributed to their insanity.

Foucault had not yet begun to construct his linguistic theories, but he did point to the new language used by doctors — a language they constructed to designate newly discovered illnesses, cures and other biological facts — 'the first and last structure of madness, its constituent form' (1965:91). Foucault's mediations between sanity and insanity, between the language of delirium and of dreams, or between doctors and their patients, were found to belong to the new scientific *Zeitgeist* which came about during the Classical Age. This dominance of science not only advanced knowledge, but also gave power to those who possessed that knowledge, so that they were in the position to increase their own status. Still, at the time, Foucault tells us in 1977, he was rather tentative:

> When I think back now, I ask myself what else it was that I was talking about, in *Madness and Civilization* or *The Birth of the Clinic*, but power? Yet I'm perfectly aware that I scarcely ever used the word and never had such a field of analysis at my disposal. I can say that this was an incapacity linked undoubtedly with the political situation we found ourselves in. It is hard to see where, either on the Right or the Left, this problem of power could then have been posed. (1980a:115)

Foucault then went on to explain how this had to do with how important political questions were being formulated — on the Right in terms of constitution, sovereignty, etc., and on the Left in terms of the state apparatus. And ideological formulation, he continued, be it of Soviet totalitarianism or of Western capitalism — both denounced in 'formulatic' ways — never allowed for an analysis of power in terms of tactics, of techniques, or of its mechanics. This task, he then stated, could begin only after 1968, after the 'fine meshes' of the web of power had begun to be visible and could be analyzed by those who 'had hitherto remained outside the field of political analysis' (1980a:116).

In retrospect, *Madness and Civilization* not only provided Foucault with the raw material for his later books, but with a new interdisciplinary, atemporal, global, and idiosyncratic approach to history, an approach that earned him much praise, and many attacks. This was a project he would soon devote much time to, and that led to the 'archeological' method he was to construct, as well as to the unveiling of the 'culture of confinement' which was said to have evolved as a corollary but subversive and unconscious element of Enlightenment thought. By uncovering the origins of existing codes of knowledge, Foucault set out to show how the whole of modern civilization was more than the sum of its parts; and how reason always incorporates 'unreason'.

The Birth of the Clinic was a much more specialized book. Whereas *Madness and Civilization* had ranged over a few hundred years, this book covered a span of fifty years, the Classical Age, from the second part of the eighteenth century to the beginning of the nineteenth. But to indicate that this was not simply a history of medicine, Foucault's preface begins by saying that:

> This book is about space, about language, and about death; it is about the act of seeing, the gaze. Towards the middle of the eighteenth century, Pomme treated and cured a hysteric by making her take 'baths ten or twelve hours a day, for ten whole months.' (1975a:ix)

How doctors, by 1816, had used language and discourse in order to learn a new *way to see*, to separate the sick organism from its disease, to use the new scientific knowledge which they argued and wrote about, with the help of what Foucault calls their *gaze* (it takes in everything all at once), is the major subject of his *Archeology of Medical Perception*, the book's subtitle. The old classificatory medicine, he notes, gave way to the anatomo-clinical method, to the 'science' we now know, and this happened as a result of many interrelations between doctors' discourses with other institutions. Foucault focuses on the changing connections between what doctors are beginning to see, how they interpret their new insights, and how they manage to get these insights accepted. He points to the reforms initiated by the fact that the implementation of the principles of the French revolution included the availability of equal medical care for all; and to ensuing expectations for public assistance, for general and teaching hospitals, medical faculties and nurses. It had become imperative that doctors learn more about diseases, that they do so quickly, and that they invent ways of avoiding epidemics. Most of all, Foucault describes how all this learning which, after all, was the means to prolong life and often to prevent death, made doctors the most powerful figures in the society. The theme of doctors and lawyers as the powers behind modern society, which Foucault addresses head on in *Discipline and Punish*, is already well articulated in this book.

Without ever stating that he is going to expose the myths of positivism, of the doctors' 'superiority' to their fellow men, or of their philanthropic nature, Foucault does just that. He never imputes evil motives to individual practitioners. Instead, he indicates how scientific explorations themselves pushed the doctors to assert what they thought correct, only to be proven wrong by others whose discoveries contradicted their own. Because, for instance, hospitals had become crowded, patient care costly and impersonal, and insanitary conditions would infect some patients with contagious diseases, expediency and empirical observations conspired to have doctors advocate home care. That home care, also, worked to the advantage of the state, in so far as the hospitalized sick (they were also poor) could eat the broth from the meat allocated to their healthy relatives, is the sort of fact Foucault uncovered from examining the various records. At the same time, as patients were cared for at home, argues Foucault, doctors began to make housecalls. This not only allowed them to observe the relationship between poverty and various illnesses, but led to a change in medical space: diseases moved out of the hospitals; hospitals became research-oriented; the state began to provide laws and funds for them, and for a 'climate for research'. This, then, led to the birth of the research hospital, where, just as inside the asylum, the poor became the guinea pigs. The practice was justified, states Foucault, because the rich subsidized their treatment, so that doctors could learn more about the relationship between human beings and the disease they carried. The consequent advance of medical science would benefit everyone.

In the process, however, doctors further strengthened their own privileged positions. Foucault shows how the sum of these changes, none of which was isolated from the others, produced new codes of knowledge and new laws favorable to medicine. Thus, examining the dead was legalized at the doctors' instigation; doctors could now 'gaze' at death when performing autopsies (1975a:96). Now the dissection of corpses allowed for the examination of dead tissues, and for 'restructuring' the disease from its corpse, so that there not only developed the new science of pathology, but also a new field for specialization. Foucault's strange and frequently ghoulish inquiries seem to pick out the unusual and weird; yet, it all appears inevitable and true. The invention of the stethoscope, for example, added ear and touch to sight (before then doctors only looked at patients who sat across from them in their clothes), and as patients undressed, religious and moral dogma about sexuality began to change as well. Consequently, the stethoscope was found to bridge moral and technological obstacles for the doctors. It differentiated them from ordinary mortals for whom the old rules still held. Patients' descriptions of symptoms eventually led to conditions which, according to Foucault, helped Freud articulate his 'talking cure'.

As noted above, Foucault was intent in 1964 on profiting from structural linguistics and on constructing his own method in order to analyze historical data within their total context. Like the rest of the Parisian intellectuals, he paid particular attention to Lacan's mediations between conscious and unconscious phenomena (themselves indebted to Saussurean dichotomies between *langue* and *parole*, and applied to the centrality of the mirror stage — the child's first and indelible apprehension of the self — because they were to facilitate his own search for the codes of knowledge with the help of his 'archival' discourse. But even though this discourse was examined with the help of structuralist oppositions, Foucault soon insisted that he was very different from all the other structuralists, neo-structuralists, or deconstructionists. In the introduction to *The Archeology of Knowledge* (1972), he indicates that the problems when relatively posed in history as well as in other fields such as linguistics, ethnology, economics, literary analysis and mythology, may be called structuralism, but 'only under certain conditions', namely when these problems originate in the field of history itself (p. 11).

The Archeology of Knowledge

In *The Archeology of Knowledge*, Foucault attempts to reorganize, to recover in controlled and methodical fashion, what he had previously done blindly (1972:17). He states that 'natural history', the 'analysis of wealth', and 'political economy' in *The Order of Things* had been considered in general terms. But he had employed the names of authors in a naive and even crude fashion, he confesses, and ought to have stayed away from individualizing them and from using names. Instead, an author, too, is to be conceptualized as belonging to his culture, to his time and place. Beckett's 'What matter who's speaking' was to supply the direction (1977:115). Thus the author simply becomes a function of discourse, performing his job of 'author-function'. This de-subjectivation required a complex method, as did the question of periodization. Conventional history of ideas either stresses continuities or discontinuities, he argued, but within a specific period, within a culture, the same form of history is operative in the economic, political, social, or religious spheres. It is the change from one way of doing history to another that concerns Foucault.

Consequently, he examines more directly the epistemological breaks that are said to usher in every new era of knowledge. Because knowledge is expressed through language, he proceeds systematically to look at each aspect of spoken and unspoken language in order to uncover 'autochthonous' transformations; that is, the emergence of new knowledge. Foucault refutes both history as a study of continuities and the examination of its structural discontinuities trying to get away from cultural totalities. He wants to 'impose the forms of structural analysis on history itself', so that historical analysis will be 'freed of anthropology'. Foucault (1972:17) attempts to locate new meaning at a 'particular site defined by the exteriority of its vicinity'. Global history is meant to make room for this general history — a history examining series, ruptures, limits, chronological specificities and types of relation. The latter are said to operate from anti-anthropologist, anti-humanist, and anti-structuralist premises. In sweeping statements, Foucault spans the entire intellectual universe, cuts through 'historical successions that exist behind revolutions, governments and famines, to other pasts, hierarchies and networks whose internal coherences constitute and maintain themselves' (1972). Because the method is said to be evolving along with the codes of knowledge, Foucault says that he requires a 'presystematic system' to accommodate this history of thought and knowledge, of philosophy and literature. In the process, he accumulates 'stratified ensembles' and 'discursive regularities' and unites 'discursive strategies' for the sake of order between objects and concepts, choices and enunciations. The smallest unit of analysis is the *enonce*. This concept is roughly the equivalent of Lévi-Strauss's constituent unit in myth.

These enunciative units are said to produce relations and a play between relations and are defined without reference to their foundation. They are dominated by the rules of discursive practice. Thus the doctor, for instance, is placed at his 'institutional site', is part of his object-centered discourse inside his enunciative field — a field subject to a strategy with its own ideas and ideality, a strategy that is to be circumvented through linguistic rules. This means that doctors constructed their own mystifying and scientific lingo, by separating the symptom from the sickness, the signifier from the signified.

The construction of this theory gets more and more murky, as Foucault tries to show how his enunciative unit becomes a part of 'verbal performance' and of the 'ensemble of signs produced by a natural or artificial language'. The problem is complicated, because he wants to account for both verbal and written language and to interpret the relationships of every sign with every other sign. He also wants to do this theoretically, so that all future signs will fit in. Hence, an ensemble of signs is hard to recognize; it facilitates 'the transcendental ends of a form of discourse that is opposed to all analysis of language'. Yet, as Foucault gazes into the depths of consciousness and of 'un-thought thought' and into the relations and roots of every thought, he continues to insist that he must also free himself of the limits of linguistic structure.

Since the archives of a culture emerge only in fragments,

Foucault postulates a general horizon for them all — his 'archeology'. This archeology is chiefly described by what it is not. It is 'neither a search for beginnings' nor a geology that attempts to define discourse itself. It is not a history of ideas, because it is not interpretive, does not look for transformations, and has no slow progressions; it does not try to grasp moments on its horizon, nor does it attach itself to sociology, anthropology, psychology, or creation. It never reconstitutes what was thought, wanted, or proven, but is the systematic description of a discourse-object itself.

Foucault explains that systems such as Darwin's, Saussure's, or Keynes's operate in different fields of 'enunciative regularities that characterize enunciative formation', even though they use the same grammar and logic. This would demonstrate enunciative homogeneity between three systems operating during the same epoch. Still, this does not mean that archeological observation has a 'deductive schema' or that it attempts any sort of 'totalitarian periodization'.

Foucault gives many examples of irregularities and contradictions in language, on many levels, tying them to coherences that are said to indicate similarities between chronological discourse (such as *Madness and Civilization* or *The Birth of the Clinic*) and lateral discourse (such as *The Order of Things*). But he does not try to reconstruct a total picture, he tells us, only wanting to 'reveal' the relations between various well-determined sets of discursive formations. Consequently, he can talk of the Classical age even as he denies the Classical spirit; his archeology refutes symbolic projection, expression, and reflection, and, once more, he rejects traditional history with its emphasis on causality in favor of an archeological analysis:

> If archaeology brings medical discourse closer to a number of practices, it is in order to discover . . . far more direct relations than those of causality communicated through the consciousness of speaking subjects. It wishes to show not how political practice has determined the meaning and form of medical discourse, but how and in what form it takes part in its conditions of emergence, insertion, and functioning. This relation may be assigned to several levels. (1972:163)

150

Relying on his insights into medical practices, practitioners and their spheres, Foucault reaches for the most hidden meanings of language, and reiterates that his archeology 'disarticulates the synchrony of breaks', does not use the epoch, the horizon or its objects as basic unities, 'but only as discursive practice'. Any social event can be examined with the help of his archeology. The French Revolution, for example:

> does not play the role of an event exterior to discourse, whose divisive effect one is under some kind of obligation to discover in all discourses; it functions as a complex, articulated, describable group of transformations that left a number of positivities intact, fixed for a number of other rules that are still with us, and also established positivities that have recently disappeared or are still disappearing before our eyes. (1972:177)

Clearly, these are the observations of a macro-theorist, of one who expects to account for phenomena, events, scientific and social change by examining how these have been, and are, apprehended.

Only in the last chapter of *The Archeology of Knowledge* does Foucault directly address the relation of science and knowledge to ideology. Since his archeology is said to exist as a sort of unconscious grid, it does away with the customary distinction of science vs. non-science. Both of these 'cultures' are distinguished in terms of their functions rather than their values. Foucault's archeology contains literary and philosophical texts as well as scientific ones. This means that science is one discursive formation among many others and its ideological function is open for examination. But, he adds, non-scientific knowledge is not to be judged as one would judge science. This is an allusion to Althusser's theoretical break between scientific and humanist Marxism, that is between the 'early' and the 'late' Marx, and is aimed at those intellectuals who believed Foucault's 'epochs' to be somewhat related. In fact, Foucault's explanation that the knowledge of a new age already has its beginning at the end of the old one, as we know, is taken directly from Marx and distinguishes itself from the sudden Althusserian ruptures.

But does that make Foucault a Marxist? And if so, what type of Marxist? In *The Archeology of Knowledge* he skirts the issue. For after saying that the fear which makes him seek 'the great historico-transcendental destiny of the Occident is rooted in politics', he immediately drops the subject. But not for long.

Toward a focus on power

The events of May 1968 drastically changed Foucault's focus. Reflecting on them in a conversation with Gilles Deleuze in 1972, he says that:

> the intellectual discovered that the masses no longer need him to gain knowledge: they *know* perfectly well, without illusion; they know far better than he and they are certainly capable of expressing themselves. But there exists a system of power which blocks, prohibits, and invalidates this discourse and this knowledge, a power not only found in the manifest authority of censorship, but one that profoundly and subtly penetrates an entire social network. Intellectuals are themselves agents of this system of power — the idea of their responsibility for 'consciousness' and discourse forms part of the system. (1977:207)

That neither the so-called structuralists, nor the 'Marxists', nor the other intellectuals had foreseen this near-revolution was 'proof', for Foucault, that intellectuals no longer could be thought of as a vanguard. But given Foucault's own interests, it was even more astonishing that he had been so oblivious to the emergence of new power centers, that while discussing how the medical practitioners and legal authorities cooperated to set themselves up, he did not focus on power itself. Sheridan (1980:116), certainly one of Foucault's admirers, says that this omission of the role of power in his archeology led Foucault to drop the term altogether, along with all its other 'panoply of terms', and to adopt, unashamedly, the Nietzschean notion of 'genealogy'. But in his subsequent works, Foucault does compensate. Re-examining the period from the end of the Middle Ages to the nineteenth century, but focusing on other subjects, he emphasizes the domination of power/knowledge, and the conscious and unconscious use of knowledge to exert power. His involvement in prison reform, itself connected to his writing of *Discipline and Punish*, catapulted him into political debates. Given the prominence of French Marxism and Communism with all the factions and followers, he was often questioned about his leftism.

If Foucault can be called a Marxist, this can be done only in the most general and idealist manner. He is as critical of repression in the Soviet Union as elsewhere. Furthermore, he avoids Marxist rhetoric, always employing Marx's own means of analysis, focusing on empirical facts, yet forgetting about the progression of history or the expected revolution. It has been possible by some, however, to interpret Foucault's predictions about the end of our age as vaguely paralleling the 'impending' Marxist revolution. In any event, the project of Foucault's archeology which was to serve as a framework able to account for all the contradictions in advanced industrial society, including communist society, was carried on in his subsequent works dealing with power.

Culture and social change

As we have seen, Foucault does not talk of culture *per se*, or of cultural change. Instead, he examines the changes that have occurred, expecting to shed light on what made them happen, how they influenced the lives of individuals of every strata, and how particular individuals came to be in or out of power. His focus on the shifts from classical to modern culture, on how culture was produced in relation to the creation of knowledge, or to the emergence of the subcultures of economics, politics, history, etc., all are evidence of his concern with social change. In fact, he goes further than most sociologists and historians, when he predicts the end of our 'age of man', as a result of the historical trends he has observed, trends that seem to have been getting more obvious from *Madness and Civilization* to *The Birth of the Clinic* and to *Discipline and Punish*. What is striking again is how Foucault's idiosyncratic method differs from all others, how he emphasizes cultural dynamics, the relation of these dynamics to perception, to how individuals' views themselves reflected social changes; and how all these changes were linked to prevalent knowledges. Foucault looks at meaning structures that have become facticities, even though these were not consciously willed or articulated by specific individuals. Whereas Peter Berger (1967:18), for instance, would ask 'How is it possible for subjective meaning structures to *become* objective facticities', Foucault sees meaning as emerging from the interplay of subjectivities in their relationships to institutions, technologies, and changing social needs. Such a theory, it would seem, does not allow for a 'customary' theory of the self, because any importance attributed to a 'self' would contradict his domain assumptions, and would be contrary to Foucault's project: to the idea that even an author is no more than an expression of the relationship between his work, his era, and his own talent; and to the notion that deviance, for the most part, depends upon its social definition rather than upon individual performance. Again, the intellectual filiation can be traced to both Marx's concept of *false consciousness* and to Durkheim's concept of *anomie.*

Evolution of the human sciences

The book that more than any other directly addresses cultural change is *The Order of Things* — an examination of the origins of language and discourse. Foucault had argued, initially, that contrary to existing beliefs, historians of science were more capable of reporting objective truth than social scientists, who were likely to suffer from subjectivity, human superstitions, and prejudicial attitudes. But realizing that scientists were as prone to peer influence as others, he hypothesized that intellectual activities during any given period are dominated by specific codes of knowledge which depend on available beliefs, technologies and social arrangements. Thus, when he examined the period from the end of the Renaissance to the end of the nineteenth century, he attempted to locate specific discourses about human beings, about language, and about wealth. In addition, he asked to what extent the periodization emerging from the study of medicine and madness would influence these three types of discourse. If he were to find common 'deep' structures alien to previous and subsequent discourses in each of these three areas prevalent during a specific time, he assumed that he would also discover underlying rules which may have helped fashion these discourses. The common, and hidden, structures which were responsible for the possibilities of a discourse in the first place, were said to be found on the archeological level. By deciphering this level, that is by getting to it through a backward tracing of all discourse, Foucault expected to uncover his archeological system. Because hidden, however, this was an as yet unconscious system, a system to be articulated.

Its articulation was to be found through examination of a particular sort. As Foucault explains in the introduction to *The Order of Things*:

> This book first arose out of a passage in Borges, out of the laughter that shattered, as I read the passage, all the familiar landmarks of thought — *our* thought, the thought that bears the stamp of our age and our geography — breaking up all the ordered surfaces and all the planes with which we are accustomed to tame the wild profusion of existing things and continuing long afterwards to disturb and threaten with collapse our age-old distinction between the Same and the Other. This passage quotes 'a certain Chinese encyclopaedia' in which it is written that 'animals are divided into: (a) belonging to the Emperor, (b) embalmed, (c) tame, (d) sucking pigs, (e) sirens, (f) fabulous, (g) stray dogs, (h) included in the present classification, (i) frenzied, (j) innumerable, (k) drawn with a very fine camelhair brush, (l) *et cetera*, (m) having just broken the water pitcher, (n) that from a long way off look like flies.' In the wonderment of this taxonomy, the thing we apprehend in one great leap, the thing that, by means of the fable, is demonstrated as the exotic charm of another system of thought, is the limitation of our own, the stark impossibility of thinking *that*. But what is it impossible to think, and what kind of impossibility are we faced with here? (1970:xv)

Put simply, Foucault is telling us that cultural factors limit our thinking, that even the most imaginative individual functions within his or her language, that the individual's imagination itself is sparked by the age he or she lives in, and that each age has its own codes of knowledge. Time and space thus predetermine the individual's scope of thought and action and, therefore, figure prominently in Foucauldian analyses.

Inevitably, Foucault's theoretical explorations flow from his empirical investigations of madness and medicine. But now he looks more directly at the languages that were created, largely because new inventions had to be named, new cures and symptoms to be described; and because doctors as well as other new professionals had to 'prove' they knew something ordinary individuals were not privy to. The languages and discourses of the new scientific disciplines reflected the new *Zeitgeist*, as well as the importance of the medical profession, and of all the other expert fields being created, from economics and sociology to law and administration. Yet all the emerging exigencies, argues Foucault, were not only addressed consciously: they evolved from the many relationships within institutions, between institutions and individuals which themselves were in flux, and were subject to change with every new technique, invention, description, and reaction. In other words, needs and responses to these needs brought forth other needs and responses which, in turn, led to more research, to the alteration of other social and scientific facts, and to far-reaching repercussions. This is part of the history of science, but Foucault's approach is unusual. Customary practice, on the one hand:

> traces the progress of discovery, the formulation of problems, and clash of controversy . . . [and] analyzes
> . . . the processes and products of scientific consciousness
> . . . But, on the other hand, it tries to restore what eluded that consciousness: the influences that affected it, the implicit philosophies that were subjacent to it, the unformulated thematics, the unseen obstacles; it describes the unconscious of science. This unconscious is always the negative side of science — that which resists it, deflects it, or disturbs it. What I would like to do, however, is to

reveal a *positive unconscious* of knowledge: a level that eludes the consciousness of the scientist and yet is part of scientific discourse, instead of disputing its validity and seeking to diminish its scientific nature. What was common to the natural history, the economics, and the grammar of the Classical period was certainly not present to the consciousness of the scientist; or that part that was conscious was superficial, limited, and almost fanciful; but, unknown to themselves, the naturalists, economists, and grammarians employed the same rules to define the objects proper to their own study, to form their concepts, to build their theories. (1970:xi)

Foucault then continues to tell us that during the Classical period, that is in the fifty years covered by *The Birth of the Clinic*, there evolved a theory of representation: certain sciences were suddenly and thoroughly reorganized; corresponding transformations occurred in 'the appearance of biology, political economy, philosophy, a number of human sciences, and a new type of philosophy' (1970:xii). By opening his discussion with Borges — as an example of thinking antithetical to the Classical age as well as to us — or continuing it with Don Quixote — as the character whose 'adventures form the boundary [which] mark[s] the end of the old interplay between resemblance and signs and contain[s] the beginnings of new relations' — Foucault (1970:46) gives literary examples paralleling the scientific ones. Actually, Foucault perceives *Don Quixote* as the literary masterpiece which, more than any other, embodies both the old interplay of signs of resemblance (these held together the world of the Renaissance) and already contains the seeds of the new era. For in *Don Quixote*, maintains Foucault, written words no longer are representations, language gets separated from words, and he is shown to be both mad and wise. Thus he still belongs in the sixteenth century, when natural phenomena, magic, scripture, discoveries of the ancients, etc. were interpreted as signs created by God. And he is already part of the Renaissance, when distinctions began to be made between the signs themselves, what they designated, and the similitudes that connected them. Until then, resemblance had constituted the sign's form and its content, and had operated as of a piece. But during the seventeenth century a separation occurred: language began to exist apart from the things it signified, so that it acquired an existence of its own:

> From an extreme point of view, one might say that language in the Classical era does not exist. But that it functions: its whole existence is located in its representative role, is limited precisely to that role and finally exhausts it. Language has no other locus, no other value than in representation. (1970:79)

Analyzing this representation in relation to speaking, to general grammar, to articulation, to verb theory, to designation, and to derivation, Foucault (1970:115) concludes that there are four basic theories — of the proposition, of articulation, of designation and of derivation which form, as it were, the segments of a quadrilateral. Essentially, he takes nothing for granted, as he strips away linguistic representations and games, dissecting language in order to get at the underside of discourse and at the structures of knowledge. He 'unveils' the strategies that sanction the 'conceptualizing rituals', expecting to find their unconscious rules. To that end, Foucault postulates a quadrilateral of language, with two axes that intersect at the center. One axis cuts across the whole quadrilateral; and it is along this line that the state of a language is marked off: its articulative capacities are determined by the distance it has moved along the line of derivation; such a reading defines both its historical posture and its power of discrimination. The other diagonal runs from the proposition back to the origin, that is, from the affirmation at the heart of every act of judgment to the

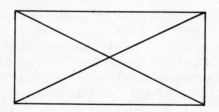

designation implied by any act of nomination (1970:116). Foucault then goes on to explain the functions of these axes at their various points, and to locate the *names* at the center, that is at their intersection. Naming places things and thought in the language, and related it to representation within the general table of classification. Addressing commentators who note the similarity of this scheme to Lévi-Strauss's 'anthropological quadrilateral', Foucault responds that Lévi-Strauss defines ethnology as the study of societies without history, and this remains within Descartes's and Kant's categories of thought. Furthermore, Lévi-Strauss's scheme, because based on nondeveloped societies, he argues, is asleep in so far as science has not yet been developed there.

A number of passages have been quoted here to give the flavor of Foucault's language, and to indicate the intricacies of his theories, and their derivation from structural linguistics in the emphasis on oppositions, transformations, adjacencies, analogies, etc., which he uses in order 'to determine in what condition language could become the object to a period's knowledge, and between what limits this epistemological domain developed' (1970:119). In this scheme, the simplest element of analysis is Foucault's *episteme* — a different one is said to dominate each epistemological age, which is very distinct from its preceding and subsequent age. The classical age was governed by the ascendance of science, and by problems of order and of measurement. Sheridan summarizes it well:

> Having analyzed the mutation in the Western *episteme*
> that took place in the mid-seventeenth century, from a
> general theory of signs and resemblance to one based
> on signs and representation, Foucault is in a position to
> embark on his detailed analysis of the Classical theories
> of language, classification, and money. No culture is able
> to grasp in its coherence the general system of knowledge
> that generates and constricts its more visible forms of
> knowledge. In this respect, however, the Classical age was
> particularly percipient at seeing the connections between
> the various branches of empirical knowledge. Writers in
> one field frequently wrote, with equal authority, on
> others. (1980: 54)

Foucault, of course, also writes about all fields of expertise, making the point that the fragmentation which goes back to the beginning of the Classical age must stop, or rather, that we must again look at the many fragments as part of the whole. By taking in the entire culture, he finds, for instance, that analysis of commodity and wealth was replaced by analysis of monetary systems so that economic knowledge, too, changed its space, became discontinuous, and broke with its past. By locating the discontinuity in economic knowledge rather than in economic conditions, Foucault by-passes the inevitability of Marx's potential revolution and Althusser's Marxism, although he increasingly emphasizes economic factors as crucial. Foucault also connects economic conditions to how people now learned to understand their own situation, and to the way in which capital and labor, production time and wages, were being related to new means of production. Although he does not directly address alienation as such, it too appears to be a knowledge that 'surfaces' at the end of the Classical age.

In *The Order of Things* language is the central means to apprehend change. Foucault traces it from archaic analyses of inflection and cries, through language development, to general grammar, because language was itself created along with the ideologies and the biases it incorporated. Addressing the philosophical discussions of the time, Foucault argues that the Kantian critique that questioned its own limits brought us to the threshold of modernity, where positivism had to give way to the modern *episteme*; and that after Fichte, Hegel's phenomenology led us back to the interior of consciousness, which could then reveal itself as spirit. Thus Hegel is said to have paved the way for Husserl and for all subsequent phenomenological reflections on subjectivity.

Foucault, however, must reject subjectivity. Authors and their works, along with language, are all said to be the objects of his search for the underlying logic which is independent of grammars, vocabularies, synthetic forms, and words. For man becomes the subject of his own discourse — both the object of knowledge and the subject that knows. This theme is exemplified, for instance, by Velasquez's painting which shows how the king is both slave and sovereign; seen through a mirror, his real presence is excluded, and his 'finitude is heralded' in so far as he knows that the painting both immortalizes him and anticipates his death (1970:313-14). This is where Foucault places the beginning of modernity, as 'the human being begins to exist within its organism, inside the shell of its head, inside the armature of his limbs, and in the whole structure of his physiology; when he [is] the center of his labour; ... [and] when he thinks in ... language much older than himself' (1970:318).

From here on Foucault takes on the philosophers and writers, such as Bataille and Artaud, to show that thought cannot be theoretical only, but has its own consequences. His search for the ultimate explanation of our universe ends in 'three faces of knowledge': mathematics and physics; the sciences of language, life, production and distribution of wealth; and philosophical reflection. The human sciences are said to exist at the interstices of them all, because they lend relevance to the others and follow three constituent models, based on biology, economics, and language, which operate in interlocking pairs: function and form, conflict and rule, signification and system. History is postulated as the environment for individuals and for the human sciences, an environment to be examined in relation to its dominating knowledge; that is, to nodal periods rather than to chronological events. And this centrality of history also is the nodal point for attacks: 'conventional' historians are outraged at this new conceptualization which invalidates their own, while philosophers, literary critics, or anthropologists prefer to place their own approaches above Foucault's even when they appreciate his ideas and use some of them.

For Foucault, language is the key to understanding the development of Western thought and society. It provides a means of ordering signs with the help of *significations* and *systems*. It is how he apprehends culture. Like the anthropologists, Foucault does relate language to the creation of symbols, but symbols are not seen as representing abstract connections. Instead, as previously indicated, language is dissected to undercut already existing symbols, to re-examine signs in their most pristine form. Myths are not much analyzed as such, or even in relation to the functions they perform for a particular society, but are considered more as productions of a specific time from the perspective of language. Potentially, everything said or written is mythical, and thus myth is part of the totality that needs to be explained. The same is true for religion: its value for individuals and groups changes in relation to everything else; it has no special place in Foucault's theories.

The evolution of confinement

As we have seen, Foucault's focus on language, sparked by the general ascendance of structural linguistics in his own cultural milieu, which was pursued further in *The Archeology of Knowledge*, receded because the unconscious structures of knowledge remained elusive, and because the events of 1968 'pushed' intellectuals to address the sudden changes within their own society. Foucault, as we would expect, continued to look at the present through the past; and he did so by focusing on deviance, thereby picking up the theme of *Madness and Civilization*. But in *Discipline and Punish* he examined the treatment of prisoners, their punishment, etc., in relation to prevalent beliefs about right and wrong, in relation to who had power, and whether this power was overt or covert.

The opening of this book is so striking that almost no reviewer has failed to comment on it, either to remark on Foucault's brilliance, or on his unerring sense of showmanship:

In March 1757 the regicide was condemned 'to make the *amende honorable*' . . . he was taken and conveyed in a cart, wearing nothing but a shirt, holding a torch of burning wax weighing two pounds, to the Place de Grève, where on a scaffold that will be erected there, the flesh will be torn from his breasts, arms, thighs and calves with redhot pincers, his right hand, holding up the knife with which he had committed the parricide, burnt with sulphur, and on those places where the flesh will be torn away, poured molten lead, boiling oil, burnt with sulphur, burning resin, wax and sulphur melted together, and then his body drawn and quartered by four horses and his limbs and body consumed by fire, reduced to ashes and his ashes thrown to the winds. (1979:3)

This dramatic passage (and Foucault goes on to elaborate how the order was carried out, how the quartering of the body did not proceed smoothly, and how the crowd came out to watch) was chosen to illustrate that, whereas in the eighteenth century criminals were punished bodily, this was soon changed: since then, punishment, primarily, has become psychological. In Foucault's words, we move from 'punishment of the body to that of the soul'. Leaning once more on the historical evidence, and using it to sharpen his concept of epistemological ruptures, he focuses on the location, treatment and importance of crime, of criminals, and of their 'keepers'. Mediating between crime and punishment to demonstrate that they were public rather than secret, physical rather than mental, and violent rather than 'civilized', he shows crime as yet another solidarizing element within society — a part of the new system that needs and produces deviance, for and by judges, lawyers, police and public, that evolved in relation to all the other changes connected to industrialization and the thinking it induced.

Until the turn of the eighteenth century, states Foucault, punishment for crime had been a theater of torture and pain that destroyed the body and served as social control. But attitudes changed; pseudo-leniency replaced cruelty; the attendants and professionals in penal institutions now judge from a psychological perspective; and ball and chain have been replaced by new and more insidious means of control. Whereas previously crime was punished in relation to the damage it inflicted on society, the authorities now use psychiatric knowledge to chastise. This is not to say that judges have become more qualified, he notes, but only that they are now able to justify their sentences by applying the laws they have helped write: it absolves them of responsibility, and it veils their power. (Naked power, however, still reigns inside the prisons.) By hiding behind psychiatric knowledge, the authorities can justify and strengthen their own concealed power, as they effectively mask it under legal codes they themselves create. Foucault explains this as a *new* technology of power, which serves *new* social, political, and economic ends. Just like the mad, the unemployed, the vagabonds, and all other deviants, the criminals are shown to provide a supplementary work force which constitutes civil slavery. Foucault frequently points this out, as he indicates how the new industrial society in creation used what cheap labor it could get. (This is another Marxist theme which is constantly present, but rarely spelled out.)

Although psychoanalytic notions are more clearly addressed in his subsequent *The History of Sexuality*, Foucault uses enough psychoanalytic and psychological theory to show how psychological punishment is an important element in maintaining the new legal system which, itself, incorporates psychiatric and medical knowledge in order to legitimate its own legal power. For the acceptance of psychological knowledge, also, makes it possible to reconstruct a crime, to produce psychological evidence by both sides, and thus to set the stage for confessions of 'truth' which may or may not be true. In other words, Foucault stresses how truth is produced to provide the 'proper' punishment or to avoid it, a truth which really is a construction of lies fitting the facts, but which enables the criminal to 'confess'. For confession of a crime is supposed to indicate at least a first step towards repentance, and repentance to legitimate the rehabilitative assumptions of all the 'experts'.

Foucault (1977:206) put this notion more simply in an interview in 1972, when he had not yet written the book, but had begun to visit prisons. He had wanted to undercut all the experts' knowledges, to find out what was really going on inside prisons, and to create a situation which would allow him to formulate his theories in relation to what criminals said rather than to what was said and accepted about them. By adding this data to available information in criminology, law, psychology, psychoanalysis, mental health, penology, etc., he set about constructing a larger 'horizon of crime'. New rituals are being compared to old ones, arbitrary rules are constrasted to the new 'egalitarian' laws, and old-style executioners to efficient and anonymous electric chairs. He even describes at length how people solidarized against hardened criminals; that is, how they judged a hierarchy of crimes and differentiated them from the post-revolutionary delinquencies — delinquencies investigated by a new class of inspectors and police. With the increase in property crime, he finds that these are being distinguished from blood crimes, and notes how much more fascinating the latter are to the masses. The people now composed lyrics about criminals and their executions, which, in effect amounted to posthumous glorification. He also describes how the universalization of punishment, that is, how the application of equality, became codified, so that crimes were being differentiated in order to have similar transgressions punished in the same way. That is what necessitated the construction of a system of punishment. An offender's intent, Foucault states, was judged along with the crime, and 'the length of pain was integrated to the economy of pain'. But whereas previously torture — days of pillory, years of banishment, or hours on the wheel — had been prescribed, now the condemned would expiate his or her crime through work. Foucault talks of the productions of crime and punishment which were becoming a 'knowledge tied to manipulable guilt'. Guilt, however, changed only the 'quality' of crime and punishment.

Because more people had to be punished, new prisons had to be built. Foucault (1979:127) describes how these prisons were organized rationally, and thus were modeled after the Walnut Street prison in Philadelphia. In great detail, he describes the functions and organization of the Panopticum. Scientific rationality was applied to the allocation of space (hierarchically organized in line with the offense), and spatial arrangements were meant to help control both the prisoners' guilt and their work, and to modify their behavior. Foucault compares this control in prisons to similar arrangements in schools, in the army, and in the factory: time was to be strictly organized, surveillance was to be efficient and uninterrupted. In the prisons, however, the rules and obligations became part of a new apparatus of knowledge which, contrary to all intentions, never deterred crime but merely regimented criminals.

Foucault brilliantly illustrates how these practices perfected punishment rather than society. He describes the machinery of punishment, its concomitant coercion, docility, and regimentation that gradually reduced people to cases. Hierarchic surveillance became the norm; power became functional and anonymous. The new disciplinary system 'celebrated' the child, the deviant, the mad, and the criminal, because individualization proceeded by singling out differences, defects, childish traits, or secret follies. But it all conspired to hide a disciplinary society in which a centralized police force was attached to political power. Foucault, of course, is not the only one, nor the first one, to describe the total institution, the solitary confinement, the accompanying disciplinary measures, coercions, and ideologies, or the total power of the staff. But what he adds to all the other theories is the notion that confinement is a central propellant of the social order. As he moves from comportment to isolation, from pain to work, from education to control by 'specialists', from words to language, from the dialectics between language and thought to those between conscious and unconscious, his 'transformational interactions' reconstruct the social system from a novel perspective. And as the rules of the penitentiary are connected to the process of incarceration, and are compared to many other practices outside the prisons, the comparisons Foucault provides are convincing enough to have the reader accept his 'culture of confinement'.

Foucault is particularly ironic when he relates how the control of prostitution by the police generates financial profit from illicit sexual pleasure which then is funneled back into the society legally and in a regulated way. Pointing to relationships between informers and participants, he shows that just at the time when moralization increased morals were lost and that a 'delinquent milieu was in complicity with an interested puritanism' in setting a price for pleasure and in making a profit on the repressed sexuality. He demonstrates how illegalities and crime were supported by the hypocrisy of the bourgeois pretensions which themselves fostered them. Such pretension, together with political expedience, and with power itself, 'constantly mixes up the art of rectifying with the right to punish' (1979:310). Legal and medical experts together are said to confuse legality and nature and to have created the knowledges and norms they then judge to be 'normal'. In this situation, judges are bound to 'indulge their enormous appetites for medicine and psychiatry . . . which in turn allows them to babble about the criminology they forget to judge' (1979:310), and to hand down therapeutic verdicts and readaptive sentences that help to perpetuate the norms of corrupt power along with the crime.

To exemplify how this system established itself, he chose one case of murder, *I, Pierre Rivière, having slaughtered my mother, my sister, and my brother . . .*, and studied it, with the help of some of his students. This edited work, based entirely on documents (from 3 June 1835 to 22 October 1840) that include Rivière's own tale of the crime, is a marvelous social history as well. Parricide was not rare at the time, Foucault found out when he decided to undertake this project, but he chose Rivière's case because it was unique: Rivière had written an account of his crime, including why and how he had committed it (after he was apprehended) and this made the question of his guilt especially interesting. Half of the experts (six lawyers and six doctors) found this ignorant and odd peasant insane while the other half found him to be a murderer. That the lawyers and the doctors themselves were split evenly was further proof for Foucault that the newly instituted codes about insanity were not as rational as they claimed to be.

Rivière used a pruning bill to kill his mother, his sister and his brother, in order to 'deliver his father from all his tribulations', from the demands his mother kept making on him. He carefully planned his act, committed it at high noon, and donned his Sunday clothes for the occasion. After the crime, he wandered about the countryside, and when apprehended admitted his deed. Before the trial, in prison, he produced the document of the crime. Since he must have known that premeditated murder was being punished more harshly than a *crime passionel*, why did he provide evidence against himself? Only an insane person would do so, argued some. On the other hand, the document was coherent, and could an insane person write a coherent account, especially a person who had been deemed illiterate and was not used to writing? The jury was hung. Rivière was put in prison for life rather than executed, but he committed suicide a few years later.

Foucault's concern, of course, was not with the story itself, but with what insights he might gain from seeing it in its larger context. Rivière provided the 'excuse' to examine power structures and social institutions, to pinpoint how doctors and lawyers started the co-operation in the eighteenth century which induced the confusion of values and beliefs that are still with us. Because Rivière's memoir was so unique, and because it made 'the murder and the narrative of the murder consubstantial' (1975b:20), while serving, also, as an 'exhibit in evidence', Foucault was able to relate it to much of what was going on among French peasants after the Revolution. Though he never passes judgment, he gets to judge by showing how the distribution of land to the formerly landless, for example, made for avarice, complicated family situations, and (limited) financial independence (Rivière's father had to cultivate his own piece of land as well as that of his wife, located in another village; and owning land near his own mother kept him close to her). In other words, he 'reads' the entire social fabric as one would a text, jumping from one field of expertise to another. But his controlled free associations make sense, in so far as they are grounded in Rivière's life, and in his memoir.

In 1967, Foucault had published 'Nietzsche, Freud, Marx', and in 1971, 'Nietzsche, la généalogie, l'histoire' (1977). The importance attributed to these three intellectual giants, and the examination of their contributions in relation to each other, was not unique to Foucault during the late 1960s and the early 1970s. The revival of their thought, in fact, still dominates Parisian intellectual life. But for Foucault, the turn to Nietzsche was particularly evident in the increasing emphasis on power, and on the power/knowledge matrix. He states that:

> development is not tied to the constitution and affirmation of a free subject; rather it creates a progressive enslavement to its instinctive violence. Where religions once demanded the sacrifice of bodies, knowledge now calls for experimentation on ourselves, calls us to the sacrifice of knowledge. (1977:163)

What better statement could be found to demonstrate the

connections between loss of religion, belief in science, knowledge, individualism, and their institutionalization? Still, it would be as much of a mistake to call Foucault a Nietzschean as it is to call him a Marxist. By 1975, he already stated that he had become tired of people studying Nietzsche, or other writers, in order to produce commentaries on them:

> For myself, I prefer to utilize the writers I like. The only valid tribute to thought such as Nietzsche's is precisely to use it, to deform it, to make it groan and protest. And if the commentators say that I am unfaithful to Nietzsche that is of absolutely no interest. (1975c:33)

But in *I, Pierre Rivière . . .* , and in *Discipline and Punish*, Nietzsche's ideas did help formulate Foucault's apprehension of the origins of the social order we still live in.

During Rivière's time, psychoanalytic knowledge had not yet been outlined so his deed could not yet have been interpreted as the acting out of arrested Oedipal development — an act of insanity. Some neighbors, townspeople who had watched Rivière grow up, and some journalists, however, had reached the conclusion that only a madman could have committed such a beastly act. Lawyers were writing laws that would punish parricide as seriously as regicide. The latter was more reprehensible than an ordinary murder should sanity be proven. These beliefs were all being codified with the advice of doctors. Essentially, Foucault expected to reconstruct the unscientific beliefs that went into constructing our 'scientific' laws. So he looked at the forces which pitted madman vs. animal, the power of medicine vs. law, or extenuating circumstances vs. rationality, and many more, and ridiculed their pretensions of scientificity. Rivière's fate was in the hands of these new 'experts', and, as Foucault shows, their preoccupations with all the 'Rivières' created more expertise.

The evolution of repression

In his examination of the uses of deviance, Foucault had increasingly alluded to the growing attention sexuality was receiving. After finishing his two books on crimes and prisons which had led him to expose the latent consequences of confinement and to elaborate on the impact of the culture of confinement on those who did the confining, he turned to repression. And being Foucault, he found repression to have begun in the seventeenth century, when:

> A certain frankness was still common, it would seem. Sexual practices had little need of secrecy; words were said without undue reticence, and things were done without too much concealment; one had a tolerant familiarity with the illicit. Codes regulating the coarse, the obscene, and the indecent were quite lax compared to those of the nineteenth century. It was a time of direct gestures, shameless discourse, and open transgressions, when anatomies were shown and intermingled at will, and knowing children hung about amid the laughter of adults: it was a period when bodies 'made a display of themselves'. (1978:3)

The display of bodies was a central theme in *The Birth of the Clinic*, as was the supervision of individuals' physical functions in the other works. But most of all, the connection between sexuality and behavior was referred to in *Madness and Civilization*, where women had been found more susceptible to nervous disease than men who were 'more robust, drier and hardened by work', and were more prone to melancholia and bad humors, allegedly because these states derived from the uterus, which also was found to be the seat of hysteria. But unlike feminists, who point out these beliefs to document discrimination against women, Foucault shows these notions to be connected to other changes. First of all, they emanated from the new scientific elite, that is, from the doctors and lawyers who were adapting sexuality to fit their own purposes. According to Foucault, the mores of the Victorian bourgeoisie transformed previous sexual freedom by restricting it to the marital relation, to the parental bedroom alone, banning it from speech and thought — it was silenced. And when it could not be contained, it was declared illicit and relegated to brothels or insane asylums.

This confinement of sex is compared to other institutions of confinement, although Foucault notes how, in our century, we also have attempted to reverse this tendency to confine. Still, the many behavioral prescriptions led to repression, and repression, as Freud was able to demonstrate, could induce conversion hysteria or neurosis. For sex had become a subject of secrecy, preferably in the dark and for procreation alone. And even psychoanalysis could not alleviate the damage done by the belief in the 'sinfulness' of sexuality. Circumspection, medical prudence, and the 'scientific guarantee of innocuousness' brought sex to the psychoanalyst's couch, to 'yet another whispering on a bed' (1978:5). Even exposing the conformist and adaptive tendencies of psychotherapy could not eliminate the repressive components of twentieth-century discourse. Sanctions against sexuality, or its strict regulation, was found to be a necessary adjunct to capitalist exploitation: the pleasurable pursuit of sex, that is, sex not practiced for the purpose of reproduction, was not to interfere with production. Thus talk of sex and the repressive power structure, and even when it was made part of the left's revolutionary agenda, when sexual freedom was said to help bring about the 'impending' revolution, it nevertheless retained its repressive elements.

Hence, the affirmation of sexuality, and the exposure of the dependent relationship between sexuality and the power structure (in legal codes, the treatment of 'deviant' sexuality from homosexuality to sodomy and childhood sexuality), he argues, can never do away with the repression that is rooted in our institutions, and in the modes of behavior we have internalized. The discourse we are part of, itself, is perceived as part of the sermon against hypocrisy pervasive in Western culture, a sermon that has been passed on through generations, since the end of the Middle Ages. This 'great sexual sermon', then, belongs to our 'will to knowledge'. Thus, we have accepted and constructed a science of sexuality, and have embedded this science in our language. 'The agencies of power are determined to speak about it, to hear it spoken about, and to cause *it* [the Lacanian *id*] to speak through explicit articulation and endlessly accumulated detail' (1978:18).

Psychoanalysis through the relationship between doctor and patient was to produce truth: scientifically validated by the psychoanalyst, it could heal. Therefore, sex was 'taken charge of', tracked down, legally exposed, discussed in relation to norms; it became public and private at the same time, inviting the state to penetrate the private (and silent) bedroom. And state regulations, Foucault again reminds us, had seen to it that these sexual mores would be reinforced in the classrooms and dormitories that were being constructed — in schools, prisons, hospitals, and all other institutions set up to socialize individuals into this increasingly controlling society.

The constant discussions of sexual matters, by transforming sexuality into a discourse about it, Foucault suggests, incite, extract, distribute, and institutionalize the sexual verbosity which has become the order of the day; our civilization has both required and ordered this quantity of sexual talk. The array of sexual discourses, then, publicly exploited sexuality's secrets. Sex began to be managed. Children's sexuality was being eradicated through rules about masturbation, corrective discourses, and through the induction of guilt; perversion became codified; observation in hospitals, prisons, schools and homes saw to it that the boundaries laid down for sexual pleasure for parents, children, wives, criminals, and for every other category of individuals, were enforced. Sexuality proliferated as the power over it was extended, and as the persistence of this power took hold and spread along with the sites for sexual pleasure (more sex in more places).

But all this talk, as Freud showed, was only a screen. Foucault maintains that Freud constructed his theories about the unconscious, or about childhood sexuality, at a time when the discourse on sex had already been incorporated into two distinct areas of knowledge: the biology of reproduction and the medicine of sex. Because this division had been firmly established, and because it was riddled with scientific pretensions, he asserts, access to the truth Freud sought was barred. The public record of the experiments Charcot conducted at the Salpetriere, for instance, were found to omit many details of what had been observed; it did not include reaction provoked and solicited by the doctors themselves, thus undermining the very apparatus they were constructing for the 'production' of truth. Instead, for the sake of their science, they masked some of the truths they uncovered. From such historical evidence, Foucault deduces that 'Freud's discoveries were made against a progressive formation of the interplay of truth and sex', and that this situation led to many misunderstandings, avoidances and evasions.

Essentially, Foucault bemoans the fact that Western society, unlike China, Japan, or India, possesses no *ars erotica* — art where truth is drawn from pleasure itself, where pleasure is evaluated in terms of its intensity, its specific quality, its duration, its reverberations in the body and the soul, and then is reflected back into practice. Instead, we practice a *scientia sexualis*, a form of knowledge/power which had its origins in the confession rituals of the Catholic church — rituals that now have 'moved to the couch'.

Foucault's 'exposure' of sexuality as an instrument of control, as part of the system of controls we are born into, attempts to demolish all notions of sexual freedom. But *The History of Sexuality* was only the first of six volumes promised on this subject. While continuing his research in the archives, he continues to look at sexual practices from the Middle Ages to the present, focusing on the oddities to extrapolate to the changes in prevalent norms. Taking for granted the epistemological ages discussed above, he came upon the treatment of hermaphrodites, and found the case of *Herculine Barbin* so fascinating that he published it, though with less analysis than Rivière, in 1980. In his introduction to Herculine's memoir, to her dossier, and to a story about her, Foucault addresses our preoccupation with *true* sex. He found that:

> It was a very long time before the postulate that a hermaphrodite must have a sex — a single, true sex — was formulated. For centuries, it was quite simply agreed that hermaphrodites had two . . . In the Middle Ages, the rules of both canon and civil law were very clear on this point: the designation 'hermaphrodite' was given to those in whom the two sexes were juxtaposed, in proportions that might be variable. In these cases, it was the role of the father or the godfather to determine at the time of baptism

which sex was going to be retained . . . But later, on the threshold of adulthood, when the time came for them to marry, hermaphrodites were free to decide for themselves if they wished to go on being of the sex which had been assigned to them, or if they preferred the other. (1980b: vii–viii)

Foucault's readers are perhaps prepared for the memoir's detailed account of Herculine's experiences as teacher in a Catholic boarding school — including her love and trysts with one young girl, its discovery, and the subsequent exposure of her 'enlarged' clitoris — but are less prepared for the many descriptive details, and for Herculine's own psychological insights. The dossier gives the facts, and places the events: born in 1838, Herculine's life as hermaphrodite was dramatically changed only after she confided her 'affliction' and practices to a priest, who in turn confided in a doctor. Here, once more, Foucault emphasizes the language of sexuality, and how doctors and their scientism influenced events. Only after her medical examination was there a dossier. The medical establishment informed the legal authorities. They had advised an operation to change her sex, so that Herculine can later write:

My arrival in Paris marks the beginning of a new phase of my double and bizarre existence. Brought up for twenty years among girls, I was at first and for two years at the most a *lady's maid*. When I was sixteen and a half I entered the normal school . . . as a student-teacher. When I was nineteen I obtained my teaching certificate. A few months later I was directing a rather well-known boarding school . . . I left when I was twenty-one . . . At the end of the year I was in Paris (1980b:98).

The sex change operation led to solitude, anxiety, poverty and misery which, at the age of twenty-five, finally ended in her suicide. But the doctors' and lawyers' reports only reflect a case rather than an individual's life — concentrating on physical and biological factors. The 'case', though causing a sensation in the press, also forgot about the psychological damage, and about Herculine's isolation. By then she was called Abel. Clearly, this is the stuff of which Foucauldian history and insights are made. This is not to denigrate them, but to understand that Foucault's constant search for the irrationality of medical and other science, and for the customarily forgotten motives of conventional historians, must lead to very strong criticism of his work. For the subversiveness of his entire enterprise challenges all of our power/knowledge elites, and all our premises about Western culture, and at the same time incorporates them.

Conclusions

Without getting into the ramifications of Marxist thought in France, its ties to intellectual tradition, to a strong and politicized trade union movement, and to a fair amount of anti-Americanism, it is safe to state that many of the evils customarily associated with advanced industrialization, the French attribute to capitalism. It is unnecessary to comment on the validity of this view, except to point out that, to some extent, its premises are incorporated in Foucault's work. The very fact that both Durkheim and Marx figure prominently in Foucault's assumptions also underlines the traditional nature of French culture — a culture that values its intellectuals. Both appreciation and criticism of Foucault must be placed in this context. The overarching national/intellectual bias — a bias whose formation is attributed to the 'cultural unconscious' — must also be considered. To over-generalize, this cultural unconscious, in France, is given to sweeping statements about humanity in the tradition of the *philosophes*, whereas in America, it tends to be channeled into academic disciplines. So on this very broad 'horizon', to use Foucault's terminology, his valid and trenchant attacks against the formation of specialized knowledges also is a reaffirmation of the French philosophical tradition as well as an attack on American scientificity. Therefore, it may not be entirely accidental that Foucault's concerns with the origins of the scientific age were first formulated — in the late 1950s and in the 1960s — at a time when American scientific methods were proliferating in Paris at an astonishing pace, and thus threatened to displace humanistic traditions.

Foucault would not deny such a connection, since it is part of his project: the investigation of cultural notions and interpenetration, from local to international ones. His concern with power, it will be recalled, focuses on the knowledge/power matrix, where individuals exert control through cultural practices extending from personal relations to the institutional centers of power. That Foucault's philosophical premises are laced through with Marx and Nietzsche, then, can be looked upon as a cultural phenomenon arising out of the concerns of the Parisian intellectual milieu. Disillusionment with the possibilities of Marxist practice, and with the aftermath of the events of 1968, also allowed for the appeal of the 'new philosophers' who in various forms picked up some of Nietzsche's nihilism. Thus it should not be a surprise that 'Freud, Marx, Nietzsche' became the accepted gurus, or that Foucault refused to 'co-opt' Nietzsche in an obvious manner, 'preferring to remain silent' when asked about the Nietzschean connection — in order to discourage false interpretations.

Many commentaries on Foucault, it seems, have exaggerated his filiation through structuralism, and have not taken sufficient account of his changes in foci, or of his intent to benefit from portions of structuralist methodology and yet to reject all of its ideological baggage along with some of the Marxist assumptions. His temporary concern with Nietzsche, it seems, provided a means of separating himself, as well as a new direction. He says so in 'Truth and Power', where he concludes that: 'The political question, to sum up, is not error, illusion, alienated consciousness or ideology; it is truth itself. Hence the importance of Nietzsche' (1980a:133).

But Foucault has his own way of linking the individual to his society. Because power and politics, in a society where confinement is so dominant, impinges upon the human body on which it is exercised, power is found to be the motive for bodily activity, that is productivity. Such productivity, in turn, produces power. As Sheridan explains:

This notion of the training of the body to productive ends brings with it what Foucault calls the 'soul'. A political anatomy is also a genealogy of modern morality. Here, too, Nietzsche provides the starting-point. The hold exercised by power over the body is also a hold over the 'soul', for the more power renders the body productive, the more forces there are to control and direct . . . To the extent that man has a soul, power does not need to be applied from the outside; it penetrates his body, occupies it, animates it, gives it 'meaning'. The soul mobilizes the body, gives it consciousness and conscience. (1980:219)

Still, it would be incorrect to assume that when Foucault moved away from Nietzsche he also gave up on his ideas of history and genealogy. On the contrary, just as all of Foucault's early notions in altered form appear later on, so do those he derived from Nietzsche — as we can observe in the works on sexuality, on the discourse on pleasure and its 'deployment'.

Ultimately, Foucault's discourses come down to political beliefs, although these are hidden behind fancy philosophical rhetoric. American and British scholars who understand the French intellectual scene are able to spot this cultural meaning, but it is unlikely that other non-French academics, impressed with the verbal pyrotechnics, are able to spot the subtle nuances and the political thrusts; these are embedded in French cultural history, a history full of allusions and loaded meanings.

Until recently, Ango-Saxon contributions on Foucault have been explanatory; they have examined his thought from a cultural or a sociology of knowledge perspective; and literary theorists have done textual analyses (e.g., Lemert, 1979; Kurzweil, 1980). But these are not 'practical' applications, such as have more recently been attempted. The latter ought perhaps to be avoided, for they falsify Foucault's basic premises in so far as they sacrifice his openness, or 'freeze' his deconstructions. Still, Foucault's very brilliance is also his shortcoming, in so far as he frequently lets his imagination run away with him. This has become most pronounced in his recent writings, so that the acceptance of *The History of Sexuality* depends to some extent on our tolerance for 'structuralist' textual readings and abstractions. Foucault's alliterations and metaphors at times make better sound than sense. Marvelous insights are mixed with mystifications. Serious points may culminate in puns, so that the reader may wonder whether he is put on, put upon, or missing the point. For Foucault, in attacking repression and the discourse of our scientific age, has created his own imaginative discourse addressed to French intellectuals who allegedly have forgotten to speak for themselves, since they have become accustomed to listening to the language of crime, illness, deviance, madness, erotics, etc., and most recently, to the language of sexuality. These provocative texts, which we know are really about power/knowledge, do provide us with many fascinating bits of knowledge, with many memorable throw-away sentences, even though they have not yet unearthed the archeology of knowledge Foucault has promised for the last twenty years.

5 The critical theory of Jürgen Habermas

The lineage of Habermas's ideas is particularly difficult to trace because his work not only exhibits eclecticism at every point, but with each new installment it attempts to incorporate insights from an ever-broadening range of scholars, most of whom have themselves been responsible for elaborate theoretical systems. Some of Habermas's underlying concerns and assumptions about the nature of culture have roots in Kant and Hegel; others reflect his exposure to the work of Heidegger and Husserl in phenomenology and his debates with Gadamer concerning the hermeneutic method. In his work on culture he has borrowed from Mead and Goffman in social psychology, from Parsons in sociology, and from Piaget and Kohlberg in psychology. He has quoted extensively from Peter Berger, critically addressed the limitations of structuralism and commented on the work of Foucault, cited theological perspectives with which he feels comfortable, and drawn widely from empirical studies characterizing economic, political, and cultural conditions (cf. Bernstein, 1976; Geuss, 1981; Giddens, 1977b; Held, 1980; McCarthy, 1978; Skinner, 1982).

The scope of Habermas's knowledge is genuinely encyclopedic. He has familiarized himself with a broad range of European and American social philosophy, political theory, and social science, addressing much of this work critically in his published essays. He has also sought to synthesize ideas from all of this work on an encompassing scale as grand as that of Hegel or Marx. It is this vision of a new theoretical framework, coupled with the fact of his erudition and analytic capacities, that makes his work exciting. At the same time, he stands in close proximity to many whose work on culture is better known than his own.

Intellectual assumptions

It is particularly important to understand the nature of Habermas's agreements and disagreements with Marx, Weber, and Freud, and the extent to which he has borrowed from critical theory and from structural linguistics. Each of these traditions has had a significant influence on his orientation toward culture.

The classical heritage

Habermas shares interests with the Marxist tradition in the evolution of capitalism, its contradictions, and its consequences for social and personal life. His criticisms of science and technology and his analyses of crises in advanced capitalism have made his work appealing to Marxists. Because of his exposure to Marxism and, less directly, the Frankfurt school's links to this tradition, he has been regarded as a Marxist himself. He nevertheless rejects Marx's basic premises and has called for a reconstruction of historical materialism.

In *Theory and Practice*, he sets forth four historical developments which for him 'form an insuperable barrier to any theoretical acceptance of Marxism' (p. 198). First, the state is no longer separated from the economy as it was under *laissez faire* capitalism, but is fused with the economy and plays an important role in guiding and regulating the economy. Thus, it no longer makes sense to regard the economy as the sole determinant of the state nor to distinguish sharply between the so-called materialist infrastructure and the superstructure of society. Rather, the functioning of the state itself must be given close attention. In so doing, questions inevitably arise about the legitimation of the state which, in turn, require that attention be paid to the cultural forces affecting legitimation. Moreover, new contradictions between state and economy require rethinking the laws of motion of

180

the capitalist system which were formulated by Marx. Second, the rising standard of living in advanced societies has changed the character of oppression in ways not fully foreseen by Marx. Increasingly oppression consists of psychological and ethical constraint rather than economic deprivation. This development necessitates rethinking the life situation of the working class; specifically, the cultural milieu in which the working class attempts to find meaning and a satisfactory self-identity. Since the proletariat no longer experiences the kind of destitution that once drove it to become a revolutionary force, Habermas wishes to identify an alternative mechanism to bring about revolutionary social change — to reconceptualize the proletariat's needs in such a way as to clarify the nature of its subjugation and inspire it to take 'revolutionary' action. His efforts to specify the manner in which political and economic concerns have penetrated the natural life-world of individuals, and his attempt to develop more effective mechanisms of reflection and communication are inspired by his conviction that an alternative force for human emancipation must be discovered. Finally, his ambivalence toward Marxism stems partly from reservations about its application in the Soviet Union. While the Soviet Union may not of itself invalidate the purely theoretical principles of Marxism, it nevertheless raises doubts for Habermas about the relevance of these principles for bringing about social change of a desired kind. He regards the Soviet Union as a bureaucratic monopoly aimed at foreshortening the transition from an agrarian to an industrially advanced economy, not as a prototype of the ideal classless society as Marx envisioned. He believes convergence between the Soviet system and advanced capitalist societies toward a kind of welfare state will occur, but convergence will not solve the dangers of international war, atomic annihilation, or dehumanized bureaucratic domination. Indeed, the emergence of a welfare state system on an international scale threatens to carry the warped principles of capitalism and instrumental thinking into new realms of life, rendering human emancipation all the more difficult to attain. This prospect lends urgency to his efforts to develop an alternative theory of culture in order to clarify the conditions under which values and societal goals can themselves become subject to self-conscious discussion.

Given his reservations about Marxism, Habermas turns frequently in his theoretical essays to Weber (especially 1971b; 1977b). Weber is one of the principal sources of his writings on the nature of rationality and Weber's view of cultural evolution is one of the sources of his evolutionary perspective. Habermas also stands loosely within the Weberian tradition methodologically, assuming that knowledge produced by the social sciences is historically limited and that there is a subjective dimension in human life to which the social sciences must pay heed. Nevertheless, he rejects two of the fundamental premises of Weber's perspective.

Weber assumes that people pursue goals and rationally select courses of action that permit them to realize goals effectively and efficiently. This assumption deeply influences Weber's (1963) comparative analysis of world religions, in which he identifies alternative 'soteriologies' or theories of salvation as the focal point for his comparisons, then draws on these alternative beliefs to make predictions about specific types of action likely to be pursued by individuals. In a well known metaphor, Weber suggests that religious systems function as 'switchmen', guiding action along different tracks. For Habermas, this view is too atomistic; it fails to illuminate the collective processes involved in the selection of values, focuses on isolated individuals, overemphasizes the competitive struggle of individuals for scarce resources to achieve personal goals, and fails to specify the importance of interactive relations that could promote co-operation and consensus.

Weber's rational-purposive model of human action also produces a social science that focuses on how well alternative courses of action lead to the attainment of prespecified values. Weber claims this approach is advantageous since it allows the social sciences to be 'value free'. Habermas argues to the contrary that Weber's approach is not value free at all, but poses its own version of rationality as the highest value of all. He charges Weber with having created a social science that exhibits the very kind of rationality which Weber himself predicted would become an 'iron cage'. Habermas wishes to construct a theoretical perspective that takes into consideration the communication processes leading to consensus on values. He hopes to bring values back into the province of social scientific investigation, not as goals to be judged in terms of absolute truth, but as goals for which the process of negotiation can be examined.

Like Weber, he recognizes the importance of 'intersubjective' understandings shared among people as they interact with one another. For Weber, the existence of these understandings or implicit agreements was the reason for emphasizing *verstehen* or empathetic understanding between the social scientist and persons under observation. Habermas accuses Weber, however, of failing to incorporate adequately the realm of intersubjectivity into his theoretical framework. Weber's concept of *verstehen* leaves this intersubjective realm primarily at the level of individual intuition or pure subjectivity. What Habermas has attempted to do, in contrast, is to raise these implicit agreements to the level of consciousness in order to examine them and subject them to criticism. For this reason, he has been keenly interested in the processes of communication that give behavioral content to these implicit understandings.

Habermas's indebtedness to Freud stems from this effort to make conscious the implicit understandings conveyed through communication (1970a, 1971a; McIntosh, 1977). Freud's work was oriented toward the practical, emancipatory goals that have also been of inspiration to Habermas. Moreover, Freud claimed to have developed a theory that was empirically grounded; indeed, a theory purporting to generate scientific laws about the nature of the inner, subjective realm. Habermas's attraction to Freud, however, does not stem from faith in Freud's ability to have actually generated such laws through psychoanalysis. The appeal of psychoanalysis for Habermas is rather that it serves as an example of a mechanism oriented toward greater self-consciousness in the communication process. In other words, the relationship between therapist and patient is concerned with overcoming barriers to communication and the purpose of psychoanalysis is to arrive at some consensus between patient and therapist concerning the interpretation of significant events. The theory of psychoanalysis, which the therapist brings to the communication process, is not so much a set of abstract laws based on empirical observation, but an *a priori* perspective the purpose of which is to give clues about the nature of communication that can facilitate the search for consensus.

Where Habermas parts company with Freud is over the question of how much improvement in the human condition can be expected from analyzing communication. For Freud, fundamental laws of nature limit this capacity for improvement in that the patient may overcome certain personal difficulties through the therapeutic process, but must nevertheless live within fairly narrow biological limitations set by laws of nature. Habermas places greater store in the prospect of cognitive evolution being able to bring about major improvements in the human situation. In this respect he gives considerably greater weight to the importance of culture than did Freud. Through reflection on the communication process, Habermas believes it is not only possible to circumvent temporary barriers to human interaction but to effect a permanent advance in human evolution.

Structural linguistics

Because of his interest in communication, Habermas borrows heavily from recent work in the field of linguistics. One contribution in this area is the work of Noam Chomsky (1957, 1965; Leiber, 1975). Chomsky assumes that universal rules can be found which organize the use of language — rules that correspond with biological structures in the human mind. This assumption has been much disputed and appears to be inherently untestable; however, the more important contribution of Chomsky as far as implications for the study of culture are concerned is his argument for the importance of examining rules or patterns of language. Traditional approaches to language sought to discover the *meanings* of words and were, therefore, engaged in a subjective enterprise, since meanings lay in the inner thought life of individuals, and words inevitably carry connotations unique to each person's experience. These approaches produced classifications of commonly shared meanings of words, but did not generate generalized principles of language. Chomsky's alternative shifted away from meanings to the rules, patterns, and structures within language that make the usage of particular words *meaningful* or possible. This perspective freed the study of language from having to make claims about the meanings of words and allowed it to focus on the observable content of language and its usage.

Habermas has adopted ideas similar to Chomsky's, although he claims to be uneasy with Chomsky's assumptions about the genetic predetermination of grammar (1979a:20). For this reason, he has drawn mainly from sources other than Chomsky, particularly the work of John R. Searle (1969) on philosophy of language. Searle takes 'speech acts' as the basic unit of analysis, examples of which include making statements, giving commands, asking questions, and making promises. He assumes there are rules governing the use of speech acts and that these can be discovered by examining speech acts themselves. He is also careful to assert that the connection between speech acts and what the speaker really means to say is never perfect; that is, the speaker may fail intentionally or unintentionally to disclose fully what he or she means. Thus, the subjective intentions, feelings, and meaning of the speaker ultimately remain unknown and do not in themselves comprise an appropriate focus for investigation. Nevertheless, one of the features characterizing speech acts is an attempt by the speaker, usually resulting in a set of observable cues, to communicate that what has been said has also been meant. In other words, speech acts contain clues about subjective meanings — clues that can be subjected to investigation. The primary purpose of examining these clues is not to make guesses about the nature of subjective meanings, but to discover the conditions required to communicate meaningfully. This idea is evident in Searle's effort to distinguish the 'propositional content' or substance of what is spoken from what he terms the 'illocutionary force' of a speech act, the latter referring to implicit messages about the relationship between speaker and hearer. These messages are separate from the actual content that is explicitly communicated. For example, if a man commands his child to 'Go bring me the newspaper before you forget it', the propositional content of this utterance is limited largely to the fact that the newspaper is to be retrieved, but the statement also carries messages about the relationship between man and child. By virtue of the tone in which it is spoken and the fact that it is framed tersely as a command, as well as the implication that the child's memory is weak, the statement dramatizes the man's authority as father of the child. This is the illocutionary force of the statement. These messages contribute to the *meaningfulness* of the statement by dramatizing characteristics of the speaker and the setting in which the statement is uttered.

Habermas (1979a:1–68) extends Searle's discussion to culture more generally, arguing that speech acts convey messages not only about the formal structure of language but also about the patterns of culture that organize thought and social interaction. With Searle, he asserts the value of basing investigations on observable facts such as the clues contained in utterances rather than purporting to have probed into the subjective meanings held by individuals. And he borrows directly from Searle's discussion of illocutionary force. It is the existence of these implicit messages about the intentions of the speaker and about the speaker's relation to the hearer that gives Habermas hope for discovering principles of communication leading to more effective social interaction.

Critical theory

In his work on culture Habermas also draws heavily on the assumptions of his predecessors in the Frankfurt school of critical theory (cf. Held, 1980; Jay, 1973; Slater, 1977). Along with Horkheimer and Adorno, he regards the modern split between social science and political practice with disapproval. The objective of critical theory as formulated by the Frankfurt school was to develop a *single* theoretical framework in which scientific investigation and the political implications of these investigations could be united. Critical theory requires the investigator to take his own position *vis-à-vis* the society into account rather than attempting to suppress it in the interest of discovering universal scientific laws. Habermas's conception of the proper linkage between

186

scholarship and politics is not, however, that of applied social science or government-sponsored policy research, such as that which has been common in the social sciences since the 1960s. This type of research is oriented primarily toward more effective manipulation of the technical world — how to improve the standard of living, how to design cities and transportation systems, how to supply medical care to the elderly, and so on. While these activities have value, they cannot substitute for a more general perspective in the social sciences that permits broad criticisms to be made of the entire cultural epoch. The purpose of critical theory is to inform the very processes by which such programs as these are selected — to contribute knowledge useful for initial decisions about social priorities. Rather than letting implicit assumptions rooted largely in the prevailing system of political domination dictate the choice of social priorities, Habermas wishes to create a body of knowledge that will permit values to be discussed and selected on a more rational, consensual, egalitarian basis. This goal, which reflects fundamentally his training in the Frankfurt school, underlies many of his more specific assumptions about the analysis of culture.

Habermas's own program for the analysis of culture stems from a desire to unmask and transcend the blinders built into the structure of modern thought. He has attempted to advance his critique of modern culture by building loosely on the work of Adorno and others such as Horkheimer, Lukács, and Marx, and has carried out this agenda simultaneously on two fronts, on a philosophical front, reflecting his early training in philosophy at Göttingen, and on a sociological front, reflecting his indebtedness to Marx and a concern with linking the critique of cultural forms to concrete developments in the economic and political realms. On the philosophical front, his work bears marks of Hegel, Heidegger, the Frankfurt school, and more broadly the phenomenological and hermeneutic traditions. He has sought to spell out a philosophical basis for his theoretical perspective while critically analyzing the suppositions of standard social scientific perspectives. On the sociological front, his work has concentrated on developing an approach to culture that can be defended in terms of a general theory of cultural evolution and an appraisal of contemporary economic and political crises.

The problems of greatest concern to Habermas, according to his own account (Honneth *et al.*, 1981), have been developing a rational theory of communication, and relating this theory of communication to social conditions. The first has involved him in an effort to clarify types of action and knowledge and to find a way to set the study of culture on an empirical footing. The second has led him to a theory of cultural evolution.

The basic conceptual distinction in Habermas's work on culture is between 'rational-purposive action' and 'communicative action'. Rational-purposive action is characterized by an instrumental orientation toward the material environment, manipulatively concerned with transforming that environment (1979a:116–23). Rational-purposive action refers to what is commonly known as 'work' or 'labor'. An activity can be characterized as work if it is directed at the physical world and treats the physical world as a means toward an end rather than an end in itself — as an object to be manipulated for the attainment of some goal. Habermas also includes within this category of action any type of behavior towards other people that is primarily concerned with organizing their relations to the material world in an instrumental way. Thus, managing a force of, say, coal miners is as much an example of rational-purposive action as is the act of mining coal itself. The reason for describing this kind of behavior as *rational*-purposive action is that it is organized and evaluated according to a particular type of criteria. Since the goal of such action is the manipulation of the material world, one of the clearest criteria of evaluation is whether the particular means chosen are the most *efficient* means of accomplishing this goal. A second criterion is whether the means chosen are *consistent* with one another. This criterion refers to the question of whether or not the various activities that must be put together to achieve a goal are compatible with one another; also, to the question of whether any principles are invoked in organizing these activities. If actions are rationally organized according to these two criteria, they should result in behavior or knowledge that is useful for attaining goals.

Much of the knowledge produced in modern society is rational-purposive knowledge, consisting of factual information about the material world, technical information about the efficiency and effectiveness of alternative techniques for manipulating the world, and administrative ideas about how best to make technical decisions and how best to organize people for instrumental goals. Knowledge of this type is regarded as being 'true' if it actually 'works' in manipulating the material world. This is the criterion of truth that is used to judge natural scientific knowledge, technological information, and most of the social scientific knowledge that is produced and applied in decision-making, administrative, and governmental settings.

Habermas recognizes the tremendous contribution that rational-purposive knowledge has made to the development of modern civilization. While he is critical of this type of knowledge, he is nevertheless thoroughly modern, seeing no possibility of pushing back the advances that have been made, nor does he desire to see this happen. Nevertheless, he believes there are serious problems in modern society that cannot be dealt with entirely on the basis of rational-purposive knowledge. Indeed, to attempt to do so only perpetuates and deepens the severity of these problems. The motive force in Habermas's work is to find some way of piecing back together 'the decayed parts of modernity' (Honneth *et al.*, 1981:28); that is, of rediscovering ways to live together in harmony and mutual dependence, while respecting individuals' autonomy, but without sacrificing the advances of modern technology.

In many respects, the motive force in Habermas's work is no different from that which inspired the great sociological theorists of the nineteenth century. There is a similarity between Habermas's concern about the limitations of rational-purposive action and Marx's emphasis on the alienating aspects of labor. The parallel with Weber is even closer, since Habermas's concept of rational-purposive action is very much akin to Weber's idea of functional rationality. Indeed, the criteria of efficiency, consistency, and manipulative utility that characterize rational-purposive action are to be found in Weber's discussion of the advancing 'iron cage' of rationality as well. There is also an affinity, which Habermas has explicitly addressed, between his own work and Durkheim's; specifically, Durkheim's struggle to discover a mechanism for sustaining moral community in the face of rampant individualism is one that Habermas perceives to be directly related to his own analysis of modern culture. Where Habermas departs from the classical sociologists is in his diagnosis of the proper direction for theoretical work to be focused. His 'intuition', as he has described it, is that the key to advancing beyond the constraints of rational-purposive knowledge is to focus on *communication*. It is, in his view, the 'web of intersubjective relations' among people that makes possible both freedom and mutual dependence, and this web of relations is necessarily involved in distributing the products of labor, as well as providing the basis from which values are derived and internalized and the condition necessary for arriving at consensus concerning collective goals. This interest in communication is the basis for his emphasis on the distinction between rational-purposive action and 'communicative action'.

Communicative action is not evaluated according to the same criteria as rational-purposive action; its validity cannot be assessed by examining whether the world of material objects was successfully manipulated, but depends on whether or not individuals are able truthfully and sincerely to express their intentions to others, and whether or not acts of intended communication accurately express the background consensus that exists among actors concerning norms of communication. Communicative action is governed by implicit rules governing the articulation of conflict, by 'world-views' or patterns of thought, and by the self-concepts of groups and individuals. This is the stuff of which culture is primarily comprised, and much of Habermas's work is concerned with describing the character and functioning of these phenomena in an effort to more fully understand the basis of human communication. The concept of communicative action, therefore, is one that runs through the entire corpus of Habermas's work.

The second intellectual construct that deeply influences Habermas's critical theory of culture is the idea of evolution (1979b). He sets his subject matter within the context of a general view of long-term social and cultural change, distinguishing broadly the earliest and presumably least differentiated forms of human culture from more developed but still traditional civilizations. He further distinguishes the modern period from all that preceded it. This broad comparative framework gives Habermas a basis for determining what is unique about the cultural conditions of the present and allows him to make choices as to what problems are most pressing to discuss. This framework gives his work a sense of timeliness and importance that would not otherwise be present. Moreover, it is this schema which buttresses his conviction that modern culture, on the one hand, is in the throes of an acute crisis and, on the other hand, has developed the potential to progress toward a higher stage in the evolutionary process.

The function of critical theory, as Habermas conceives it, is to contribute to the understanding of communicative action and thereby to facilitate progress toward a higher stage of cultural evolution. Although his version of critical theory has obvious links to the work of Adorno, Horkheimer, and others preceding him at Frankfurt, he has taken a somewhat ambivalent stance toward this earlier work. On the one hand, he has suggested that most of the general orientations were well worked out by his predecessors and that his own work has been concerned more with developing a systematic theory of communication than with extending or reformulating critical theory itself. On the other hand, he has argued that little existed even as late as the middle 1950s in the way of a self-conscious, systematic body of critical theory *per se* and that much of what is now regarded as critical theory represents a reconstruction of his predecessors' ideas.

Habermas's critical approach to the analysis of culture is deeply rooted in the scientific tradition. He is skeptical of theory that has no obvious reference to the condition of observable social events. His interest lies in raising phenomena to the status of observable objects which can then become the focus of reflection and criticism. While it is necessary in this quest to posit certain unobservables, he is reluctant to make these unobservables the focus of his theory or to accept their existence on the basis of faith alone. He has also devoted

191

considerable effort to the refinement of concepts in his framework and to systematically relating them to one another. He regards it of value to construct a unified theory of human culture, rather than admitting that different theories may be of value in different situations.

Compared with many of his contemporaries, his approach to culture extols the virtues of rationalism, but he is not an advocate of the kind of rationalism that characterizes positivistic philosophy or the Popperian version of the scientific method. Indeed, he has been a fierce critic of this variety of rationality. In his view, the concept of reason has been seriously distorted over the past one hundred and fifty years by the advance of science. Reason has come to be understood merely as a subjective adjunct to the empirical method and is now regarded as little more than the capacity to formulate empirically testable hypotheses. Reason is now that type of thought which assists in pragmatically selecting alternative means for the most efficient attainment of a given end. The broader rationalistic agenda that inspired the *philosophes* during the Enlightenment, by way of comparison, has been lost. This agenda was to develop a philosophical critique of the prevailing assumptions of the age, a critique that was empirically grounded, yet capable of contributing to higher levels of human freedom. This is the vision that inspires Habermas: he believes a relation between reason and human values can be rediscovered; articulating this relation is the objective of his critical theory.

Habermas's perspective on culture

The term 'culture' is one that Habermas has come to take for granted in more recent writings. During the 1960s he was at pains to distinguish culture as a separate province of inquiry from the natural sciences. Having accomplished this distinction to his satisfaction, he has now moved on to more specific discussions of various problems associated with the analysis of culture, including cultural evolution, the internalization of culture, and crises at the level of culture. Certain themes run consistently through his treatment of culture, particularly his emphasis on language and communication.

In other ways, however, his thinking on culture has undergone serious revision. Tracing these developments provides a means of grasping the distinctive features of his approach to culture.

Meaning and language

In his chapter on 'The Self-Reflection of the Cultural Sciences' in *Knowledge and Human Interests* (1971a:161–86), Habermas argues that the task of the cultural sciences is to understand the meanings attributed to objects and events by individuals in concrete historical circumstances. He sharply distinguishes the cultural sciences from the natural sciences. Whereas the natural sciences attempt to construct lawlike regularities applicable to all times and places, the cultural sciences focus on knowledge specific to historical situations. This distinction gives an important clue to his understanding of culture at this stage in the development of his theory. Following both the Weberian and phenomenological traditions, he identifies culture as a set of subjective meanings held by individuals about themselves and the world around them.

To understand the meanings that individuals may attribute to objects and events, the analyst must reconstruct the subjective perceptions of individuals in specific situations and discover the prevailing understandings that are shared by individuals in the situation but taken for granted by them. Not only are these difficult tasks, they are essentially non-cumulative, since each situation is different. Habermas assumes that meanings and the rules by which meanings are constructed differ from one situation to the next. Thus, it is impossible to construct universal laws describing the construction of meanings.

In emphasizing the situational variability of meanings from situation to situation, Habermas borrows heavily at this juncture from the hermeneutic or non-positivistic tradition in the social sciences. He asserts that meanings are sufficiently idiosyncratic to prevent approaching them from the standpoint of scientific criteria, including canons of verifiability and reliability. Instead, the observer must take the role of participant, actual or vicarious, and in this way discover the meanings implicit in that situation. Furthermore, the observer brings preconceived models of interpretation to the situation. Thus, it is less accurate to say that the observer 'discovers' meanings than to recognize that these meanings are 'reconstructed'.

At this stage in his theorizing, Habermas denies any possibility of discovering universal rules for the construction of meanings such as those associated with the construction of language. He distinguishes the study of cultural meanings from the study of linguistics. Nevertheless, language is of special interest to him even at this phase in the development of his perspective. Language, he argues, provides a key to the analysis of culture. Even though the individual attributes unique personal meanings to objects and events, language must be used to express these meanings to anyone else. Moreover, the individual uses language to codify these meanings for self-reflection. It is by analyzing the generalized or universal properties built into language, therefore, that the cultural analyst comes to some understanding of the meanings associated with particular situations.

Habermas also recognizes the limitations that language imposes on meanings. The rich connotations and implicit understandings present in any concrete situation are never captured fully or expressed adequately in language. For this reason, the analyst who relies on language as a primary source of evidence and as a medium for expressing conclusions necessarily engages in an act of interpretation. The analyst does more than simply observe and report the meanings which individuals ascribe to their circumstances. The analyst reconstructs these meanings according to certain rules implicit in language itself. Nevertheless, Habermas tends to be relatively less concerned about the biases inherent in language than others have been. In comparison with Susanne K. Langer (1951), for example, who regards the discursive or narrative form of language itself as a serious distortion of meanings, Habermas is relatively sanguine about focusing on language to understand culture. Clearly he pays less attention to alternative modes of symbolic expression, such as mythic or artistic forms of communication, than does Langer.

One reason why Habermas is content to focus on language is that his interest in the cultural sciences stems primarily from a desire to extend rational cognitive knowledge. He approaches culture as an observer and interpreter, not as an actor within the situation itself. For the observer, language is the only medium available for learning about the situation and for transmitting this information to other settings. Unlike many who have written on culture, Habermas does not approach the subject with the intention of enriching individuals' intuitive sense of meaning and purpose. Rather, his concern is discovering more effective mechanisms of communication about *shared* interests and problems.

A second reason for his interest in language is his view of scholarship, the goal of which he defines as human emancipation through enhanced capacities for reflection. These, he believes, come about only through language. It is through language that any event, experience, or subjective perception becomes sufficiently objectified to reflect critically upon it. He recognizes that there is a gap between the intuitively felt meanings that individuals construct as they go about their daily lives and the more generalized expressions of these meanings that are possible in language, but this gap, he argues, should not deter the analyst from examining language. The analyst's role should be to narrow this gap, a task accomplished by investigating, on the one hand, the nature of language and, on the other hand, the actions in which individuals engage. In this process the subjective meanings attributed to objects and events remain hidden, but the observer can, through examination of observable utterances and activities, begin to decipher the rules and conditions necessary for meaningful communication to take place.

The subjective 'understandings' held by an individual in any concrete situation may, of course, not be held at a conscious level. Consequently, these understandings may not be ascertainable even from sustained questioning of the individual. At this point, Habermas is willing to assume, however, that these implicit understandings tend to surface as a part of the individual's utterances and actions. Whether the individual intends to reveal them or not, clues are built into the manner in which language is constructed and used. Thus, the utterances an individual makes serve, in Habermas's work, as 'an indication of how seriously something is meant, whether the communicating subject is deceiving itself or others, to what degree it wants to or may identify itself with an actual expression of its own life, and how broad is the spectrum of connotation, concealment, or contrary intentions' (1971a:167).

If the cultural sciences are destined to focus on specific situations and cannot construct valid universal laws like the natural sciences, how then can their results be evaluated? In answering this question, Habermas again stresses the role of language and communication. He rejects both the argument of positivist philosophers who claim that valid knowledge in the cultural sciences can be achieved only by imitating the natural sciences and the argument of historians who assert that only an interesting rendition of particular events can result from the cultural sciences. In place of either of these arguments, he suggests an alternative that stems directly from the general perspective of his critical theory. The results of the cultural sciences, he suggests, must be evaluated in relation to 'practice', that is, in terms of their contribution to the capacity of individuals to engage in self-reflection and effective communication. To the extent that cultural analysis enhances these capacities, its results can be claimed to have 'validity'. This type of validity, of course, is situationally and historically specific. Thus, cultural analysis cannot claim to produce a single correct rendition of the meaning of any object or event. Any number of practically useful renditions are possible. Still, this number is not completely unlimited; testing alternative renditions in the communication process itself, the analyst and other participants gradually learn more about the nature of communication and culture.

The development of more effective models of communication and culture is apparently an iterative process. Models are formulated, applied, and evaluated again and again in the context of social interaction. This process necessarily occurs gradually, but it is no different in substance from the experimental method in the natural sciences. There, too, knowledge is accumulated gradually through the juxtaposition of models and data. In the cultural sciences, however, no prospect of arriving at a fully generalizable description of communication is held forth, since the social exigencies setting constraints on communication also vary over time. The process of testing out theories of culture, therefore, involves the analyst as an active participant in the construction of cultural interpretations. This process, nevertheless, does not consist simply of a vicious circle in which all interpretations are equally valid. That would be the case if language alone were subjected to scrutiny and interpretation, and these interpretations were subjected to further interpretation, and so on, without any reference to actual instances of social interaction. Nothing would be accomplished by this process. By the same token, repeated inductive examinations of interactive situations would also be fruitless. Thus neither pure philosophical speculation nor pure empiricist induction is sufficient to advance the study of culture. Only as language is used to interpret situations will progress be made toward an understanding of the workings of culture.

This formula for arriving at valid knowledge is disarmingly simple, resembling the desiderata set forth in social science texts of linking theoretical reflection with empirical observation. At one level, Habermas's proposal sounds very much like standard social science studies of culture, in that it resembles studies in which attitudes and beliefs are related to empirical evidence on social circumstances. Yet, in practice, his proposal has not been widely implemented in the social scientific study of culture. Symbolism and belief systems tend to be examined without reference to social structure or, alternatively, social structure is studied without paying attention to its symbolic-expressive dimensions. Few studies have seriously considered the connections between language and social experience.

The perspective revised

In his more recent writings, Habermas has advanced considerably beyond the perspective on culture outlined in his earlier work. There, the cultural sciences were distinguished from the natural sciences chiefly on the basis of self-reflection being an important component of knowledge about culture. Thus, the distinguishing feature of culture was the presence of subjectivity. Even though subjective meanings remained largely hidden from direct observation, they were the central aspect of cultural studies. Moreover, subjective meanings were the reason to engage in cultural studies. By elevating them to consciousness they could be communicated more effectively and subjected to critical reflection. The result, he assumed, would be greater freedom from domination. But what this approach did not provide was a firm empirical footing for the cultural sciences. If subjective meanings remained opaque to the observer, no possibilities existed for arriving at objective knowledge. This problem was the reason for his growing interest in language and communication. Evidence about subjective meanings became available to the observer only through language. But two serious problems remained unresolved: first, language was conceived of as an expression of subjective meanings, but this connection was simply posited rather than being defended theoretically or tested empirically; second, the concept of language itself remained vague, its components and the methods by which it was to be examined left unspecified.

Habermas has largely resolved the question of language's relation to subjective meanings by distinguishing more sharply between the two. In broad epistemological terms subjective meanings continue to serve as the basis for differentiating the cultural from the natural sciences and subjectivity remains as a rationale for wanting to produce knowledge that can be used for self-reflection, but he no longer appears to regard language *primarily* as an indicator of subjective meanings. In his more recent work, language has acquired greater stature in its own right (1979a), being only partially important as a medium for expressing subjective intentions. In addition to this function, it serves other purposes as well, such as legitimating social norms, conveying facts about the world, and above all, rendering communication possible. Habermas has come to regard language increasingly as an inherently *social* phenomenon which transcends and precedes the thoughts of individuals. Thus, language has objective status as a fact of social life, and can be observed and examined as an object in its own right, not merely as an indicator of subjective meanings. Significantly, language also appears to operate according to rules and in relation to particular kinds of constraints that Habermas appears to regard as universal.

By studying language generalizable knowledge can be obtained. This knowledge, to be sure, remains limited: it does not provide an account of the specific interpretations that individuals ascribe to their situations. Instead, the product of cultural analysis is knowledge about the conditions that must be satisfied in any situation for competent communication to occur. In short, cultural analysis is concerned with conditions and rules rendering acts of communication *meaningful*, not with the specific meanings that these acts may convey.

Habermas has also begun to specify in greater detail what is meant by 'language'. Rather than treating it simply as a broad generic phenomenon, he has come to emphasize the importance of paying attention to specific utterances or speech acts which can include written (and presumably behavioral) as well as verbal modes of communication. The speech act provides a tangible unit of culture that can be examined objectively to determine the conditions rendering its use meaningful. Speech acts themselves vary from the relatively simple to the more complex. A single sentence or phrase may be regarded as a speech act for certain purposes, while in other cases it may be more appropriate to examine an entire conversation, book, or episode. The issue is not so much the level of complexity or specificity at which speech acts are examined, but the fact that speech acts themselves are taken as the unit of cultural analysis.

Since speech acts are observable forms of behavior, culture becomes a behavioral phenomenon. It is a type of behavior in the same manner that riots, suicide rates, ethnic groups, and social movements are types of behavior and can be studied with as much objectivity as these other forms of behavior. Thus, Habermas's concept of culture differs radically from commonsense usages of the term. Culture is not a subjective phenomenon comprised of attitudes, beliefs, ideas, meanings, and values, as it has often been thought of in the social sciences, but consists of communicative behavior.

As presently formulated, the criteria that must be met in order for something to be considered a speech act remain somewhat ambiguous. From the examples Habermas gives, it is clear that his own thinking has concentrated primarily on verbal or written utterances in which formally codified language is employed. His preference for this type of speech act stems partly from the fact that generalized rules of communication may be easiest to observe when language is present, and partly from his conviction that rational communication involving the use of language is likely to be necessary for resolving social crises (cf. Alford, 1979). Thus, there is both a methodological and a practical reason for focusing on speech acts involving language. Nevertheless, it remains conceivable that other modes of communication can also be fruitfully considered. Physical gestures, dramatizations, art, music, ikons, even the symbolic-expressive aspects of ordinary behavior such as eating, voting, or participating in strikes — all might be regarded as communicative acts.

In choosing to focus on speech acts, Habermas is less concerned with the content of these acts themselves than with using them to generate assertions about deeper patterns in culture. He distinguishes the propositional content of utterances from the implicit rules of interaction that are conveyed by these utterances. These rules, he assumes, are most likely to reveal universal patterns and are of greater practical value to understand, since they remain largely implicit.

When Habermas discusses world-views, self-concepts, patterns of moral reasoning, norms of legality, and patterns of legitimation, he is considering these primarily as 'structures' or sets of rules influencing the nature of communication. The existence of these structures is indicated by the implicit messages present in communicative acts. It is important to emphasize again that these structures, in Habermas's view, do not necessarily exist in the subjective consciousness of individuals, but are abstractions that the observer constructs by observing symbolic-expressive behavior.

The internalization of culture

While Habermas conceives of culture as an objective phenomenon external to the individual, he also asserts the importance of individuals' internalizing culture. Only through the subjective internalization of culture does the individual learn to become an effective member of society. How does this process of internalization come about?

Habermas deals neither fully nor systematically with the question of internalization. Compared with Peter Berger, for example, he pays little attention to discussing the socialization processes involved in transmitting symbolic worlds to children nor does he examine the ways in which individuals construct subjective realities. What he has emphasized primarily are points of convergence in the literature on child psychology which serve as a basis for his own views of internalization (1979a:69–94).

He assumes that learning occurs in a series of irreversible, inevitable, discrete, and increasingly complex stages of development. Each stage supplies necessary patterns of rationality for the individual to proceed to the next higher stage. The transition from one stage to the next does not occur smoothly. Crises are associated with each transitional phase. Patterns learned in the preceding stage partially break down resulting in some degree of individual regression before the next stage is achieved. As higher stages of development are eventually reached, the individual becomes more autonomous, gains personal independence, is more capable of solving problems, can take different perspectives on the external world, and feels a greater sense of personal unity and psychological consistency. At the same time, the individual also internalizes more complex, abstract dimensions of the cultural environment into his or her subjective consciousness, including rules for organizing and manipulating the cultural environment. As a result, the individual becomes more thoroughly competent as a 'speaker' or social actor.

The attractiveness of these assumptions for Habermas is that they characterize the internalization of culture as a *rational* process. An orderly hierarchical sequence of development leads to greater degrees of personal competence at higher stages. A progression of this kind is important to Habermas because of his desire to discover mechanisms leading to more competent communication about common human needs. The presence of an identifiable developmental sequence gives him confidence that such mechanisms can be found and that they can be disseminated to individuals capable of learning them.

201

Habermas's emphasis upon rationality and competence as features of the internalization process distinguishes his approach from other perspectives. In contrast to theorists working in the tradition of phenomenology, particularly, he is interested in the need to enhance rational, self-conscious reflection about the internalization of culture. This interest stems from the fact that he is less confident than are phenomenologists about the stability of the taken for granted reality of everyday life. Whereas phenomenologists (including Peter Berger) have argued that everyday reality maintains and encompasses the meaningful existence of most individuals most of the time, Habermas asks what happens when this everyday world breaks down. Indeed, he suggests that everyday life-worlds are becoming increasingly precarious due to encroachments upon them by the modern state and crises inherent in the modern economy. Thus, it is imperative to Habermas that individuals' capacities to rationally communicate about their life-worlds be examined.

In further contrast to phenomenology, Habermas pays less heed to the subjective needs of the individual than to the interactive needs of social groups. More specifically, he pays virtually no attention to the problem of personal meaning that has preoccupied much of contemporary thinking about culture. He does, however, pay close attention to a problem which may on the surface appear to be simply another way of discussing the issue of personal meaning. This is the problem of *motivation* (1975:75–91). Crises of motivation stem from an erosion of cultural values which make sense of contemporary social, economic, and political conditions. As such, they represent a kind of psychological malaise which results in inaction or indecision on the part of the individual. This malaise bears a certain resemblance to the problem that other theorists have variously identified as anomie, meaninglessness, or lack of purpose. Habermas is not interested in the constellation of feelings and attitudes of which this subjective state may be comprised, however, except to acknowledge its existence and its experiential relevance for the individual. His concern is instead with the behavioral manifestations of this subjective state.

Two such manifestations are of particular importance.

One consists of an overwhelming fascination on the part of many individuals in contemporary culture with family concerns, leisure time, and consumption. The other is what Habermas terms 'civil privatism', connoting a lack of interest and participation in the process giving public (especially political) institutions legitimation. Thus, the upshot of his discussion of motivation crises is to point again toward communication and interaction. The serious result of motivation crises is not so much a lack of subjective personal meaning but an inability or unwillingness to participate effectively in the public realm.

The most specific aspect of Habermas's discussion of internalization is his attempt to delineate actual stages of cognitive and moral development characterizing the internalization process (1979a:100–2). These are derived largely from Piaget but represent reconceptualizations more in keeping with Habermas's own theoretical orientations. He identifies four stages characterizing the typical developmental process involved in the internalization of cultural patterns and the attainment of competence to speak and act: *symbiotic*, *egocentric*, *sociocentric-objectivistic*, and *universalistic*.

The *symbiotic* stage occurs primarily during an infant's first year of life. During this period the infant is apparently unable to differentiate clearly its own body or its internal states from the world of surrounding objects. The child remains completely dependent upon reference persons and the physical environment. The *egocentric* stage takes place for the typical child during the second and third years of life. In this stage the child gains a capacity to differentiate between self and environment, recognizing its own corporal existence and can identify objects in the external world, albeit without sophistication as to the complexities of the physical and social worlds. The child, however, remains unable to perceive the environment except from his or her own vantage point and, indeed, judges the relevance of external objects almost exclusively in terms of personal needs and feelings. The *sociocentric-objectivistic* stage lasts from years four or five until the onset of adolescence. During this stage the child learns to differentiate more fully among a variety of complex and abstract categories. Specifically, the child learns to differentiate symbols, meanings, and the objects they represent; the world of things versus the world of thoughts; and his or her own perceptions versus the perspectives of others. These developments go hand in hand with greater mastery of communication and social interaction. The *universalistic* stage, finally, comes about for most individuals during adolescence. It includes the capacity to think hypothetically and to reflect critically upon one's self-identity and assumptions. During this stage the individual gains relative autonomy from the dogma of particular subgroups in which he or she has been reared. This autonomy comes about from personal or vicarious participation in a greater variety of social settings, from critical reflection, and from learning processes oriented toward universalistic values.

Habermas has done little to elaborate the discussion of these stages or to indicate their relevance to the study of specific cultural issues. It is noteworthy, however, that the stages themselves are distinguished primarily in terms of differences in cognitive sophistication, particularly the capacity to make more refined differentiations among categories of the physical, social, and cultural world. Thus, it is implied that variations in cultural styles among particular groups or strata may be attributed chiefly to differences in the cognitive functioning of their members. These differences, in turn, can be traced both to aspects of the social structure and to broader stages of cultural evolution.

Culture and social structure

The relation between culture and social structure figures prominently in Habermas's work and, of course, has been heatedly debated in the literature on culture. On the one hand, theorists have argued that cultural patterns are shaped decisively by the social arrangements in which they are produced; on the other hand, social scientists have been accused of reductionism, of explaining away cultural patterns by attributing them to social arrangements rather than attempting to understand the internal structure of these patterns in their own right. Habermas has been caught up by this debate, as well, but his perspective offers a potentially important resolution to the controversy.

His theory of culture shares some of the reductionistic assumptions of the Marxist tradition from which he has borrowed. In this tradition, cultural elements tend to be regarded as mere reflections of other, more fundamental features of the social world. Accordingly, in his (1975) discussion of the crisis tendencies inherent in advanced capitalism he appears to regard the crises which most closely involve culture (legitimation and motivation) as secondary manifestations of more basic crises produced at the economic and political levels by the advancement of monopoly capitalism and its increasing dependence on the state. This view is also evident in his work on legitimation. While his interest in culture stems from a desire to understand the nature of legitimation, this aspect of culture is closely associated with the state and is problematic primarily because of functions performed by the state in advanced capitalist societies. He is not concerned, at this level, with culture as a phenomenon of interest in itself, but with legitimation as a tangible product of culture which bears on the decision-making capacities of the state.

The advantage of viewing culture in close connection with social structure is that culture ceases to be reified as a purely abstract set of norms and values. For Habermas, the problem of legitimation is never solved through values and norms alone; it involves the dynamic interaction of social classes, class factions, prophetic and messianic movements, and state agencies. The values and norms espoused by these various actors must be seen in conjunction with the institutions that articulate them and translate them into collective behavior.

Habermas's treatment of culture differs, nevertheless, from those that have approached this subject from a Marxist perspective. He sets forth a framework that explicitly guards against the danger of explaining away culture or of perceiving it as a mere reflection of social activity rather than treating it as a phenomenon of importance in its own right. This framework is articulated most clearly in his essay on 'universal pragmatics' (1979a:1–68). In this essay, he poses the question of what conditions influence the likelihood that any attempted act of communication will actually communicate effectively.

This question is remarkably similar to the more specific issue concerning ideology that has been addressed in the Marxist tradition. The question of what produces ideology, in Marx's formulation, is answered primarily with reference to the class struggle. Ideology is produced by the ruling class in its struggle for domination, masking the interests of the ruling class and promoting false consciousness among both rulers and ruled. Genuine understanding of ideology, therefore, must concentrate on the structure of class conflict, not on the content of ideology itself. Habermas's treatment of effective communication, in comparison, is more complex in that he distinguishes four types of conditions influencing the effectiveness of communication, each of which represents a distinct domain of reality.

First is the *world of external nature*, consisting of all objects, both animate and inanimate, that are accessible to sensory perception. This domain is a world of objects that can be manipulated. Any act of communication will be affected by its symbolic relation to this domain, being judged meaningful or effective in so far as it accurately represents the facts. Speakers and actors accordingly make claims about the 'truth' of their assertions in relation to this domain. Other things being equal, the closer the level of correspondence between these claims and facts observable in the external world, the more likely it is that a specific act of communication involving these claims will be regarded as meaningful.

The second domain is the *world of society*. This domain includes the usual array of interpersonal relations, institutions, traditions, and values that social scientists commonly associate with the idea of society. These can be recognized by the actor as external objects or simply taken for granted as features of life incorporated into the actor's perspective. In either case, they consist of pre-existing norms or symbolic patterns — objects created through processes of social identification and interaction (e.g., the concept of a nation, the value of freedom, the feeling of love). The fact that any act of communication takes place in relation to this domain, in addition to the domain of external nature, means that its effectiveness or meaningfulness is influenced by its relation to social norms. Communication can be judged as legitimate or illegitimate in relation to these pre-existing norms, and for this reason, speakers build clues into the content of their speech acts that make claims about the 'rightness' or 'legitimacy' of their assertions.

The third domain is the *internal world* of the person communicating — the realm of subjectivity. This domain includes feelings, wishes, and intentions. Only the person has access to this realm, but it influences the effectiveness of communication. Assumptions tend to be made in judging communication about the relation between what has been uttered and what the speaker really thought or felt internally. Other things being equal, communication will be more effective if it is judged to have accurately expressed the speaker's intentions. The speaker, therefore, is likely to shape communication in such a way that it can be judged to have contained 'truthful', or sincere, statements.

Finally, communication takes place within the domain of *language*. Consequently, its effectiveness depends in part on the linguistic medium in which it is framed. To the extent that an act of communication conforms to the grammatical, semantic, and syntactical rules of the language in which it is expressed, it may be said to be 'comprehensible' and, therefore, more likely to achieve its intended results.

All of these domains (see Figure 1) must be taken into account to fully assess the conditions influencing communication. Different academic disciplines may have more to offer toward understanding some of these conditions than others; thus, it may be useful for specific investigations to focus on, say, the linguistic component or the social component at the exclusion of the other domains. But the schema specifies that no one of these approaches can claim to have provided a complete explanation of cultural forms, nor can charges of reductionism be justified if investigations are conceived of within this framework.

In contrast to the Marxist perspective, work done on the social determination of culture within Habermas's framework must acknowledge the limitations of its claims. This work may shed valuable light on the *social* conditions affecting the legitimacy of various cultural forms, but such findings say nothing about the objective truth of these cultural forms, the sincerity of persons responsible for them, or the role of language in making them comprehensible. Habermas's approach, in short, provides for connections between social structure and cultural patterns, while obviating being able to 'explain away' the latter in terms of the former.

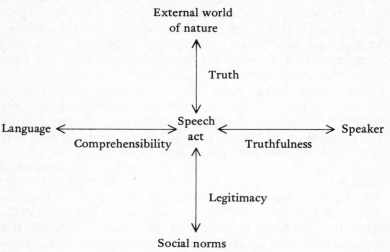

External world
of nature

Truth

Language ← Comprehensibility → Speech act ← Truthfulness → Speaker

Legitimacy

Social norms

Figure 1

This perspective on culture represents a clear departure from classical treatments of the relation between culture and social structure. Classical discussions of this relation grew from a positivistic orientation rooted, in turn, in conceptions about the nature of objects and their relations to the subjective world of the social actor. The quest for positivistic knowledge in the social sciences led to an emphasis upon external objects, since these appeared more amenable to empirical observation. Accordingly, the social sciences stressed the study of such 'objective' phenomena as interaction patterns, work, suicide rates, incomes, and group memberships, but attached less significance to the realm of culture. This realm, conceived as beliefs, attitudes, feelings, and values, was regarded as a manifestation of subjective states of the individual, which were less amenable to empirical observation. As a whole, culture remained a shadowland of non-objective moods and mental fabrications, compared with the objective world of social structure. To those who retained an interest in the social scientific study of culture, therefore, there was a strong tendency to develop 'explanations' purporting to give scientific accounts of cultural forms by revealing their dependence on the more objective patterns of social structure. This approach largely accepted the notion that culture was subjective, unlike the concrete world of social facts.

In contrast to this traditional view, Habermas denies the desirability of approaching the social world as if it were purely an external set of objects to be manipulated. Thus, communication and the sharing of ideas, feelings, and values take on primary significance in his perspective on culture. He regards it of little value to explain away ideas and beliefs in terms of presumably more objective social phenomena. Rather, it is important to understand the nature of culture itself. His conception of communication as an integral feature of culture also means that he is not concerned with the subjective aspects of culture, such as attitudes and beliefs. The unit of culture is essentially the speech *act*, meaning that culture takes on objective, social characteristics. Furthermore, there is no sharp distinction in his approach between culture and social structure. The domain of society itself is defined as patterns of symbolically structured events and expectations. Therefore, the study of culture no longer consists of relating culture to social structure, as traditionally conceived, but of relating *specific* symbolic acts to the broader symbolic *environments* in which they occur.

Habermas's perspective on the relations between culture and social structure is most clearly pronounced in his efforts to reformulate the Marxist theory of historical materialism (1979a:130–77). These efforts consist primarily of an attempt to recast Marx's concepts in more abstract terms in order to render them applicable to the modern situation. In so doing, communication and culture come to occupy a more central place than in Marx's own version of the historical process. The basis of Marx's theory was the observation that human-kind engaged in productive labor to earn its subsistence. Habermas characterizes production as 'instrumental action'; that is, action concerned with the manipulation of the material (physical, objective) world. This mode of action is governed by norms of purposiveness and efficiency. In Marx's view production is also characterized as *social* activity, since labor itself is typically organized into collective forms and the products of labor require social interaction for purposes of distribution. These features of production became the basis for Marx's discussion of the social relations of production and his identification of the disparity between socially produced profits and individually accumulated wealth as a basic contradiction in the capitalist mode of social organization.

Habermas's reformulation of Marx suggests that the social relations of production be regarded as a distinct type of behavior, as 'communicative action', governed by rules concerned with the distribution of goods and the processing of ideas about interests and expectations. Communicative action is by definition concerned with the symbolic expression of meanings and expectations, including both verbal and behavioral modes of communication. He also challenges the conventional Marxist view of the relation between culture and social structure by arguing that this view was originally meant to apply only to those periods in which society was passing into a new developmental level. Marx's view of culture as 'superstructure' dependent upon the economic and political spheres, Habermas argues, was not meant to be a general theorem applicable to all times and places (1979a:143). Instead, the economic and political base of society periodically poses problems which demand resolution if society is to evolve to a higher level. Accordingly, the base of society determines the nature of cultural events only during transitional phases to new levels of evolution.

Habermas further complicates the Marxist argument by suggesting that the social base need not be the economy in all stages of societal development. The economy did in fact serve as the basic determinant of society during the transition to capitalism. For this stage Marx was correct in focusing on economic conditions and classes as determinants of cultural forms such as religion and political ideology, but in primitive societies the kinship system fulfilled this function and in precapitalistic civilizations it was fulfilled by the political system. Habermas also cites discussions of 'post-industrial society' to suggest that science and education may come increasingly to function as dominant social institutions (1979a:144). These are, of course, primarily concerned with the production of culture and give rise to Habermas's belief that the symbolic-expressive realm itself may come to play an increasing role in the further evolution of society.

Culture and social change

As in the writings of the more prominent classical social theorists (including Comte, Spencer, Marx, and Durkheim), a strong evolutionary perspective runs through Habermas's theory of culture. His theory corresponds in many respects to contemporary theories of social evolution, such as the theories of Robert N. Bellah, Gerhard Lenski, and Edward O. Wilson. It is distinguished, however, by the subtlety of its relation to his overall philosophical perspective. Although he has outlined his assumptions concerning cultural evolution at a number of points, he has not to date presented a full length statement of these views as a single coherent treatise. It is necessary, therefore, to draw on a number of his briefer expositions in order to arrive at a description of his theory of cultural evolution.

The evolution of culture

Theories of evolution tend to be regarded as descriptive generalizations about the patterning of historical events and the transitions over time from one such pattern to another. One can, for example, equate the stages of evolution identified in many evolutionary theories with specific historical periods and events, such as the Middle Ages, the Reformation, and the Age of Absolutism. At this level, questions about period-ization, the relation of specific events to historical stages, and the relative adequacy of competing theories for understanding specific historical developments take priority. Habermas, however, is careful to distinguish these 'historical narratives', as he calls them, from theories of evolution (1979b).

Historical narratives are attempts to describe concrete empirical events and to identify a developmental logic that accounts for the sequencing of events. In contrast, theories of evolution are highly general abstractions developed to describe structures in human consciousness and general principles of social organization that set broad limits on the events, institutions, and social crises likely to occur. A theory of evolution is not meant to specify an actual or exact sequence of historical events. Reversals of such sequences can occur and specific events can take place outside of the possibilities prescribed. The purpose of an evolutionary theory is not to provide a concise account of what took place or did not take place, but to identify in probabilistic terms the limiting conditions and limiting modes of thought making overall patterns of events more or less likely.

The gap between narrative history and evolutionary theory is sufficiently broad in Habermas's view to make doubtful the possibility of rejecting or accepting competing descriptions of historical events on the basis of theory alone or, conversely, of testing competing theories against specific accounts of historical events. This is an important concession. It means that Habermas is not proposing a theory of cultural evolution that can be accepted or rejected on the basis of historical facts. In this sense, his theory is not an empirical theory at all. The purpose of such a theory, rather, is to provide an *orientation* for research — an orientation suggesting the importance of a certain set of problems on which research can be conducted. This research agenda may be sufficiently productive that the theory will be judged to have been fruitful, but the theory itself can neither be proven nor disproven by research alone. To take an example from Habermas's own work, the concept of 'technical reason' — associated by critical theorists with the modern or advanced capitalist period of evolution — serves primarily as a sensitizing concept, orienting the researcher to a set of problems deemed to be of general significance as far as the overall development of human culture is concerned, and highlighting problems such as the influence of technology on planning activities of the state or the structure of thought associated with technological work. But the concept of technical reason itself, and specifically the assertion that it predominates in the modern era, may be ultimately untestable.

212

Habermas's theory, at a more substantive level, identifies four distinct stages of cultural evolution: *neolithic societies*, *archaic civilizations*, *developed civilizations*, and *the modern age* (1979a:104, 106, 183–8). These stages are characterized by different principles of organization determining the kinds of institutions possible, the extent to which productive capacities will be utilized, and the capacity of societies to adapt to complex circumstances.

In *neolithic* societies actions are judged entirely in terms of consequences. No distinction is made between a person's motives and the consequences of that person's actions: a person who kills another is judged guilty of punishment without regard to the mood or intentions of that person. Human action is, in turn, an enactment of mythological world-views, and these world-views do not differentiate sharply between human and divine action, between natural events and social phenomena, or between tradition and myth.

Archaic civilizations are organized around a centralized regime or state, and the world-views associated with this stage provide concepts legitimating the state's domination. These world-views tend to be more complex and more rationally organized than those associated with neolithic societies. A concept of linear time is now present, allowing different time periods to be distinguished. Myth can be distinguished from tradition and the latter can be used as legitimation for the state. Motives are differentiated from the consequences of action, resulting in possibilities for a more elaborated system of law and punishment. The purpose of law is geared more closely to making determinations about personal intentions. Punishment is designed more for retaliation than to compensate for damages. There is also a greater degree of differentiation at this stage between the world of society and the world of nature, permitting a greater degree of calculation for purposes of manipulating and controlling nature.

In *developed* civilizations myths and narrative stories about tradition are replaced by cosmologies and higher religions. Knowledge is codified around concepts and moral principles, making it more readily disseminated and requiring a professional priesthood for its maintenance and transmission. The world-view itself becomes more unified, picturing the

213

world as a single orderly schema of things. This universalistic outlook makes possible the formulation of abstract legal and moral principles held to be universally true, and political organization must now be legitimated with reference to these principles, the highest of which are held to be indisputably true, subject neither to argumentation nor to objections. Rulers, therefore, are dependent upon these principles for legitimation and social conflicts must be resolved ultimately in conformity with these principles rather than on the basis of arbitrary or pragmatic considerations alone.

The *modern* age, marked by an erosion of confidence in the validity of higher order principles, coincides roughly with the period since the Reformation in which religious faith itself has become more self-conscious and reflective. While the modern world-view continues to assert the existence of unity, order, and coherence in the world, this unity no longer consists of a taken for granted set of absolute laws concerning God and nature, but inheres only in the nature of reason itself. So there are efforts to reflect upon and to demonstrate connections between concrete behavior and what is known about reason. There is also a greater degree of differentiation between statements referring to nature, truth, and morality, on the one hand, and the norms or procedures used to derive these statements and to validate them, on the other.

It is instructive to observe that these stages pertain primarily to cultural models or world views rather than to institutional arrangements or forms of social organization. It is primarily the complexity of alternative world-views that distinguishes the four stages, each incorporating a new level of differentiation not present in the preceding stage: archaic cultures contain a greater degree of differentiation between society and nature, tradition and myth, and motives and actions than do neolithic cultures; developed cultures differentiate between universalistic principles and narrative traditions more so than do archaic cultures; modern cultures, in turn, differentiate universalistic principles from the processes of reason used to arrive at conceptions of these principles. Each stage logically precedes the succeeding stage and learning occurs at each stage, making possible the next level of evolution.

In choosing to focus on cultural factors as the defining elements of his theory of evolution, Habermas is, of course, making a radical departure from the Marxist tradition in which modes of production are the operational criteria for distinguishing different stages of historical development. He (1979b) cites a number of empirical problems with the Marxist schema, particularly, difficulties arising out of variations observed among primitive societies, questions of periodization for pre-modern modes of production, and incompatibilities among theories emphasizing different aspects of the production process, such as technology, labor, and markets. The principal grounds on which he rejects the Marxist formulation is its lack of universality. No single dimension of comparison runs through the entire Marxist typology of societies; it is based largely on *ad hoc* observations of specific historical cases. His solution is to propose concepts at a sufficiently abstract level to apply to all the stages with which he is concerned. These concepts refer primarily to *principles* of organization rather than to actual types of social organization, and are conceived of primarily at the level of learning, cognition, and world view. This is not to say that Habermas has replaced Marx's materialistic conception of history with an equally narrow form of cultural determinism, for he is not concerned with the historical description of concrete cultural symbols or systems of belief, but with stages pertaining to structural *patterns* or principles of differentiation which subsume both specific cultural forms and specific modes of production.

Although careful to avoid carrying the analogy too far, he suggests there is a parallel between stages of cultural evolution and those through which an individual progresses in the process of maturation. Specifically, the individual must learn to make progressively more refined differentiations, first, between himself or herself and the external world and between his or her own actions and the motives behind these actions; then between specific experiences or roles and universalistic principles of behavior or values; and finally, between these values and his or her own thoughts about them, as well as the processes of communication giving rise to these thoughts. These levels correspond roughly to the types of differentiation

215

that become evident with successive stages of cultural evolution.

What is the driving force in this evolutionary scheme? What pushes culture to evolve from one stage to the next? Habermas answers that at each stage problems arise that cannot be successfully resolved without progressing to the next higher stage. It is not inevitable for any particular society or civilization to effectively make this transition; indeed, societies and civilizations have failed to do so, resulting in social disintegration or fixation at a certain level of development. Habermas's argument is simply a logical one: that cultural learning of the type described *must* come about in order to say that the main problems of the preceding stage have been resolved. These problems arise primarily in the economic and political realms, imposing strains on prevailing world views, including religion, philosophy, morality, and law. It is in *transitional* epochs that the material base of society exerts pressure on cultural patterns. It is within the cultural patterns themselves, however, that learning occurs permitting evolution to advance to a higher stage.

The specific problems arising in each cultural epoch, and creating pressures leading to successive epochs, differ from one epoch to the next. Those in neolithic societies appear primarily to be problems of subsistence — problems associated with the society's capacity to extract from nature the necessary provisions with which to sustain itself. This necessity produces pressure in neolithic cultures toward greater differentiation between the realms of nature and society, and permits activities to be consciously organized for purposes of manipulating nature. An apparent consequence of this activity, in turn, is the emergence of a more centralized or rationally organized system of governance. This governing regime requires legitimating beliefs in order to justify its domination over the social realm. This requirement becomes a major problem in archaic civilizations, since legitimation strictly on the basis of tradition, retaliation, coercion, or pragmatic success in manipulating nature is at best tenuous. The evolution of world-views in which higher order principles are clearly differentiated from specific traditions provides a solution to this problem. Both political and economic activities can be organized on a more rational basis in relation to these universalistic principles. Then, with the geographic extension of political and economic control, alternative formulations of universalistic principles come into confrontation with one another. Particularly with the rise of capitalism and the modern bureaucratic state, social integration must occur on a level that subsumes a diverse array of absolutist principles. Thus, it becomes necessary to resolve conflicts not on the basis of unquestioned values themselves but in terms of procedures regarded as rational means for arriving at consensus. These are the problems Habermas addresses most systematically in his discussion of legitimation.

The problem of legitimation

Habermas regards legitimation as one of the most significant functions of modern culture. So he has taken up the question of what it means to call something 'legitimate' and has extended this discussion to include a sophisticated analysis of the economic and political conditions influencing the nature of legitimation problems in advanced capitalist societies (1975, 1979a:178–206). His concept of legitimacy is similar to standard social scientific definitions of the term. 'Legitimacy', he writes, 'means that there are good arguments for a political order's claim to be recognized as right and just . . .' (1979a:178). Legitimacy implies recognition, and recognition includes an evaluation which imputes justice and propriety to the situation. One of the important consequences of legitimacy is stability. This consequence has been taken to mean preservation of the *status quo*, but it is more correct to associate stability with adaptive capacity. A social system is stable to the extent that it can adapt to strains or changes confronting it. This kind of stability may encompass change, but does not include system breakdown or capitulation to crisis.

His concept of legitimacy differs from standard usages of the term in at least one important respect: it refers particularly to the type of *claim* that can be made by the state or on its behalf. If a convincing claim or argument can be made, then it may be said that the state must actually have gained widespread recognition. So, Habermas does not restrict the notion of legitimacy to situations in which public opinion at large supports the state's right to power. He is willing to focus more narrowly on the state's claims, whether these claims are broadly compelling or not. It may be that these claims are effective but not true, true but not effective, or they may appeal primarily to significant groups other than the populace itself. This view of legitimacy is consistent with his more general discussion of the types of validity claims inherent in any speech act. His treatment of the state's legitimacy may be regarded as a special application of this more general theoretical analysis. Statements made by the state or by others about the state's right to exert power are a type of speech act. As such, these statements contain implicit claims to being valid: claims of being in consonance with the world of nature, of expressing the sincere intentions of the speaker, of properly subscribing to conventional linguistic rules, and most importantly, of being correct in relation to social norms.

Habermas restricts his discussion of legitimacy primarily to the state, asserting specifically, for example, that 'multi-national corporations or the world market are not capable of legitimation' (1979a:179). The special position of the state derives from its role as a corporate actor, not only making decisions affecting the whole society, but doing so in the name of society itself. More specifically, the state purports to guarantee the viability of society through its decisions, and this guarantee constitutes an important basis of the state's claim to power. In other words, the state's right to make binding decisions — tantamount to exercising coercive power — is rooted in its ability to prevent social disintegration. But understandings of disintegration are dependent on collective values. Therefore, the state's legitimacy depends ultimately on culture.

These arguments are restricted further to the *modern* state. In traditional societies questions arise about the state's right to exercise power, but these questions can be answered with reference to coherent religious or philosophical world views specifying absolute values. Political conflicts can be resolved by messianic or prophetic movements asserting new values as sources of legitimacy. In contrast, the modern state derives legitimacy from procedural norms concerning the legality and constitutionality of decisions. Political opposition tends to be institutionalized within the political structure of the modern state itself. Parties and factions ready to oppose an existing regime are ever-present. Questions about legitimation, therefore, are permanent features of modern societies.

In contrasting modern and traditional societies this way Habermas deviates from one of the more familiar views of legitimation in American social science: the work of Robert N. Bellah (1970, 1975) on civil religion. In Bellah's view, the basis of legitimation in American society, and apparently in others as well, continues to be a set of absolute values including notions about God (in the American case) which were built into the American tradition from the beginning and have been carried on to the present day by religious groups. Bellah acknowledges the importance of rationalistic, utilitarian norms, traceable to the Enlightenment and ultimately to Roman law, norms that come close to Habermas's description of legitimation, but Bellah treats them as absolute values, akin to but conflicting with the Puritan tradition, rather than norms differing qualitatively from traditional values. Habermas and Bellah agree that legitimation involves claims about social integration, but Habermas gives little weight to the importance of absolute values rooted in tradition. Claims may be set forth by political leaders framed in terms of, say, absolute religious values, or opposition parties may root claims in such arguments, as in the case of religiously conservative interest groups, but in Habermas's view these do not constitute the most significant arena of legitimation. In comparison with Bellah, he is less concerned with refurbishing the traditional meanings of religious or patriotic symbolism and more concerned with advancing understandings about the role of rational communication in the political process.

The capacity of the modern state to make convincing claims about its legitimacy has been seriously eroded, Habermas asserts, by changes in the character and role of the state. Under normal conditions, the strength of the modern state lies in the fact that questions about legitimacy have been institutionalized: routine mechanisms have been established to deal with issues of propriety and legality and to resolve questions about the constitutionality of state actions; political parties also provide an institutionalized mechanism for expressing grievances. In so far as dissatisfaction with the state can be expressed through voting and support for opposition parties, problems of legitimation can ordinarily be handled through the transfer of power to an opposing regime. Nevertheless, Habermas argues that these institutionalized measures have become subject to serious limitations because of changing economic and political circumstances — circumstances deriving from the growth of advanced capitalism itself, including increased competition, dependence on technology and research, and social costs accruing from the disruptions of the economy and the need to stabilize ever-expanding markets both domestically and abroad. In developed economies the state is expected to perform an expanded array of functions, among the most demanding of which is that of buffering individuals against the ill effects of capitalism. The state is called on specifically to provide social welfare and security programs for the labor force, to compensate for structured economic inequality by providing public education and job programs, to engage in counter-cyclical financial policy in order to correct for the effects of business swings, and to provide environmental clean-up and other services associated with the by-products of industrial production. The problem encountered by the modern state in attempting to perform these tasks is not so much that the tasks themselves are difficult (although they may be), but that they engage the state in a fundamental contradiction of roles. On the one hand, the state is expected to fulfil these functions; on the other hand, it is expected to respect the autonomy of private enterprise. State and economy are sufficiently interdependent that the state is 'damned' if it does not intervene, but 'damned' also if it does because of classical free enterprise ideology. Furthermore, when the state does intervene, it is confronted with conflicting norms. As representative of the public good, it is expected to base decisions on consensual values; as economic actor, it necessarily bases decisions on instrumental interests.

The state finds its claims to legitimacy hampered further

by incompatibilities between constraints imposed by the world market and the international state system, and by traditional sentiments of national consciousness. Traditionally, the state could head off legitimation crises by appealing to national consciousness. Fascism in Europe during the Second World War was an extreme example of this tactic. More abstractly, the traditional state was able to derive legitimation by appealing to common values over against competing private economic interests. It could invoke nationalistic arguments about collective goods, such as national security and defense, and forge symbolic links between folk culture and civil law to buttress the legitimacy of legal procedures. However, growing interdependence of the world-economy, of the international state system, and of the global communications network have rendered these tactics relatively inoperable. The news media, international travel, and transnational agencies (such as the United Nations) raise to consciousness alternative values, notions about collective goods, and legal procedures transcending those of specific nations, and heightened global consciousness reveals that social integration cannot be attained on the basis of national culture alone. Hence, the state's claim to coercive power in the name of social integration falls into question.

Habermas regards the present legitimation crisis as a higher order problem than any previously confronting the state. He is careful that his usage of the phrase 'legitimation crises' not be confused with the kinds of controversies that originated as the nation-state itself emerged and which now have largely been resolved. Among the controversies he places in this category are: detaching the state's legitimacy from specific religious traditions, a process which was largely accomplished by the early part of the nineteenth century; conflicts between classical natural law and rational natural law, the latter providing a basis for procedural forms of legitimation as opposed to legitimation based on substantive values; the transition from civil rights legitimated in terms of abstract values toward theories linking these rights to the capitalistic system itself; the transition from princely sovereignty to sovereignty of the people; and the transition from elite bourgeois conceptions of citizenship to broad

221

conceptions of national citizenship. While these controversies still erupt occasionally, Habermas believes they were largely resolved *at the cultural level* during the nineteenth century and, therefore, fail to pose as serious a threat to the modern state as the legitimacy crisis it now faces.

The legitimacy of the modern state no longer rests on tradition or absolute values, but is rooted in conceptions of proper *procedure* — procedures deemed legitimate if they have been established according to norms of legality and constitutionality and if they conform to certain conceptions of citizenship and representation. They are intended to serve as mechanisms for negotiating policies oriented toward the common good. The modern period is characterized by a relatively high degree of reflection about these procedures. They are not taken for granted as the way things simply must be, but are consciously subjected to scrutiny to determine if they in fact produce desired consequences. The material contradictions associated with advanced capitalism, however, have placed these procedures under tremendous strain. No longer can they function smoothly or effectively without even greater scrutiny. The very *discourse* involved in the functioning of these procedures needs to be raised to the level of self-conscious scrutiny. So Habermas has sought to develop a more reflective theory of communication with this end in view. This theory has been worked out with particular reference to the problem of ideology.

The critique of ideology

Habermas's contribution to the discussion of ideology is distinctive in at least three respects: he has taken seriously the Marxist and Freudian perspectives on ideology, regarding it as a form of *false* consciousness; he has directed his substantive attention toward all-pervasive ideologies — science and technology — rather than limited ideologies associated with particular political interest groups; and he has attempted to go beyond the description of ideology to suggest a procedure for overcoming ideology. His approach runs counter to recent tendencies in the literature that regard ideology as any concrete *subset* of the prevailing cultural system. Clifford

Geertz (1973), in a well-known discussion of ideology, argues against linking ideology with interest groups or with social strains that give it a distorted content, preferring instead to treat ideology as any other cultural system, as symbols and meanings to be examined in their own right. For Geertz, ideology is different from other cultural systems only in terms of specificity, being concerned with patterning concrete social circumstances in order to mobilize behavior. Peter Berger and Thomas Luckmann (1966) take a somewhat more delimited view of ideology, associating it with specific groups' claims to power, but their discussion also treats ideology as a subcategory of culture differing little in substance from other machineries of reality construction. In contrast, Habermas harkens to earlier discussions of ideology put forward by Marx and Freud who sought to differentiate ideology from truthful ideas by pointing out its biased, unrealistic, delusional qualities. According to this tradition, the trouble with ideology is its tendency to distort reality. For Marx particularly, such distortion was a stumbling block impeding revolutionary progress.

These early formulations have generally been rejected because of their seemingly inherent limitations, including the tendency to neglect systematic analysis of ideology itself, turning instead to its sources in political or economic interests, or its consequences for people caught up in its delusions, and the related problem of establishing convincingly that ideology in fact distorts reality, at least in a more serious way than, say, science or philosophy. Habermas avoids the problem of focusing on causes and effects rather than ideology itself, asserting the priority of the nature of ideology. In his view, ideology consists not so much of false perceptions, but of a type of communication that affects the capacity of groups or whole societies to arrive at satisfactory agreements concerning common problems. He also resolves the problem of differentiating ideology from other, presumably less delusional ideas, albeit in a different way from other theorists. Whereas writers like Geertz and Berger suggest implicitly that ideology and science both provide appropriate constructions of reality, differing only in purpose, Habermas suggests that ideology and science both *distort* communication —

indeed, science is ideology. In making this argument, he has to specify the meaning of 'distorted communication'.

Systematically distorted communication is for Habermas (1970a) what false consciousness was for Marx: it prevents the resolution of major social crises. *Systematically* distorted communication is to be distinguished from simple breakdowns of communication stemming from misused rules of language. These are easily recognized by participants themselves, who simply fail to comprehend what others are attempting to communicate. A *systematic* distortion is more serious in that participants assume they have understood one another and have arrived at some consensus, but because of un-acknowledged interests they have engaged only in pseudo-communication, and have failed to achieve genuine consensus. Pre-existing patterns of thought have prevented them from communicating fully and effectively. These pre-existing patterns of thought are not distinguishable in terms of content, but by the level of complexity or sophistication they embody. Because of the importance of communication to the functioning of advanced capitalist societies, high levels of sophistication and self-awareness concerning communication are necessary; values and facts cannot be accepted uncritically as 'givens'; attention must be paid to the effects of communication on values and facts and to their expression in discourse. Any failure to question the nature of values and facts can lead to systematically distorted communication.

Habermas (1970c) regards science and technology as sources of systematically distorted communication. Because of their sheer pervasiveness, they are a serious form of ideology, reflecting rational-purposive action, and conflicting with communication oriented toward social solidarity and the attainment of consensus. While promoting economic growth through manipulation of the physical and social environment, they pay no attention to promoting self-conscious reflection about values. Advances of science and technology substitute manipulative rules and context-free knowledge for norms of solidarity and reciprocity, and lead to an emphasis on technical skills at the expense of roles and values defining moral obligations. In traditional societies, dominant institutions (family, ethnicity, and religion) were

224

oriented toward moral obligations, not the instrumental manipulation of nature. Now, science and technology have become the dominant institutions. Families, small groups, and intimate relationships continue to be cherished as sources of support and basic values, but the mentality of science and technology increasingly spills over into these areas, infecting them with rational-purposive styles of thought. This has taken place, not because of any ill effects intended by scientists, but by the very form of scientific thought itself. Science manipulates nature, but excludes values from consideration.

Scientific thought has also been affected by the growth of the political sector. Massive political intervention in the research enterprise has furthered the ideological domination of science and technology. The state's intervention has altered institutional arrangements that traditionally kept rational-purposive action confined to the economic sphere, leaving the state to be concerned with consensus and common values. Under the present system, these functions are now combined within the political sphere itself, giving the rational-purposive orientation of science an opportunity to prevail.

As the link between technology and scientific theory has grown closer, technological progress begins to appear inevitable. Science purports to discover fundamental laws of the universe, and technological progress, rooted in science, appears to come about because of these laws. The rate and direction of technological progress cannot be questioned. Societal goals involving technology (such as the development of nuclear energy or the exploration of outer space) should result from collective decisions in which mutual interests are taken into account. Instead, these goals are advanced as inevitable next steps in a natural sequence. Claims that technology is ready but only government incompetence prevents its implementation, or that new technology is the only way to solve problems produced by existing technologies, are examples of this type of reasoning. More abstractly, technology appears as an aspect of the external world of nature over which humans have no control, rather than a product of social communication and decision-making. Technology, therefore, becomes a source of false consciousness. As with religion in the Marxist view, technology misinterprets human

225

misery, attributing it to 'gods' over whom no control can be exerted, rather than associating it with society. In this fashion it renders objective and uncontrollable that which should be subject to collective decision.

The defining feature of ideology for Habermas is that it rules out particular topics of discussion *a priori*. The sciences do this by arbitrarily distinguishing the world of facts from the world of values. From this perspective, knowledge is useful only if it identifies regularities between causes and effects. Knowledge of this type permits the world of objects to be manipulated in order to achieve desired outcomes, but when questions arise about the desirability of alternative outcomes, the sciences answer only that some decision must be made, and they rule out the possibility of systematic reasoning being able to inform this decision. Thus, the sciences' manipulations are left to operate blindly within whatever system of irrational domination may prevail. Habermas believes modern culture is caught up in a more complex, sophisticated form of ideological domination than ever before. Technocratic consciousness increasingly pervades government and the economy, and technological progress has become indispensable to economic growth and to regimes concerned with fostering growth. The ideology of technology cannot be linked directly to the interests of one social class, nor shown to conflict with those of another, but is a pervasive mentality in which all participate; and all may perish collectively in it, since it prevents human beings from taking charge of their own values.

The solution to ideological domination is the cultivation of what Habermas has termed variously 'the public sphere', 'an ideal speech community', or in more abstract terms, 'communicative competence' (1970a, 1970b; McCarthy, 1973, 1978): a cultural context in which political decisions can be discussed. In this setting, politics ceases to be based primarily on the manipulative expertise of technical experts, but becomes oriented toward arriving at consensus and making decisions based on mutual concerns. Habermas argues that a stable society must have a mechanism of this type, but that common symbols and values cannot alone fulfill this function. Critical, conscious reflection and deliberation must be present in order to apply common values to concrete problems.

It is not always clear in Habermas's writing whether an ideal speech community has ever actually existed or whether it is truly an *ideal* to be achieved at some higher level of cultural evolution. He regards it as a practical political necessity, due to the fundamental crises he perceives in advanced capitalism, but his discussion is more concerned with specifying its theoretical characteristics than with examining historical or contemporary examples. One writer has suggested that the eighteenth-century bourgeois public sphere comes close to Habermas's view of an ideal speech community and may have served as a model for his discussion (Hohendahl, 1979:92–3). The bourgeois public sphere consisted of private persons without strong links to particular political parties or regimes, who engaged in critical discourse about the claims of the state and examined the assumptions on which political actions were based. With increasing penetration of the state into the bourgeois economy, this sphere eventually lost its autonomy and its capacity to reflect dispassionately upon the interests of the state.

Under present circumstances, it is difficult to imagine groups capable of dissociating themselves sufficiently from the throes of technocratic consciousness to satisfy Habermas's criteria for a public sphere. Still, in scattered remarks Habermas has (e.g. 1979c, 1981) suggested the possibility of grass-roots interest groups fulfilling this function — environmentalists, consumer action groups, student activists, and although Habermas has generally been distrustful of religious movements, certain types of consciousness raising or meditation groups. Such groups, arising outside of established party structures and motivated by a populist democratic spirit, enjoy a degree of critical distance from political institutions and seek to cultivate discussion about underlying values. It is perhaps significant that Habermas does not regard with optimism the likelihood of universities serving this function, except through the informal activities of students. The prospect of *any* group being able to communicate openly and effectively about fundamental values is not high because of blinders built into the structure of rational thought itself by science and technology. Vested interests attached to individuals and subgroups also remain a problem, and channels for disseminating reflective communication, particularly the mass media, are dominated by norms of technical reason. It is clear that Habermas has not yet conceived an entirely satisfactory resolution to these problems, only some tentative clues.

In his discussion of systematically distorted communication, he (1970a) discusses psychoanalysis as a model for overcoming ideological thinking. He is not concerned with its content but with the *type of discourse* that occurs between analyst and patient. Three aspects of this discourse are important: a genuine desire on the part of both participants to explore underlying motivations, to unmask false assumptions, and to arrive at an assessment of needs and capacities; an iterative process, in which insights are not achieved immediately but develop gradually as the analyst probes successively deeper layers of consciousness and the patient compares these layers with personal experience; and a preconceived theory against which experience can be examined, a theory emphasizing the structure of communication itself, including relations among words and symbols. The discourse between patient and analyst serves as a prototype for Habermas's (1970b, 1979a) more general treatment of communicative competence. Ideological distortions are gradually overcome when persons have a genuine desire to reflect upon the validity claims built into the structure of discourse itself, and this process is facilitated by pre-existing models of discourse. More specifically, effective communication requires awareness of the types of claims present in speech acts, as discussed earlier: claims of truth, legitimacy, truthfulness, and comprehensibility. Once these claims are recognized, they can be subjected to scrutiny.

The evolution of religion

Reference has already been made to Habermas's views on modern religion. Generally speaking, he has paid relatively little attention to religion, focusing more heavily on the rationalistic aspects of communication, and assuming that contemporary culture is thoroughly secular. For this reason, he has not developed a systematic treatment of religion, certainly not to the same extent as Peter Berger or Mary

Douglas. Nevertheless, he has made reference to religion on a number of occasions and some insights can be obtained from these remarks. The context in which he views religion is his theory of cultural evolution. In tracing particularly the archaic and developed stages of evolution, he finds it necessary to discuss religion; then, in discussing distinctive features of the modern period, he considers some of the limitations and possibilities to which religious sentiments are now subject.

Habermas (1975) assumes that individuals need some kind of personal integration, unity, self-identity, or meaning, and although he does not specifically spell out the reasons for this assumption, the idea of system integration can clearly be derived from his more general perspective on social systems. He suggests, further, that this sense of personal integration depends on unifying cultural norms, citing Durkheim's argument linking self-development to unified world-views provided by society (1975:117). He also quotes from Peter Berger's *Sacred Canopy*, which argues that society provides a meaningful order of existence for the individual who, without this sheltering cosmos, would experience the horror of chaos (1975:118). The way in which personal meaning is attained, Habermas asserts, has shifted dramatically during the course of cultural evolution. In the neolithic epoch, the individual fails to differentiate sharply between his actions or intentions and the world of external nature. The world of nature itself also tends to blend indiscriminately with the world of myth. As a result, the individual develops neither a sharp sense of individuality nor a distinct need for self-reflective meaning and integration. Only with the development of a more rationalized world-view, as Weber (1963) pointed out, does the need for a highly coherent sense of personal integration arise.

With the transition to archaic and developed civilizations, religious world-views become important as a source of personal integration, providing a unified understanding of group life and of the individual's role in society. He argues that religious world-views link the individual's sense of personal identity with assumptions about the larger world, and that these assumptions inevitably arise as societies struggle for survival. The confrontation with nature, over

229

which no society has perfect control, raises questions about the limits of human existence that must be answered. For the individual, these questions arise from risks involving physical well-being, as well as problems associated with social interaction, such as loneliness and guilt. Religious world-views perform a dual function: they assure the individual of his or her existence as part of some larger totality or absolute principle, thereby resolving cognitive doubts; they also promise consolation in so far as the contingencies of existence cannot be eliminated or explained away.

In this depiction of religion, Habermas draws heavily on Weber's (1963) discussion of the 'problem of meaning'. According to this argument, questions of meaning arise because of experiences, such as suffering, grief, and death, having no intrinsic value and not being desired. These experiences raise doubts about the rationality of the world, and must be dealt with by any world-view purporting to order the world according to meaningful universalistic principles. Like Weber, Habermas considers modernization to have had serious effects on traditional religious world-views, although he takes this discussion in a somewhat different direction from Weber. As societies developed, they exercised increasing control over nature and the effects of starvation, natural catastrophes, and disease gradually diminished, although they did not, of course, disappear entirely. The result was not simply a diminution of religious world-views, but the functions these world-views had performed underwent differentiation. Knowledge about the world of nature became a distinct sphere, while religious world-views focused more narrowly on questions of meaning and purpose (1975:119–20) — science and religion became separate spheres of culture. The sciences gradually monopolized knowledge concerned with interpreting and manipulating nature and with techniques for mastering the unsought contingencies of nature, making these contingencies more bearable. Religious world-views, in contrast, became limited to problems of personal meaning and to problems of social integration.

This much of Habermas's discussion corresponds closely with other treatments of modern religion. With Geertz, Habermas regards religion as a mediating link between moral action and cognitive world-views, agreeing that religion's function is to make suffering understandable and bearable. With Berger and Luckmann, he stresses that religion has become, in their terms, 'privatized' — functioning as a source of subjective integration, rather than providing a compelling description of the external world. With Bellah, he emphasizes religion's role in legitimating social integration, one manifestation of which is the notion of civil religion. But Habermas carries his own discussion one step farther.

In his view, the *social sciences* have seriously affected the functioning of modern religion. Imitating the natural sciences, they attempt to provide knowledge about the external world of *social* contingencies. In this attempt they have invaded the realm of values and social integration left to religion by the natural sciences, a realm increasingly important because of the complexity of social life. Advanced capitalism successfully exploits nature through technology, but produces economic dislocations, inequality, military conflicts, and political contradictions on a scale hitherto unseen. The social sciences have tried to resolve these problems by producing technical knowledge about the social world, but this knowledge does not address fundamental questions about values or consensus. The social sciences have remained relatively ineffective, even though they have eroded faith in traditional religion by pointing out the relativity of cultural forms, thereby challenging religious claims to absolute truth. In place of absolutes, they substitute blind faith in technical reason. Habermas admits that the social sciences have been unable to deal effectively with social problems such as loneliness and guilt, let alone offer solutions to make them more bearable. Problems of suffering and death also remain beyond the scope of consolation that the social sciences provide. We must, Habermas concludes, resign ourselves to living without consolation.

Habermas is more thoroughly secular than many of his contemporaries. Unlike Gadamer, he sees no possibility of reconstructing traditional world-views to have convincing meaning in the modern situation. Unlike Ricoeur, he is unable to adopt a post-Enlightenment stance toward religion which finds meaning in religious symbolism even though it is stripped of literal significance. Unlike Berger, he posits no possibility of discovering 'signals of transcendence' within the secular realm. Habermas remains in many respects a serious disciple of the Marxist tradition, granting sufficient credibility to the social sciences to regard all religious suppositions unworkable in the modern era. There is one special function which religion can play, however. If properly conceived, it can facilitate the process of communication. Habermas points to recent theological work by Pannenberg, Moltman, and Metz as examples. In these writings, God is conceived as an abstraction with characteristics resembling those put forth by Habermas as features of ideal communication. The concept of God symbolizes the process binding together a community of individuals striving for emancipation. God, in Habermas's words, 'becomes the name for a communicative structure that forces men, on pain of loss of their humanity, to go beyond their accidental, empirical nature to encounter one another *indirectly*, that is, across an objective something that they themselves are not' (1975:121).

Conclusions

Criticisms of Habermas's work, of which there have been many, have generally fallen into three categories: metatheoretical criticisms, usually from philosophers of science, concerned with the consistency of his assumptions about the nature of science, his criticisms of the positivistic approach to science, and the philosophical underpinnings of his critical approach to knowledge (e.g., Brand, 1976; Kortian, 1980; LaCapra, 1977; Mendelson, 1979; Misgeld, 1976, 1977, 1981); political criticisms of various kinds concerning his status within the Marxist tradition, his emphasis on culture and communication as opposed to material conditions, the adequacy of his descriptions of advanced capitalism, the political implications of his writings for the working class and for world revolution, potential elitism in his emphasis on competent communication, and the relevance for democracy of his work on the public sphere (e.g. Bernstein, 1976; Sensat, 1978; Weiner, 1981; White, 1979); and criticisms dealing specifically with his assertions about culture, particularly the role of the unconscious, rationality, and tradition in culture and the adequacy of his distinction between rational-purposive and communicative action as a basis for the study of culture. Only this final set of criticisms is directly relevant to the present discussion.

Habermas has been sharply criticized for paying too little attention to the role of the unconscious (McIntosh, 1977). The very notion of intersubjectivity suggests that definitions of reality are internalized and these definitions are likely to be internalized so well that they do not figure consciously in communication, nor is it necessary for them to be conscious to arrive at common understandings. In other words, assumptions about reality may be taken for granted, rather than requiring conscious reflection, and interaction involving values and consensus is particularly likely to rest on unconscious assumptions. In intimate communication, as between mother and child, implicit feelings are the very basis on which a relationship exists. In emphasizing the rational and cognitive dimensions of communication, Habermas pays little attention to these unconscious sentiments.

It is the case that Habermas acknowledges the unconscious in his early work on blockages inhibiting the quest for reflective communication. There, he assumes unconscious moods, feelings, and presuppositions to be significant elements of any cultural system. Nevertheless, he argues that effective communication is possible by completely circumventing these elements. His goal is to go beyond cultural systems in which the unconscious plays an important role. In more recent work, he has to some extent moved away from these earlier views. While he continues to pay little attention to the unconscious, he has articulated an approach which, in his view, justifies this omission by dealing with the implicit dimensions of communication in other ways. In particular, he assumes that many of the unconscious or implicit qualities of communication are built into the observable artifacts of speech itself. Utterances contain patterns and cues which communicate unconscious messages; these are important, but become observable only in speech. Habermas's growing interest in philosophical linguistics has enhanced his capacity to deal with these implicit patterns and cues. While it remains to be seen how well this perspective will work out, it at least admits the significance of unconsciously transmitted messages. Indeed, it suggests that *because of* such unconscious factors, the analysis of culture should focus on observable communication, rather than the subjective consciousness of individuals. His current framework also suggests an additional way of incorporating the unconscious into a theory of culture, namely, by focusing on the social context in which communication takes place. Elusive, unconscious aspects of culture from the standpoint of the individual become observable when they are understood as social norms. For example, a mother's unconscious feelings toward her child reflect social norms about relations between mothers and children. Accordingly, the observer of culture can illuminate these 'unconscious' dimensions by examining norms manifest in concrete social interaction. Habermas assumes, again, that signals will be present in the communication process from which the observer can ascertain the nature of social norms.

A related criticism holds that Habermas, by staking so much faith in the human capacity for rational reflection, is idealistic in his perspective on culture. Gadamer (1975) argues that reflection necessarily has a historical dimension: to reflect about anything requires one to recall events within a particular historical situation and to relate them to other events and situations. Reflection on one's own actions or plans also necessitates thinking about historically situated events. Gadamer argues that these historical situations are never completely or consciously recognized. It is, therefore, impossible to subject one's reflections to an entirely rational critique independent of one's historical experiences. Gadamer disputes the possibility of being able to develop an ideal speech community in which people become free of their historical experiences, roles, and cultural contexts. He also argues that Habermas neglects the role of *tradition* in his theory of culture. Tradition should be central to the study of culture, shaping the content of culture, giving meaning and continuity to life. Even to bring about cultural change, the meanings invested in traditional contexts must be understood — only by reconstructing them can they be understood.

234

Habermas objects to focusing on tradition on both substantive and methodological grounds. Substantively, his
theory of cultural evolution posits that tradition has largely
been superseded, at least as a basis of political legitimation.
If legitimation is the central issue for modern society, as
Habermas believes it is, then the study of culture promises to
contribute more by focusing on phenomena other than
tradition. Methodologically, he wishes to circumvent questions
of tradition, because these questions inevitably raise considerations about the specific content and meanings of cultural
symbols that vary so widely as to make generalizable knowledge a virtual impossibility. He regards the search for underlying patterns rendering meaning possible a more promising
approach. It is not clear that Habermas has satisfactorily
answered Gadamer's criticisms, however. In the first place,
Gadamer's term 'tradition' appears to be more encompassing
than that which Habermas refers to in his discussion of
cultural evolution. Secondly, Habermas's own consideration
of the role of social norms in legitimating validity claims
appears to introduce tradition, requiring paying some attention
to it despite the methodological difficulties this may entail.
Furthermore, his concessions concerning the historical
specificity of knowledge in the cultural sciences appear to
support Gadamer's broader assertions about the nature
of tradition.

Yet another line of criticism concerns Habermas's distinction between labor and interaction. This criticism has been
put forth by Giddens (1977b), who argues that Habermas
too readily equates labor with instrumental rationality,
on the one hand, while equating interaction with communicative rationality, on the other. Dichotomizing the world in
this manner makes it impossible to consider the kind of
labor that is required, say, to sustain interaction, or the
role that interaction may play in promoting instrumental
rationality. Giddens suggests there are really four separate
concepts in Habermas's overall schema — labor, interaction,
instrumental rationality, and communicative rationality
— and all the relations among these concepts need to be
examined, rather than dividing them into two separate
spheres as Habermas has done. Although Giddens is concerned

with broader philosophical issues in Habermas's conceptual schema, his criticisms raise an important substantive question. This is the possibility of being able to distinguish empirically between rational-purposive action and communicative action. Habermas treats the two as if they were clearly separate and designates the latter as the realm for studies of culture. Yet, as Giddens points out, reality seems not to divide easily into these categories. To what extent can it be said that driving down the highway, for example, constitutes nothing more than rational-purposive action? The very manner in which this act is performed — in accordance with traffic laws and social customs, involving traffic signals and implicit messages to other drivers — indicates that communicative action is also present. Habermas has not dealt with this criticism directly, perhaps because it suggests the need for a basic conceptual modification of his framework. Rather than concrete acts being instances of rational-purposive behavior *or* communicative behavior, both types of behavior may be mixed together in any specific act or event. The distinction between rational-purposive action and communicative action may be useful, not as a classificatory device, but as an analytic distinction highlighting different *dimensions* of behavior. Any event may contain both of these dimensions. From this perspective, the study of culture is distinguished by investigations concerned especially with the communicative dimension.

Despite the various criticisms of it, Habermas's approach provides an attractive solution to many of the concerns that have troubled the analysis of culture. It puts the study of culture on a solid empirical footing equal to that on which other studies of social arrangements are based, doing so by taking as its focus objective behavior, including utterances, acts, events, and objects that have symbolic-expressive value. It avoids conceiving of culture as subjective ideas, attitudes, and beliefs that cannot be studied scientifically or that must be related to social structure in order to be understood. It also avoids problems of reductionism, asserting that cultural elements must be related to social circumstances to discover the conditions rendering meaningful communication possible, but denying that these circumstances account

236

completely for the meanings communicated. These meanings depend on additional validity claims, including claims about truth and sincerity. Habermas has also systematized a theory of cultural evolution specifying important dimensions of culture for examination. These dimensions bear on issues concerning democracy, freedom, and communication and are grounded in an analysis of the conditions of advanced capitalism. Finally, his schema reasserts culture as a central feature of modern social life, as opposed to theories focusing mainly on economic and political conditions.

Nevertheless, Habermas's approach to culture remains largely an approach rather than a substantive theory or precise guide to empirical investigation. While it provides a general perspective, it has yet to provide direction for routine investigations of culture. Several problems, in particular, need to be resolved if this perspective is to advance the study of culture. One concerns the relation between speech acts and social norms. This relation is the most obvious focus for the social scientific investigation of culture. In order to examine the nature of legitimation, it must be investigated, and the appeals to social norms contained in speech acts must be examined in order to grasp the social dimension of culture. These appeals dramatize and maintain social relationships between speakers, hearers, and others. Yet is is not clear from Habermas what this kind of analysis should involve. Indeed, it is not evident that he has advanced the study of culture beyond asserting, as social theorists have often done, that social norms influence communication. Implicit social arrangements contribute to the meaningfulness of cultural symbols, but knowing this helps little in guiding specific investigations. To be useful in research, his theory needs to be more specific about the nature of social arrangements and the ways in which these are dramatized in symbolic-expressive acts.

Habermas also remains unclear concerning more general relations between culture and social structure. At the most general level, he distinguishes between the world of communication and the world of work, the latter concerning the instrumental manipulation of nature, leaving the former to deal with the symbolic-expressive, or cultural, aspects of social existence. In addition to the difficulties of classification to which Giddens has alluded, this distinction raises questions about the relations between these two realms. Symbolic-expressive activity does not, in fact, take place in an ideal setting of the kind Habermas envisions with rational individuals simply discussing common interests and values. It normally takes place *within the world of work*. Communication comes about naturally as people relate to the material environment, and it requires resources from that environment — time, energy, technology, and other social resources, all of which may themselves become symbols. How these resources affect communication is left largely unspecified. It is possible, of course, to investigate culture apart from its material environment. In effect, this is what Habermas proposes in discussing the relations between speech acts and social norms, since the latter are symbolic constructions as much as the former, only more general and more broadly contextual. Yet it is evident within Habermas's framework that relations between culture and the material environment must also be understood. For this relation plays a decisive role in transitional periods between stages of cultural evolution and gives the study of legitimation its practical political significance.

Finally, Habermas thus far has dealt only minimally with the problem of self-identity and its relation to culture. In putting cultural analysis on an objective footing, he has largely ignored the influence of culture on individual thoughts and feelings and has specified a loose analogy between the type of world-view present in a particular epoch of cultural evolution and the type of personal identity which individuals are likely to develop, but the processes involved in this connection have not been specified. In more traditional theories of culture, the process of internalization has been a central problem. Parsons (1951), for example, held that social norms needed to exist not only as coherent cultural systems but as internalized aspects of individual identity. Individuals needed to share an internalized commitment to abide by these norms. Hence, mechanisms of socialization and social control, and problems of faulty socialization and deviance were essential aspects of any social investigation.

Habermas largely ignores the role of social control, socialization, and deviance in social life, devoting much attention to the state and to the economy, but giving little consideration to fundamental institutions of socialization such as the family, or to schools, law, and mechanisms of repression other than the state. By way of comparison, his approach fails to include any extended treatment of the interaction between self and culture such as that embodied either in Peter Berger's work on externalization and internalization or in Mary Douglas's discussion of 'grid' and 'group'.

The implications of Habermas's silence on internalization are ambiguous. On the one hand, self-concepts can be treated like any other aspect of culture; i.e. as specific types of speech acts, observable and objectified only in communication. In this respect, the self is no longer a subjective property of individual consciousness but an objective component of culture itself. Thus, Habermas's general perspective may in fact suggest possibilities for the study of self-concepts. On the other hand, he has not provided a satisfactory answer to questions about emotions and feelings between individuals and cultural artifacts, processes involved in transformations of individual consciousness, nor the effects of creative or unpredictable individual behavior on social interaction and cultural configurations. These questions warrant serious consideration in any comprehensive discussion of culture.

As presently formulated, therefore, Habermas's treatment of culture remains incomplete, at the same time that it is highly suggestive. He has contributed significantly to laying the foundations of cultural analysis, but his writings also bear the mark of continuing development and elaboration.

6 An emerging framework

The contributions of Peter Berger, Mary Douglas, Michel Foucault, and Jürgen Habermas represent distinct alternatives for the investigation of culture. Berger stresses the personal interpretations which aid individuals in adapting to everyday reality; Douglas, the role of ritual and material artifacts in defining conceptual boundaries; in Foucault the problem of power — its reinforcement through categories of knowledge — acquires primacy; and in Habermas the epistemological bases of communicative action assume priority. Berger compellingly argues that things may not be what they seem, only constructions held in place by mutual consent; Douglas extends the argument, viewing ritual as a necessary component of reality construction; Foucault adds a historical dimension, tracing the evolution of madness, health, punishment, sexuality, and the like; and Habermas takes the philosopher's role, creating a presumptive foundation for an independent science of culture. Each body of work contains a unique conceptual apparatus for the study of culture and an elaborate metatheoretical justification for its applicability. Each perspective reflects the imprint of different philosophical, disciplinary, and national contexts. In one sense, each perspective can be seen as highlighting different aspects of cultural reality. Thus, while the strength of one perspective may be a weakness in another, together they contribute greatly to an understanding of the complex and multi-dimensioned nature of culture. To say this is *not* to imply that a syncretic theoretical perspective which draws on

240

the strengths of each is possible or for that matter desirable. Such a synthesis would ultimately be forced and would result in a bland dilution of each. The orientation of this chapter is not to perform that task or even to suggest ways in which to do it. Rather, our concern here is to explore several central issues which underpin the task of analyzing culture. The issues are the role of subjectivity, the limits of sociologistic reductionism, and the place of positivism. Beyond this task our purpose is to explore the ways in which each theorist attempts to reconcile certain long-unsolved problematics within each of these issues. The emerging framework then is not so much a repudiation of past efforts at cultural analysis but a new and distinctive approach to the analysis of culture *implied* in the attempt of each theorist to resolve these problematics. The result is ultimately suggestive of a framework of cultural analysis which departs significantly from the manner in which culture has traditionally been treated in the social sciences.

The problem of subjectivity

What is the place of subjectivity in the analysis of culture and what are the problems that occur when subjectivity is introduced into this process? Douglas and Foucault approach culture in their empirical investigations with almost no *explicit* consideration of the inner thoughts, feelings, and perceptions of culture-producing actors. Habermas brackets the subjective realm from social, linguistic, and factual considerations influencing the meaningfulness of symbolic behavior. Only Berger attaches particular significance to subjectivity and thus his work provides an appropriate place in which to explore the advantages and disadvantages of incorporating subjectivity in cultural analysis.

It should be clear that while Berger emphasizes subjectivity in his writings more than the other theorists (and logically so as one coming from the phenomenological tradition), it would be grossly inaccurate to characterize him as a subjectivist. His own perspective has clearly moved beyond the suppositions found within a traditional phenomenological approach where subjectivity is regarded of paramount and

241

nearly exclusive importance. As seen in Chapter 2, the foundation of Berger's perspective on culture rests upon an on-going dialectic between subjectivity (perception, intentionality, etc.) and an objective socio-cultural reality. Human subjectivity (in the course of social interaction) is externalized in objectified social products and, in turn, this objective reality acts back on subjectivity, influencing and even reconstituting it. Theoretically, this represents a unique balance and highly penetrating perception into the nature of social reality and further represents the very best of a theoretical approach that deliberately incorporates the subjective element in cultural analysis.

The advantages of incorporating subjectivity in cultural analysis are not insignificant. One advantage is simply the inclusion of an important dimension of the social into analysis. Cultural reality, in as much as it is a human phenomenon, is necessarily rooted at some level in human subjectivity. And while culture is clearly analytically distinct from human subjectivity, it profoundly and continuously affects human consciousness. This perspective offers one way of dealing with the factor of subjectivity in cultural analysis, allowing the latter to retain that which is *specifically* human in this human/social science. Along similar grounds the methodological advantage is seen in an implied critique of the reifying tendencies of social scientists. To incorporate subjectivity into cultural analysis provides one deterrent against the ossification of social reality into categories totally detached from the actors that individually and collectively produce them. If the issue of social science is to describe and interpret social reality, then plainly subjectivity has a place in cultural analysis. Berger's perspective, again, goes some distance to contributing to an understanding of just how subjectivity fits in.

It should be noted that Berger himself maintains these assumptions because (as suggested in Chapter 2) his philosophical agenda is concerned with broadly depicting the human condition itself. To omit subjectivity from this depiction would be to deny human freedom, the social-psychological bases of culture, and that which Berger takes to most clearly differentiate humans from other animals. These assumptions have, in fact, figured importantly among the reasons for Berger's popularity. The novice, encountering social science for the first time in *Invitation to Sociology*, discovers that seemingly whimsical moods and intuitions have a basis in society, while older hands find Berger's insistence on the subjective a refreshing challenge to deterministic social science.

Advantages notwithstanding, a variety of unresolved problems plague the task of incorporating subjectivity into cultural analysis; problems that translate into unqualified disadvantages. Empirically, this general approach argues that access must be gained to the inner ruminations of the actor in order to determine the subjective intentions in a social situation. These must be reconstructed for each unique social situation in which the actor is involved. Collectively, the intentionality of actors in a social situation becomes objectified into cultural artifacts (symbols, typifications, codes, rituals and the like) which are then analyzed and interpreted accordingly. However appealing aesthetically or necessary theoretically, such an approach is difficult to sustain on practical methodological grounds. *Practically* the collection of data through phenomenological 'thick' description largely rules out the use of codified data collection techniques, the examination of questions concerned with macroscopic social institutions, and progress toward empirical generalizations. Minimally, incorporating subjectivity into cultural analysis becomes a burdensome enterprise. For example, in Berger's case, though he maintains that individuals display a strong desire for subjective order, that they require legitimating frameworks with which to explain events to themselves, that they bracket reality into compartmentalized spheres, and that confrontations among alternative legitimating schemes erode credibility, none of these assertions rests on conclusive *deductive* evidence (even though all of these propositions are theoretically falsifiable).

Just as Berger's theory is dialectical, the methodological approach implied can also be considered dialectical. Thus, to argue that human intentionality *creates* or *becomes objectified* into cultural objects, is to simultaneously contend (as Berger does) that cultural objects (typifications, etc.) *embody* subjective intentions. Empirically this suggests that

243

we can examine cultural artifacts and therefore understand the subjective intentions of those actors who produce and reproduce them in everyday life. While this may be true, neither angle accounts very well for the fact that cultural objects or artifacts very often are *starkly different* from the desires and intentions of those involved in creating and maintaining them. Incorporating subjectivity at this point in the analysis of culture becomes theoretically and analytically problematic.

It may be argued that theories which take subjective perceptions into account are better than theories which do not. The meaning of 'better', nevertheless, depends on what is to be explained. Weber's own case for probing the subjective gained substance in the particular context of his investigations into the origins of this-worldly asceticism. At issue were comparisons of individual behavior, particularly between those whose life-styles led toward or away from capitalist accumulation. In this context he advanced the now familiar argument that additional explanatory power could be gained by considering the internalized religious convictions which generated individual motivation. Had Weber (like Durkheim, for example) been concerned with variations in suicide rates or the collective symbolization of moral order, his formulation might well have de-emphasized the subjective.

This observation brings us to the central issue which must be resolved for analyses of culture to advance — the issue of defining culture. If culture is regarded as fundamentally based in the perspective of the individual (as beliefs, attitudes, perceptions, and moods), then the subjective clearly must be taken into account in any investigation of culture. If a decisive analytic distinction is made between culture and the individuals who produce it, however, then relations among cultural elements may be examined without consideration of subjective meanings. This in fact is the perspective which allows Douglas, Foucault, and Habermas to separate cultural analysis from considerations of individual subjectivity.

The separation between culture and subjectivity is most explicit in Habermas. In his work the purpose of scholarship is not to paint a philosophical portrait of the human condition in its individual/collective sense (as it appears to be for

244

Berger), but to facilitate the capacity for human communication. Although his orientation (like Berger's) includes the humanistic goal of enhancing freedom through knowledge, it leads directly to a behavioral concept of culture and explicitly differentiates philosophical from empirical interests as far as the conditions influencing the meaningfulness of speech acts are concerned. Both social and subjective (as well as linguistic and factual) conditions enter into the determination of meaningfulness as philosophical considerations, but Habermas draws a sharp distinction between them for purposes of investigation.

Less explicitly, Douglas and Foucault make the same differentiation. Though Douglas's humanistic concerns parallel Berger's (meaning and purpose, self-identity, social order), her work focuses on culture with virtual disregard for individual subjectivity. Objective symbolic classifications, ritual dramatizations of these patterns, and their functions for social order constitute the primary topics of her investigations. Similarly, Foucault emphasizes the categories, concepts, relations, and rituals which, as he says, delimit possibilities for thought, but conceptualizes them as objectified accretions of social interaction, not as subjective elements.

Plainly a reading of Berger indicates that his formulation also provides a basis for differentiating culture from individual subjectivity. The thrust of his dialectic interpretation of the reality construction process is to emphasize the objectified character of constructed reality over against the internalized perspectives of the individual. Berger himself makes amply clear (and often in the most ironic and humorous of terms) the fact that the cultural objects are, in consequence, contrary if not opposite to the subjective intentions that produced those cultural objects or patterns. Indeed, Berger's discussion can at many points (particularly his treatments of legitimation, symbol systems, ideology, institutions, and religion) be interpreted as exclusive descriptions of cultural *objects* and critics within the phenomenological tradition have accused him of paying too little attention to subjective consciousness.

To some extent, this interpretation of Berger fails to correspond wholly with his own formulation, however, for

245

the dialectic moment of objectification acquires identity *only in reference to* the subjective perceptions of the individual who perceives culture as an object, an external reality with seeming facticity apart from his or her personal intentions. The distinction between external and internal reality which the individual perceives, in fact, serves as the foundation for Berger's entire discussion of *legitimation* in which his most familiar descriptions of culture take place. The role of legitimation, as 'second-order' constructions of reality, is to rationalize for the individual the objectively perceived world and thereby to reduce subjective alienation. In this sense, the Berger formulation, despite its roots in descriptive phenomenology remains deeply indebted to the Cartesian dualism which informed classical discussions of culture. Only with partial accuracy can it be said that the Bergerian framework permits culture to be examined without reference to individual subjectivity.

Nor can it be said that the subjective is entirely absent from Douglas, Foucault, and Habermas. In so far as culture is defined to include communicative acts, utterances pertaining to the subjective states with which phenomenologists have been concerned fall within the realm of cultural analysis. Their inclusion does not constitute a concession to the phenomenological perspective, however, since they are conceptualized as objectively observable behavior rather than dimensions of internal consciousness. The difference exists clearly in the manner in which utterances are interpreted, taken at face value rather than serving as indicators of an inner realm.

While there are certain benefits gained by including the subjective dimension in cultural analysis, much appears to be gained by excluding it from *explicit* consideration in analysis as well. The primary benefit as far as scientific advancement is concerned is that the elementary units of culture become, by definition, strictly observable. Culture acquires reality as an autonomous object of investigation rather than serving in its traditional role as an indicator of realities presumed to be structured within the subjective consciousness of the individual. Accordingly, the observer is forced to acknowledge the natural focus and limitations of the data at hand, rather than assume to make discoveries about an inner realm. Assumptions can be made about the influences of individual motivations on culture, of course, but these would be tested at the cultural level itself by examining the observable behavior of which culture is comprised.

Secondarily, the comparison of Berger, Douglas, Foucault, and Habermas suggests that cultural analyses gain theoretical flexibility when severed from considerations of subjectivity. Whereas Berger's concerns focus heavily on the cultural patterns which emerge from the subjective requirement for a sense of order and continuity, it is clear from the others that cultural patterns may also be investigated with reference to the constraints of social interaction, the state, or patterns of communication. This flexibility appears particularly valuable if large-scale systems of ideology and legitimation are to be compared.

Finally, the central problematic of cultural analysis shifts in a broadening and thus promising direction when culture is differentiated more clearly from subjectivity. As noted in connection with Habermas, the principal questions for cultural analysis now not only include the *meaning* of symbols but the conditions, patterns, and rules of use which render symbols *meaningful*. This shift in orientation has considerable heuristic value because it permits progress to be made toward empirical generalizations in the cultural sciences.

Relating culture and social structure

The intellectual pursuit we refer to as the analysis of culture crosses specific intellectual disciplines. However, it clearly has a special place within the discipline of sociology. Largely because of this historical fact, combined with the longstanding scientific goal of finding reliable causal correlations between various social phenomena, cultural analysts have long operated within the framework of a perspective which has sought scientific explanations for cultural phenomena in different configurations of social interaction — the social structure. Indeed the dominant tendency has been to reduce culture — its causes, its form and quality — to social structural considerations. This tendency has formed its closest articulation in a

247

traditional 'sociology of knowledge', which sought to demonstrate the determination of ideas by social circumstances.
This method of sociologistic reasoning has provided valuable
tools and has added important insights into an understanding
of cultural reality. None the less, it has limitations. A characteristic of recent approaches to the analysis of culture (which
signals a broadening in the scope and method of cultural
analysis generally) is the tendency to pay greater attention to
the structure of culture itself rather than the relation between
culture and social structure. The perspective now emerging
emphasizes the patterns, rules, and relations which are
evident at the cultural level itself. In this fashion, the implied
approach represents a move beyond sociological reductionism
to the supposition that culture itself is an object worthy
of study.

This new emphasis is variously pronounced in the writings
of each of the authors reviewed here. All have, to different
degrees, contributed to this development. While concentrating
heavily on the perspectival or symbolic aspect of reality,
Berger, as a sociologist, has been the one least interested
in this dimension of cultural analysis or in the obverse, the
one emphasizing the causal capabilities of the social structure
more than the others. In his discussion of 'plausibility structures' (which has been one of his more popular concepts),
for example, Berger argues that symbolic definitions of
reality retain plausibility — credibility, an aura of facticity —
only to the extent that they are reinforced by a collectivity
whose members interact with one another. Thus, it is the
presence or absence of social relations that acquires objective
status as an explanatory variable rather than culture itself.
Or, put differently, there is an asymmetry between culture
and social structure such that social structure may be conceived of as a determinant of culture to a greater extent than
culture may be conceived of as a determinant of social
structure. This position is also expressed in Berger's treatment
of the origins of culture and of cultural change. With respect
to the former, he asserts that symbols acquire meaning only
within specified social contexts; i.e. the objective character
of these contexts and the interaction taking place within
them gives rise to cultural constructions. Moreover, with

respect to cultural change, it is the evolution of the social infrastructure — industrialization, bureaucratization, urbanization — that accounts for such phenomena as secularization and deinstitutionalization at the cultural level.

A point of clarification is warranted here. It would be misleading to regard Berger's approach as vulgar reductionism. It is not. To be sure, much of his corpus is devoted to articulating a dialectic between culture and social structure. It is this dialectic (among others) that accounts for a significant measure of social change in society at both a micro-cosmic and macro-cosmic level. It is this dialectical approach which moves significantly beyond much of classical social theory. None the less, while this dialectic is evident enough, it is equally apparent that Berger views the social structural element as the dominant partner in the dialectic — indeed almost to the exclusion of cultural phenomena as causally viable. In a very real sense, one could argue that what one sees in Berger's corpus is a *functional* (and operative) *dualism* occurring within the framework of a *theoretical dialecticism.*

Berger's functional attribution of causal determination to the realm of social structure is not altogether surprising, given that he borrows so heavily from classical theories which incorporated various forms of sociological reductionism in their approach to culture. His formulations concerning alienation and world-views draw heavily on Marx and reflect the Marxist epistemology. His work on modernization is deeply indebted to Weber and Durkheim, particularly in assuming the vulnerability of culture to structural changes associated with modernization. He has also borrowed Mead's emphasis on the importance of social interaction in formulating his discussion of social psychology. In these borrowings Berger also tends to adopt the implicit dualism between the realm of objective social structure and the realm of ideas and beliefs which, as noted in Chapter 1, runs through classical social theory.

It is, nevertheless, Berger's theoretical reformulation of the sociology of knowledge that can be focused upon. It is a perspective that does depart significantly from classical reductionist arguments and, in this sense, contains hints of reorientation in precisely the direction seen more clearly in each of the other theorists. This reorientation *in practice* frees culture from the determination of social structure and permits investigations to focus on the internal patterning of cultural constructions. Parenthetically, it would appear that Berger posits the dependence of culture on social structure primarily as a 'given' rather than as a matter warranting investigation or suggestive of fruitful research endeavors. In the classical view, demonstrating that beliefs did not spring full-blown from rational argument or conviction but were shaped by powerful interests, were attributable to the arrangements of social resources, or were the product of social ties, became the *raison d'être*, as it were, of social scientific inquiry. Berger, in contrast, claims relatively little for the role of social interaction as an explanatory variable. In his view the relation between constructed realities and social contexts is exceedingly indeterminate. Judging from the manner in which he treats this relationship, it might be argued, in fact, that *any* world-view can be maintained by any particular set of interacting persons. All that is required is for interaction to be present and for this interaction to involve the verbal or behavioral articulation of constructed realities; interaction, however, need not restrict the actual content of these realities. As with his treatment of subjectivity, Berger appears to emphasize the role of social interaction as a philosophical consideration, perhaps primarily in the interest of comprehensiveness, whereas in terms of his actual discussion of concrete cases and theoretical propositions this factor appears largely irrelevant to his concerns. Berger's formulation, in short, represents a 'weak' version of the sociology of knowledge in that it fails to credit social structure with precise explanatory power.

If this interpretation of Berger is correct, it implies that culture has acquired *de facto* status in his formulation as an autonomous entity. What, then, gives shape to cultural constructions? What regularities does the observer seek to understand? For Berger, the answer stems from his larger philosophical reflections, particularly those concerning the individual's requirements for meaning and order. These needs, while untestable themselves as philosophical assertions, serve so powerfully in human thought and action that their imprint is reflected in the very patterning of culture. Indeed, a distinguishing feature of Berger's perspective is the wager that culture can best be understood with reference to these individual needs rather than, say, expressions of the contradictions of class relations (as in Marx).

At this level, we can clearly see that Berger believes that culture has an identifiable structure that is worthy of investigation and which, moreover, can be observed and therefore subjected to systematic empirical analysis. This assumption is essential for a science of cultural analysis to develop and it is clear that Berger heartily endorses this supposition in his own work. Culture consists of a relatively rational (or at least orderly) set of classifications which permit the individual to make sense of the surrounding environment and to function actively in relation to it. Berger's concepts of identity, institution, and world-view and his discussions of compartmentalized 'spheres of relevance' and hierarchically nested categories of secondary explanation serve as initial sensitizing concepts for the investigation of these classifications.

Despite considerable differences in style and conceptualization, Berger's discussion of cultural patterns actually conforms quite closely to that of Mary Douglas. She too devotes primary attention to the identification of patterns — objective demarcations and regularities — at the symbolic-expressive level itself, rather than attributing culture to ultimate determinants at the level of social structure. Hardly any of her work focuses on aspects of social life which have been associated with the idea of social structure, such as material resources, differentials in power, or population size. She has described other aspects of social structure, such as technology, goods, kinship, deviance, and the physical environment, but she treats these primarily as symbolic forms in which patterns of culture are displayed. And when she relates linguistic codes to their social environment, the environment itself is portrayed as a set of symbolically expressed relationships. Like Berger, she associates culture with the dynamics of social interaction, dramatized in ritual, in speech, and in social arrangements. These arrangements she regards as transmitters of messages necessary for the orderly conduct of social life.

251

Two characteristics, nevertheless, distinguish Douglas's perspective from Berger's in so far as social structure is concerned. First, there is no explicit analytic separation of culture from social structure in her work as there is in Berger's. From her perspective culture is not a subjectively perceived reality or world-view which can be related to social contexts or interaction — to plausibility structures — which are analytically distinct from culture. Rather than defining culture from the standpoint of the individual, she regards it as an object which can be observed by the analyst and which exists at the social rather than the individual level. Culture, then, is interwoven into the fabric of social life itself, not an attitudinal realm separated from it. Although she does not argue this point explicitly, culture is distinguished in practice in her work by the observer's treatment of social life. In choosing to inquire into those aspects of social arrangements which communicate messages about the social order, which display order among social relations, the observer focuses on culture. Others may examine the same material as evidence of social resources without expressive qualities but such investigations do not focus on culture.

Secondly, Douglas (following Durkheim) stresses the *moral* aspect of culture, as opposed to its psychological functions for the individual. The underlying philosophical reasons for the existence of culture do not derive, as they do for Berger, from the individual requirement for cognitive and emotive security, but from the necessity of having predictable behavior if social interaction is to be possible. Moral order implies that certain relations can be counted on, even taken for granted. These relations affect the flow of social resources and define subjectively felt loyalties or commitments, including ones which cannot be defended strictly in terms of rational argument or short-term utilitarian interest. Symbols of pollution typically establish external boundaries around such collective loyalties and other arrangements dramatize the relations among actors within a given social setting. These dramatizations allow actors to co-ordinate their personal activity with the activities of others, thereby accomplishing collective objectives. Because culture is so intimately

252

woven into social arrangements, Douglas does not concern herself with finding 'deeper' explanations for culture by attributing it to social structure. Again, culture is inherently an aspect of social structure.

Douglas's work focuses on subject matter which has largely escaped the attention of scholars concerned with beliefs and attitudes, on the one hand, and been neglected by empirically minded social scientists, on the other. Hers is a world of implicit symbolism, of expressivity contained neither in words nor conscious gestures but built into the arrangement of social life itself — of banquets and eating habits, of consumer goods, in pollution rituals and social movements. She emphasizes that culture consists not only of codified knowledge but of the cues inherent in all collective activity.

Foucault also rejects the dualistic approach to culture, focusing instead on patterns within culture rather than seeking explanations rooted in social structure. The possible exception to this generalization is his work on the relations between knowledge and power. In attempting to demonstrate the effect of power relations on the construction of social knowledge Foucault appears to engage in the reductionism characteristic of a traditional sociology of knowledge perspective. This interpretation misconstrues the true intent of Foucault's work, however. By joining the concepts of knowledge and power, particularly in his graphic expression 'knowledge/power', he intends to demonstrate that asymmetries of power tend to exist in the structure of knowledge itself, not as configurations whose influence on culture consists only of externalities. The dictum 'knowledge is power' is true in the most literal sense, according to Foucault.

Unlike Douglas, and to a degree considerably more pronounced than in Berger, Foucault's analyses of culture focus on *discourse*, written and verbal. It is the recorded testimony of henchmen and lunatics and the archival accretions of medical practice and the social sciences from which his observations are primarily made. In focusing on discourse, Foucault implicitly differentiates the verbal and written record from social arrangements. This differentiation allows him to seek interpretations of discourse by examining larger social arrangements as he does, for example, in considering the physician's role or the development of modern penal institutions. It runs contrary to the spirit of Foucault's 'archeological' approach, however, to suggest a sharp distinction between discourse and social arrangements. The essential task which Foucault sets for himself is to account for the co-presence of mutually existing arrangements, whether manifested as discourse or in social interaction, by discovering underlying rules of cultural construction. In this quest social arrangements become a type of discourse. As in Douglas's view, they contain an expressive aspect which dramatizes cultural patterns.

As shown in Chapter 5, Habermas has devoted the most explicit consideration to the relations between culture and social structure. He preserves the idea that social patterns may be useful in determining what constitutes meaningful 'utterances' at the cultural level and relates the evolution of cultural patterns to social conditions in his treatment of evolutionary dynamics. Nevertheless, his work incorporates an explicit proviso against sociological reductionism by differentiating social conditions from factuality, linguistic competence, and subjective intentionality, all of which bear on the interpretation of cultural patterns. Even work within the traditional sociology of knowledge perspective stands to benefit from this conceptual formulation as a reminder of the limitations of sociological explanation.

Habermas has also struggled most explicitly with the problem of differentiating the subject matter of the cultural sciences from that associated with the study of social structure. In his view it is important to distinguish behavior concerned with the communication of social values from that oriented toward manipulation of the physical world. Culture, therefore, consists of patterned relations among actors which emerge from their efforts to engage in communication.

This formulation parallels the interest expressed by Douglas, Foucault, and Berger in discourse, conversation, and expressivity as essential ingredients of culture. Though variously conceptualized, each theorist regards culture as a type of behavior, rather than mere ideas about behavior. Habermas implies, moreover, that this type of behavior is of principal concern in the contemporary epoch since it must be more fully understood for deliberation of basic societal goals to take place.

Unfortunately, Habermas's formulation contains an ambiguity which limits its usefulness as a heuristic for defining the scope of cultural analysis. This ambiguity occurs because of Habermas's failure to distinguish clearly between the subjective intentions of the actor and the perspective of the observer in defining different types of human behavior. As a result, it remains unclear in his discussion whether communicative action is so defined because it is objectively oriented toward communication as perceived by the observer or because it is intended as communication by the actors in the situation itself.

The preferable resolution of this ambiguity as far as cultural analysis is concerned is to define communication as an analytic aspect of human behavior from the standpoint of the observer; hence, behavior can be regarded as having expressive qualities whether its intended purpose is primarily communication or not. In these terms cultural analysis becomes the examination of the symbolic-expressive aspect of behavior, whether that behavior is oriented primarily toward the discussion of values or the rational-purposive manipulation of the material world.

This definition of culture affords a perspective on the relations between culture and social structure which is compatible with the common emphases of Berger, Douglas, Foucault, and Habermas. As the symbolic-expressive dimension of behavior, culture subsumes not only the verbal discourse with which Foucault and Habermas have been most concerned but also the dramatizations of everyday life and the ritualized aspects of social arrangements with which Berger and Douglas have been concerned. Having defined culture in these broad terms, a primary task of cultural analysis is to identify recurring features, distinctions, and underlying patterns which give form and substance to culture. It is also clear that culture does not encompass all that is implied by the concept of social arrangements, since these may also be regarded as stores of differentially distributed resources (incomes, populations, modes of production, etc.)

apart from their symbolic-expressive significance. Consequently, possibilities for relating culture and social structure continue to exist, not in any reductionistic or causally *a priori* order, but as mutually influencing aspects of behavior. In particular, the role of available resources in shaping symbolic-expressive communication and the role of communication in regulating the control and distribution of resources warrant investigation as general tasks in the social scientific study of culture.

The issue of positivism

According to some social scientists, cultural analysis has been inhibited by a reluctance to play by the rules of positivist science. There has, in fact, been a strong tendency for social scientists in other areas to take a dim view of work on culture for this reason. Since the same theorists who have made significant contributions to the study of culture have also challenged the philosophical premises of positivism, there has been some justification for questioning the scientific basis of cultural studies. Of the four theorists, Berger and Habermas have been most outspoken in criticizing positivism, but Foucault's work also differs from the positivist tradition and even Douglas appears to have gained a greater following among non-positivists in the humanities than among social scientists.

The roots of Berger's dispute with positivism lie in phenomenology. The same relativisitic perspective that permits visualization of the constructedness of everyday reality forces an acknowledgment of the arbitrary nature of scientific evidence. Others working from this perspective have argued that scientists negotiate definitions of reality through the strategic use of language, symbolism, and discourse, just as ordinary persons do in daily life. In the phenomenological perspective, therefore, any possibility of discovering purely objective scientific laws is denied and the role of the observer in interpreting reality is emphasized, especially where human interaction is involved. Habermas also rejects positivism, but on grounds that value considerations are neglected in this approach. In his view the test of evidence within the realm of social science lies in its capacity to facilitate discussion of values, rather than strict correspondence with objective reality. Foucault, while working within the tradition of empirical historians, also stops short of claiming evidence conducive to positive scientific generalizations, preferring instead to characterize his conclusions as 'interpretations' of history concerned with unmasking relations of power. And Douglas, despite close reliance on anthropological methods and materials, has adopted at least some of the anthropologists' distance from modern positivistic methods, acknowledging the possibility of equally valid knowledge from sources such as ritual and myth.

The question arises, therefore, of whether it is possible to construct cultural analysis on a basis capable of producing verifiable social scientific knowledge at all, or whether the study of culture necessarily remains a speculative venture. Barring hope of producing verifiable knowledge, the task of cultural analysis becomes hermeneutics — giving meaning enriching interpretations to discrete events. If, on the other hand, the critique of positivism leads to a more qualified position, then the thrust of cultural analysis can focus valuably on the search for empirical generalizations.

Taking clues again from each of the four writers, it is apparent that the critique of positivism need not rule out a search for empirical generalizations about culture. The principal reservation about positivism that characterizes recent work on culture is the assumption that all knowledge, including scientific evidence, is mediated by culture. Thus, empirical facts are 'known' only through the filtering lens of available language. Furthermore, the kinds of knowledge produced and considered of value clearly depend on cultural circumstances. As Habermas has suggested most clearly, the possibility of evolution to a higher cultural epoch poses considerations of entirely different needs as far as empirical knowledge is concerned. This restriction on the positivist perspective does not, however, rule out the application of normal scientific methods of verification. It requires only that the usual canons of provisionality concerning scientific truth be emphasized, taking into account explicitly the personal, cultural, and historical predispositions of the scientist. Within this limitation, cultural analysis can function as an empirical science.

In Berger's work, the bases for an empirical science of culture have been advanced considerably beyond the traditional suppositions of phenomenology. Speculations about the nature of being in its transcendent or ultimate sense, which are implied in Berger's philosophical underpinnings, can be bracketed largely from his assertions about culture. The method advanced for the analysis of culture consists chiefly of eliciting evidence from the discourse and everyday behavior of interacting subjects. Douglas's work, as observed previously, focuses on the empirical artifacts of culture as expressed in ritual and ceremony. In rendering interpretations of the structure and function of these materials, the observer is required to present evidence and must refrain from making assertions about ultimate or purely subjective meanings of these events which lie outside the realm of disconfirmation. Foucault relies similarly on empirical evidence; indeed, has sought to expand the usual varieties of evidence which are taken together in the construction of historical interpretations. Criticisms of his work have been possible on the basis of this evidence, focusing on its adequacy rather than its presence or absence. Habermas has been least devoted to empirical investigations, but in his epistemological arguments he too has outlined an approach, resting largely on the analysis of discourse, which provides empirical tests of theoretical adequacy. His efforts to distinguish between theoretical arguments and empirical generalizations (particularly in relation to cultural evolution) have led to charges that his framework is basically alien to normal canons of scientific evidence. But these charges merely fail to heed Habermas's own warnings. While his conceptual apparatus is *explicitly* beyond empirical confirmation or disconfirmation, this apparatus is intended only as a framework within which to select problems for investigation.

The uneasy stance that cultural theorists have taken toward positivism, therefore, does not rule out the possibility of pursuing cultural analysis as a rigorous empirical science. Because of its orientation toward the role of ideas in social life, cultural analysis is perhaps a somewhat more perceptive vantage point from which to recognize the biases inherent in scientific investigation itself. The analyst of culture is of necessity forced to acknowledge the interpretive impact of his or her own suppositions on the data and to recognize the value of these interpretations within particular cultural contexts despite their relativity. But this admission does not foreclose the possibility and desirability of seeking empirically verifiable generalizations about the patterning of cultural phenomena. A word about these patterns is in order in concluding.

Cultural analysis

In brief summary, the emerging framework evident in the work of Berger, Douglas, Foucault, and Habermas identifies culture as a distinct aspect of social reality, the patterns of which are subject to observation and theoretical interpretation. As a more formalized distillation of this framework, cultural analysis may be defined as the study of the symbolic-expressive dimension of social life. As such, one of its chief aims is to identify empirical regularities or patterns in this dimension of reality and from these regularities to specify the rules, mechanisms, and relations which must be present for any particular symbolic act to be meaningful. The subject matter of cultural analysis is readily observable in the objective acts, events, utterances, and objects of social interaction. The appropriate level of analysis is the patterns among these artifacts of interaction, rather than efforts to reduce culture either to the internal states of individuals or to the material conditions of societies. As a systematic body of inquiry, therefore, cultural analysis becomes distinct from related disciplines such as social psychology or sociology in that it concerns a unique aspect of human behavior.

As with any nascent orientation to the study of human behavior, the question arises of whether cultural analysis of this sort can be a productive enterprise and, if so, what the most fruitful strategies of investigation may be. The answer to this question is as yet far from clear, but some clues can be identified. For example, the method of focusing on deviance to make the ordinary seem less obvious has been of strategic value in the work of both Foucault and Douglas. Madness, disease, torture, imprisonment, sexual misconduct — all serve as sources of fresh insights about culture. Deviance tends to prompt discourse (including historical transcripts) which can be analyzed. It also serves a theoretical purpose, as Douglas has argued, in that deviant acts dramatize cultural boundaries and, conversely, acts which violate cultural boundaries become defined as deviance. Deviance, therefore, is a special category for understanding the general properties of cultural meaning.

Deviance takes on significance within the larger context of *symbolic boundaries*, an idea that gains expression most clearly in Douglas's approach but which has value more generally as an elementary construct in the study of culture. Boundaries dramatize order. As Berger has emphasized, order is fundamental for the individual; it is also necessary for the conduct of social affairs. It can safely be assumed, therefore, that some level of orderliness or pattern will be evident within culture. Or, put differently, culture will exist only in a limited variety of forms relative to the immense, perhaps infinite, variety of forms in which it conceivably might exist. It is this delimitation of forms that makes a science of culture possible and which gives purpose to such an endeavor, namely, to specify the conditions or rules under which different patterns emerge and are sustained. The study of patterns, however, requires some initial understanding of what these patterns may entail. The answer is given by Douglas — that order (patterns) exist only in so far as there are symbolic boundaries.

What does this argument imply? An elementary task of cultural analysis must be the study of symbolic boundaries, for these constitute the essence of cultural order. Symbolic boundaries separate realms, creating the contexts in which meaningful thought and action can take place. Moreover, that which is separated by symbolic boundaries may also be joined by them. It is in the experiences of marginality, as Douglas and Berger have observed, that one is able to move (physically and figuratively) from one realm to another. Generally speaking, boundaries also constitute the basis for examining the nature of cultural differentiation (e.g. as specified in Habermas's theory of cultural evolution), for differentiation means a differentiation of realms, of categories, separated and joined by symbolic boundaries.

Regarding culture as an observable aspect of human behavior lays emphasis on the realities of symbolic boundaries. Not only do they exist as conceptual distinctions in persons' minds; they are publicly visible in the manner in which social interaction occurs, in discourse, and in tangible objects. Resources are expended in creating and maintaining them and many social activities may be understood as efforts to sharpen eroded boundaries, to redefine cultural distinctions, or as symptoms of ambiguous frameworks. Identifying these activities is a concrete task to which cultural analysis can be applied.

Which patterns, of the many, are most worthy of examination? Another lesson from these theorists is that a metatheoretical perspective on the nature of modern culture is essential to guide the selection of concrete problems for investigation. Indeed, the attraction of these theorists lies as much in their efforts to conceptualize such a framework, as in their substantive insights. Each theorist's concept of cultural change specifies a distinct set of problems with which modern society is faced. These range from the problem of competing definitions of absolute reality (Berger) to Douglas's emphasis on the decline of group identity, and from Foucault's concern with the growing penetration of the state into the personal realm to Habermas's treatment of legitimation. The differences in perspective are often considerable and rest on assumptions about the course of history which are not themselves subject to empirical examination. The point, however, is that some framework of this kind is indispensable for the selection of problems to investigate. The analysis of culture can be pursued with explicit reference to one or another of these (or other) metatheoretical frameworks; or it can be conducted blindly with only tacit recognition of its presuppositions. In either case, a selective process will be evoked. As a practical guide, therefore, cultural analysis needs to include discussion of the merits of alternative conceptions of history.

It is apparent that the concept of symbolic boundaries

bears a close relation to the macroscopic problems identified in the different theorists' conceptions of history. In each case it is a particular cultural boundary which is at issue — between alternative conceptions of the absolute, between self and community, state and self, state and economy, and so on. Thus, the practical analysis of contemporary cultural problems can be extended by exploring the manner in which these boundaries have been defined and have served as symptoms of conflict and cultural redefinition.

Finally, the fact that each theorist has emphasized discourse and has drawn on theories of language is suggestive of fruitful lines of investigation. Just as formal language exists according to identifiable patterns, so the 'language' of tacit communication in ordinary social life more generally may conform to observable rules. Schutz (and Berger *a fortiori*) drew on the fact of different styles of language within different contexts as a basis for identifying discrete provinces of meaning. In Berger's own extension of this work the hierarchical nature of language ranging from the specific to the general is regarded as a basis for classifying modes of secondary legitimation. Douglas has borrowed from Bernstein in developing the concepts of grid and group as general principles of classification; Foucault has sought parallel structures in different varieties of discourse; and Habermas has considered the presence of 'illocutionary' or status-defining cues within speech as a key to the social conditioning of culture.

These beginnings appear productive of further insights in the study of culture. For example, the binary structure of language, exploited most fully by Lévi-Strauss, may be important to explore in other contexts. Though perhaps not as universally as Lévi-Strauss believed, the maintenance of any conceptual category requires its opposite: dark/light, good/evil, freedom/necessity. The symbolic boundary as well as the balance between each pair represents significant material for investigation. Activities which alter the balance or which violate symbolic boundaries are likely to be of special interest. Or for another example, the capacity of cultural systems to change — to adapt to new situations — bears similarities to the capacity of languages to generate new variations, the problem to which Chomsky has devoted considerable attention. Just as there are 'generative mechanisms' (e.g. 'and', 'or', etc.), which enhance the capacity for new manifestations of language to appear, so there are undoubtedly such mechanisms at the cultural level more generally. The idea of individual autonomy which essentially decouples the thoughts and commitments of one individual from those of another is one example. The idea of cultural relativism, allowing different beliefs to exist in different situations is another.

At this juncture the study of culture stands poised at the threshold. The shortcomings of traditional approaches, hewn from Cartesianism and incorporated enthusiastically into classical social theory, appear starkly evident. It has taken the sustained effort during the past quarter century of such writers as Peter Berger, Mary Douglas, Michel Foucault, and Jürgen Habermas to reveal this fact and to suggest alternative formulations. The task of consolidating these insights into fruitful avenues of inquiry now lies ahead.

Bibliography

Alford, C. Fred (1979), 'Review of Jürgen Habermas' *Communication and the Evolution of Society*', *New German Critique*, 18:176–80.

Anderson, Perry (1976), *Considerations on Western Marxism*, London: New Left Books.

Barthes, Roland (1964), *Essais Critiques*, Paris: Editions du Seuil.

Barthes, Roland (1968), *Elements of Semiology*, New York: Hill and Wang.

Baum, Gregory (1980), 'Peter L. Berger's Unfinished Symphony', *Commonweal*, 263–70.

Bellah, Robert N. (1970), *Beyond Belief*, New York: Harper & Row.

Bellah, Robert N. (1975), *The Broken Covenant*, New York: Seabury.

Berger, Peter (1961a), *The Noise of Solemn Assemblies*, Garden City: Doubleday.

Berger, Peter (1961b), *The Precarious Vision*, Garden City: Doubleday.

Berger, Peter (1963a), *Invitation to Sociology*, Garden City: Doubleday.

Berger, Peter (1963b), 'A Market Model for the Analysis of Ecumenicity', *Social Research*, 30:75–90.

Berger, Peter (1964a), 'Marriage and the Construction of Reality' (with Hansfried Kellner), *Diogenes*, 46:5–22.

Berger, Peter (1964b), 'Social Mobility and Personal Identity' (with Thomas Luckmann), *European Journal of Sociology*, 15:331 ff.

Berger, Peter (1965), 'Reification and the Sociological Critique of Consciousness' (with Stanley Pullberg), *History and Theory*, 4:198 ff.

Berger, Peter (1966), *The Social Construction of Reality* (with Thomas Luckmann), Garden City: Doubleday.

Berger, Peter (1967), *The Sacred Canopy*, Garden City: Doubleday.

Berger, Peter (1970), 'On the Obsolescence of the Concept of Honor', *European Journal of Sociology*, 11:373–80.

Berger, Peter (1972), *Sociology: A Biographical Approach* (with Brigitte Berger), New York: Basic Books.

Berger, Peter (1973), *The Homeless Mind* (with Brigitte Berger and Hansfried Kellner), New York: Vintage.

Berger, Peter (1974), *Pyramids of Sacrifice*, Garden City: Doubleday.

Berger, Peter (1977a), *Facing up to Modernity*, New York: Basic Books.

Berger, Peter (1977b), 'Secular Theology and the Rejection of the Supernatural', *Theological Studies*, 38:39 ff.

Berger, Peter (1978), 'On the Conceptualization of the Supernatural and the Sacred' (with Hansfried Kellner), *Dialog*, 17:36 ff.

Berger, Peter (1979a), *The Heretical Imperative*, New York: Doubleday.

Berger, Peter (1979b), 'Religion and the American Future', pp. 65–77 in S. Lipset (ed.), *The Third Century*, University of Chicago Press.

Berger, Peter (ed.) (1980), *The Other Side of God*, Garden City: Doubleday.

Berger, Peter (1981a), *Sociology Reinterpreted* (with Hansfried Kellner), Garden City: Doubleday.

Berger, Peter (1981b), 'New Attack on the Legitimacy of Business', *Harvard Business Review*, October: 82–99.

Bergesen, Albert (1977), 'Political Witch-hunts: The Sacred and Subversive in Cross-National Perspective', *American Sociological Review*, 42:220–33.

Bergesen, Albert (1978), 'A Durkheimian Theory of Political Witch-hunts with the Chinese Cultural Revolution of 1966–1969 as an Example', *Journal for the Scientific Study of Religion*, 17:19–29.

Bergesen, Albert and Warr, Mark (1979), 'A Crisis in the Moral Order: The Effects of Watergate Upon Confidence in Social Institutions', pp. 277–95 in Robert Wuthnow (ed.), *The Religious Dimension*, New York: Academic Press.

Bernstein, Richard (1976), *The Restructuring of Social and Political Thought*, Oxford: Basil Blackwell.

Bolaffi, Angelo (1979), 'An Interview with Jürgen Habermas', *Telos*, 39:163–72.

Brand, A. (1976), 'Interests and the Growth of Knowledge: A Comparison of Weber, Popper and Habermas', *The Netherlands' Journal of Sociology*, 13:1–20.

Braudel, Fernand (1966), *The Mediterranean*, 2 vols, New York: Harper & Row.

Breyspaak, William A. (1974), 'Toward a Post-Critical Sociology of Knowledge: A Study of Durkheim, Mannheim, Berger, and Polanyi', Ph.D. Dissertation, Duke University.

Bruner, Jerome S., Oliver, Rose R., and Greenfield, Patricia M. (1966),

Studies in Cognitive Growth, New York: John Wiley & Sons.

Burnham, James (1972), 'Selective, Yes. Humanism, Maybe. Reply to Berger: Two Paradoxes', *National Review*, 513 ff.

Cairns, David (1974), 'Thought for Peter Berger', *Scottish Journal of Theology*, 27:181.

Chomsky, Noam (1957), *Syntactic Structures*, The Hague: Mouton.

Chomsky, Noam (1965), *Aspects of the Theory of Syntax*, Cambridge, Mass: MIT Press.

Clanton, Gordon (1973), 'Peter Berger and the Reconstruction of the Sociology of Religion', Ph.D. dissertation, Union Theological Seminary.

Cooper, Barry (1981), *Michel Foucault: An Introduction to the Study of His Thought*, New York: Edwin Mellen Press.

Coser, Lewis (1974), *Greedy Institutions*, New York: Free Press.

Crittenden, Ann (1979), 'A New World Disorder', *New York Times* (February 4).

Douglas, Mary (1957), 'Animals in Lele Religious Symbolism', *Africa*, 27:46–58.

Douglas, Mary (1963), *The Lele of the Kasai*, Oxford University Press.

Douglas, Mary (1966), *Purity and Danger: An Analysis of the Concepts of Pollution and Taboo*, New York: Pantheon Books.

Douglas, Mary (1970), *Natural Symbols: Explorations in Cosmology*, New York: Pantheon Books.

Douglas, Mary (1978a), *Implicit Meanings: Essays in Anthropology*, London: Routledge & Kegan Paul.

Douglas, Mary (1978b), *Cultural Bias*, Royal Anthropological Institute of Great Britain and Ireland, occasional paper no. 35.

Douglas, Mary (1982a), *In the Active Voice*, London: Routledge & Kegan Paul.

Douglas, Mary (1982b), 'The Effects of Modernization on Religious Change', *Daedalus* (Winter):1–19.

Douglas, Mary and Isherwood, Baron (1979), *The World of Goods: Towards an Anthropology of Consumption*, London: Allen Lane.

Douglas, Mary and Wildavsky, Aaron (1982), *Risk and Culture: An Essay on the Selection of Technological and Environmental Dangers*, Berkeley: University of California Press.

Dreyfus, Hubert L. and Rabinow, Paul (1982), *Michel Foucault: Beyond Structuralism and Hermeneutics*, University of Chicago Press.

Durkheim, Emile and Mauss, Marcel (1963), *Primitive Classification*, University of Chicago Press.

Erikson, Kai T. (1966), *Wayward Puritans*, New York: Wiley.

Foucault, Michel (1965), *Madness and Civilization: A History of*

Insanity in the Age of Reason, New York: Random House.

Foucault, Michel (1970), *The Order of Things: An Archeology of the Human Sciences*, New York: Random House.

Foucault, Michel (1972), *The Archeology of Knowledge*, New York: Random House.

Foucault, Michel (1975a), *The Birth of the Clinic: An Archeology of Medical Perception*, New York: Random House.

Foucault, Michel (1975b), *I, Pierre Rivière, Having Slaughtered My Mother, My Sister, and My Brother . . . A Case of Parricide in the 19th Century*, New York: Random House.

Foucault, Michel (1975c), 'Entretien sur la prison: le livre et sa methode' (with J. J. Brochier), *Magazine littèraire*, 101:33.

Foucault, Michel (1977), *Language, Counter-Memory, Practice*, New York: Cornell University Press.

Foucault, Michel (1978), *The History of Sexuality, Volume I: An Introduction*, New York: Random House.

Foucault, Michel (1979), *Discipline and Punish: The Birth of the Prison*, New York: Vintage.

Foucault, Michel (1980a), *Power/Knowledge*, New York: Pantheon.

Foucault, Michel (1980b), *Herculine Barbin*, New York: Random House.

Gadamer, H. G. (1975), 'Hermeneutics and Social Science', *Cultural Hermeneutics*, 2:307–16.

Geertz, Clifford (1973), *The Interpretation of Cultures*, New York: Harper & Row.

Geuss, Raymond (1981), *The Idea of a Critical Theory*, Cambridge University Press.

Giddens, Anthony (1977a), *Studies in Social and Political Theory*, London: Hutchinson.

Giddens, Anthony (1977b), 'Habermas' Social and Political Theory', *American Journal of Sociology*, 83:198–212.

Goffman, Erving (1967), *Interaction Ritual*, New York: Anchor.

Habermas, Jürgen (1970a), 'On Systematically Distorted Communication', *Inquiry*, 13:205–18.

Habermas, Jürgen (1970b), 'Towards a Theory of Communicative Competence', *Inquiry*, 13:360–75.

Habermas, Jürgen (1970c), *Toward a Rational Society: Student Protest, Science, and Politics*, Boston: Beacon.

Habermas, Jürgen (1971a), *Knowledge and Human Interests*, Boston: Beacon.

Habermas, Jürgen (1971b), 'Discussion of Parsons's Interpretation of Weber', in Otto Stammer (ed.), *Max Weber and Sociology Today*, New York: Harper & Row, pp. 59–66.

Bibliography

Habermas, Jürgen (1973), *Theory and Practice*, Boston: Beacon.
Habermas, Jürgen (1974), 'The Public Sphere', *New German Critique*, 3:49–55.
Habermas, Jürgen (1975), *Legitimation Crisis*, Boston: Beacon.
Habermas, Jürgen (1977a), 'A Review of Gadamer's *Truth and Method*', in F. Dallmayr and T. McCarthy (eds), *Understanding and Social Inquiry*, Notre Dame: Notre Dame Press, pp. 335–63.
Habermas, Jürgen (1977b), 'Hannah Arendt's Communications Concept of Power', *Social Research*, 44 (Spring):3–24.
Habermas, Jürgen (1979a), *Communication and the Evolution of Society*, Boston: Beacon.
Habermas, Jürgen (1979b), 'History and Evolution', *Telos*, 39:5–44.
Habermas, Jürgen (1979c), 'Conservatism and Capitalist Crisis', *New Left Review*, 115 (May-June):73–84.
Habermas, Jürgen (1980), 'The Hermeneutic Claim to Universality', in Josef Bleicher (ed.), *Contemporary Hermeneutics: Hermeneutics as Method, Philosophy and Critique*, London: Routledge & Kegan Paul, pp. 181–212.
Habermas, Jürgen (1981), 'New Social Movements', *Telos*, 49 (Fall): 33–7.
Habermas, Jürgen (1983), *The Theory of Communicative Action*, 2 vols, Boston: Beacon.
Hammond, Phillip (1969), 'Peter Berger's Sociology of Religion: An Appraisal', *Soundings*, 52:415 ff.
Hart, Jeffrey (1972), 'Peter Berger's "Paradox": reply to Berger, Two Paradoxes', *National Review*, 511–13.
Harvey, Van (1973), 'Some Problematic Aspects of Peter Berger's Theory of Religion', *Journal of the American Academy of Religion*, 41:75.
Heidegger, Martin (1959), *Introduction to Metaphysics*, New Haven, Conn.: Yale University Press.
Held, David (1978), 'The Battle Over Critical Theory', *Sociology*, 12: 553–60.
Held, David (1980), *Introduction to Critical Theory: Horkheimer to Habermas*, Berkeley: University of California Press.
Hjelmslev, Louis (1959), *Essais Linguistiques*, Copenhagen: Nordisk Sprog-og Kulturforlog.
Hohendahl, Peter Uwe (1979), 'Critical Theory, Public Sphere and Culture: Jürgen Habermas and His Critics', *New German Critique*, 16:89–118.
Honneth, Axel, Knödler-Bunte, Eberhard, and Widman, Arno (1981), 'The Dialectics of Rationalization: An Interview with Jürgen Habermas', *Telos*, 49:5–31.

Horkheimer, Max and Adorno, Theodore (1972), *Dialectic of Enlightenment*, New York: Herder & Herder.

Horster, Detlev and van Reijen, Willem (1979), 'Interview with Jürgen Habermas, Starnberg, March 23, 1979', *New German Critique*, 18:43.

Jacobson, Roman (1971), *Selected Writings*, The Hague: Mouton.

Jay, Martin (1973), *The Dialectical Imagination: A History of the Frankfurt School and The Institute of Social Research, 1923-1950*, Boston: Little, Brown.

Jones, Hugh (1978), 'Spirit of Inquiry and the Reflected Self', *Scottish Journal of Theology*, 31:201 ff.

Kanter, Rosabeth Moss (1968), 'Commitment and Social Organization: A Study of Commitment Mechanisms in Utopian Communities', *American Sociological Review*, 33:499-517.

Kortian, Garbis (1980), *Metacritique*, Cambridge University Press.

Kurzweil, Edith (1980), *The Age of Structuralism: Lévi-Strauss to Foucault*, New York: Columbia University Press.

LaCapra, Dominick (1977), 'Habermas and the Grounding of Critical Theory', *History and Theory*, 16:237-64.

Langer, Susanne K. (1951), *Philosophy in a New Key: A Study in the Symbolism of Reason, Rite and Art*, New York: New American Library.

Leiber, Justin (1975), *Noam Chomsky: A Philosophic Overview*, New York: St. Martins.

Lemert, Charles (1979), 'De-Centered Analysis: Ethnomethodology and Structuralism', *Theory and Society*, 7:289-306.

Lévi-Strauss, Claude (1963), *Structural Anthropology*, New York: Basic Books.

Lévi-Strauss, Claude (1966), *The Savage Mind*, University of Chicago Press.

Lévi-Strauss, Claude (1968), *Tristes Tropiques*, New York: Atheneum.

Lukács, Georg (1971), *History and Class Consciousness*, Cambridge, Mass.: MIT Press.

McCarthy, Thomas (1973), 'A Theory of Communicative Competence', *Philosophy of the Social Sciences*, 3:135-56.

McCarthy, Thomas (1978), *The Critical Theory of Jürgen Habermas*, Cambridge, Mass.: MIT Press.

McIntosh, Donald (1977), 'Habermas on Freud', *Social Research*, 44:562-98.

Marcus, Alfred (1980), 'Environmental Protection Agency', pp. 267-303 in James Q. Wilson (ed.), *The Politics of Regulation*, New York: Basic Books.

Martinet, André (1960), *Elements of General Linguistics*, London:

Faber & Faber.

Mendelson, Jack (1979), 'The Habermas/Gadamer Debate', *New German Critique*, 18:44–74.

Misgeld, Dieter (1976), 'Hermeneutics and Critical Theory: The Debate Between Habermas and Gadamer', pp. 164–84 in J. O'Neill (ed.), *On Critical Theory*, New York: Seabury.

Misgeld, Dieter (1977), 'Discourse and Conversation: The Theory of Communicative Competence and Hermeneutics in the Light of the Debate Between Habermas and Gadamer', *Cultural Hermeneutics*, 4:321–44.

Misgeld, Dieter (1981), 'Science, Hermeneutics, and the Utopian Content of the Liberal-Democratic Tradition: On Habermas' Recent Work, A Reply to Mendelson', *New German Critique*, 22:123–44.

Nicholson, Linda J. (1980), 'Why Habermas?' *Radical Philosophy*, 25:21–6.

Parsons, Talcott (1951), *The Social System*, New York: Free Press.

Searle, John R. (1969), *Speech Acts: An Essay in the Philosophy of Language*, Cambridge University Press.

Sensat, Julius (1978), *Habermas and Marxism: An Appraisal*, Beverly Hills: Sage.

Sheridan, Alan (1980), *Michel Foucault: The Will to Truth*, New York: Tavistock.

Skinner, Quentin (1982), 'Habermas' Reformation', *New York Review of Books*, 29:35–9.

Slater, Phil (1977), *Origin and Significance of the Frankfurt School*, London: Routledge & Kegan Paul.

Swanson, Guy E. (1964), *The Birth of the Gods*, Ann Arbor: University of Michigan Press.

Van den Berg, Axel (1980), 'Critical Theory: Is There Still Hope?' *American Journal of Sociology*, 86:449–78.

Van Gennep, Arnold (1969), *The Rites of Passage*, University of Chicago Press.

Weber, Max (1963), *The Sociology of Religion*, Boston: Beacon.

Weiner, Richard B. (1981), *Cultural Marxism and Political Sociology*, Beverly Hills: Sage.

White, Stephen K. (1979), 'Rationality and the Foundations of Political Philosophy: An Introduction to the Recent Work of Jürgen Habermas', *Journal of Politics*, 41:1156–71.

Wilson, John (1969), 'The De-alienation of Peter Berger', *Soundings*, 52:425 ff.

Wisdom, J. O. (1973), 'The Phenomenological Approach to the Sociology of Knowledge', *Philosophy of the Social Sciences*, 3:257–66.

Index

Index

272